ЃONGA

A SAFE ABODE IN
THE WILDERNESS

BARRY BABCOCK

ISBNs: 979-8-9873191-4-7 (pb);

979-8-9873191-5-4 (hc);

979-8-9873191-4-7 (eBook)

Book Cover Design: The Book Cover Whisperer, OpenBookDesign.biz

Interior Book Design: Inanna Arthen, inannaarthen.com

Maps by Philip Schwartzberg, Meridian Mapping

Library of Congress Control Number: 2023937532

First Printing: 2023
Printed in the United States of America

Names: Babcock, Barry, author.
Title: Bonga : a safe abode in the wilderness / by Barry Babcock.
Description: [Bemidji, Minnesota] : [Barry Babcock], [2023] | Includes bibliographical references.
Identifiers: ISBN: 979-8-9873191-5-4 (paperback) | 979-8-9873191-6-1 (hardcover) |
979-8-9873191-4-7 (ebook) | LCCN: 2023937532
Subjects: LCSH: African Americans--Minnesota--History. | Fugitive slaves--Minnesota--History. |
Ojibwa Indians--Minnesota--History. | Indians of North America--Minnesota--History. |
Racially mixed people--Minnesota--History. | Fur traders--Minnesota--History. |
Minnesota--History. | BISAC: HISTORY / General. | HISTORY / United States / General. |
HISTORY / Indigenous Peoples in the Americas.
Classification: LCC: F615.N4 B33 2023 | DDC: 977.600496073--dc23

Dedicated to the memory of Henry "Hank" Bonga

Also by Barry Babcock

Teachers in the Forest: New Lessons from an Old World
Riverfeet Press, 2022

Table of Contents

"It is my fear that if we allow the freedom of the hills and the last of the wilderness to be taken from us, then the very idea of freedom may die with it"

– Edward Abbey

"And with a sincere analysis that contained no hint of irony nor sarcasm, Sir Robert Peel told Parliament: 'The United States has been rapidly undergoing a change from a republic to a mere democracy. The influence of the executive—the influence of the government—has been daily less and more power has consequently been vested in the hands of the people. And yet, in that country, there is land uncultivated to an extent almost incalculable—there is no established church, no privileged orders—property exists on a very different tenure from that on which it is held in this country; therefore let not the people of England be deceived, let them not imagine from the example of the United States, that because democracy has succeeded and triumphed there, it will also succeed and triumph here.' Such were a few of the drifts of thought and action at work in Europe in the year 1831 and years just before."

– Carl Sandburg, *Abraham Lincoln: The Prairie Years*

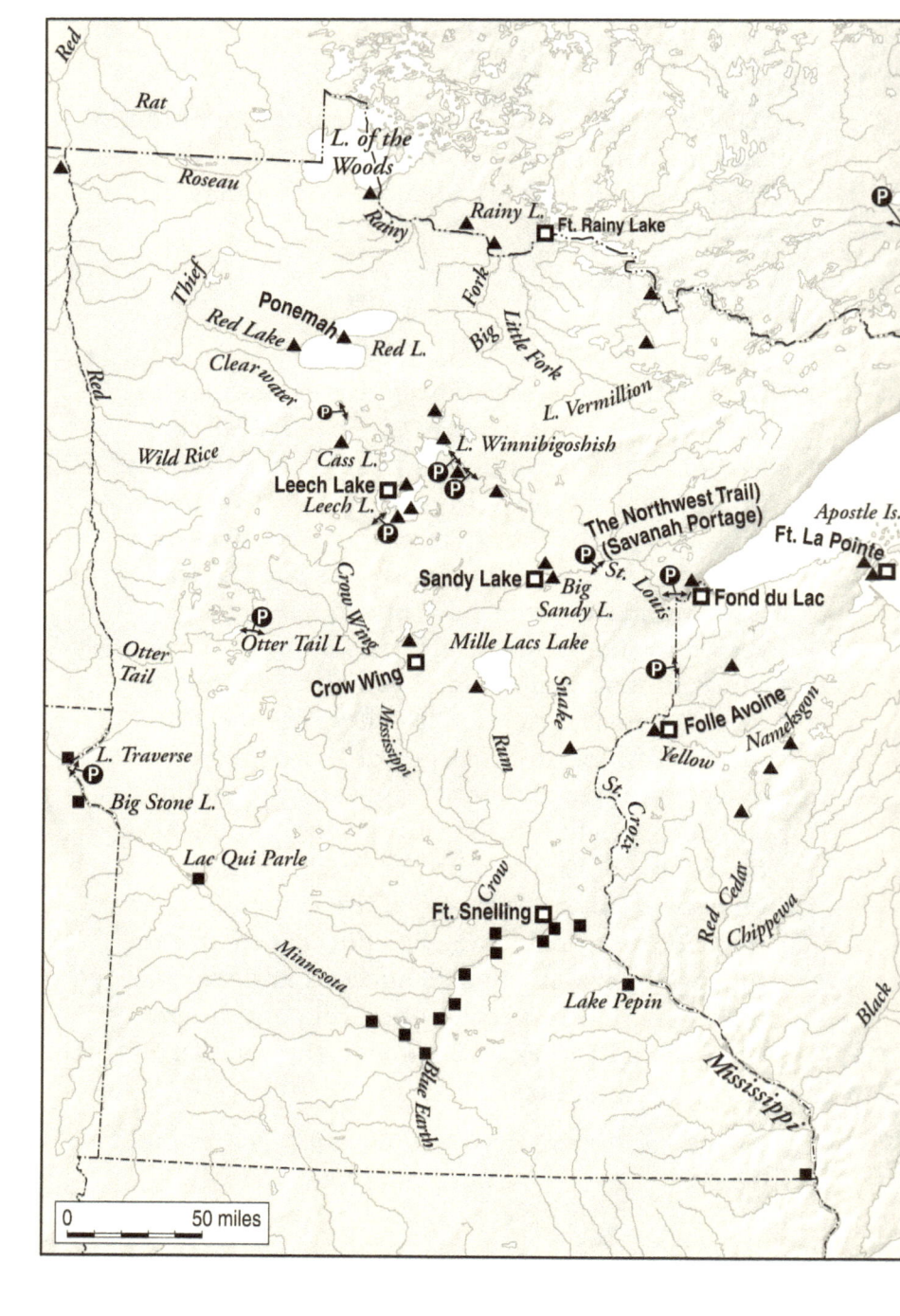

Red

Rat

Roseau

L. of the Woods

Rainy L. Ft. Rainy Lake

Rainy

P

Thief

Ponemah

Red Lake

Fork

Red L.

Clearwater

Big

Little Fork

P

L. Vermillion

Red

Wild Rice

Cass L.

L. Winnibigoshish

Leech Lake P

Leech L. P

P

The Northwest Trail)
(Savanah Portage)

Apostle Is.

Ft. La Pointe

Sandy Lake P

Big Sandy L. *St. Louis* Fond du Lac

Crow Wing

P

Otter
Tail

P

Otter Tail L.

Mille Lacs Lake

Crow Wing

P

Mississippi

Snake

Folle Avoine

Nameksgon

Yellow

Rum

L. Traverse

Big Stone L.

St. Croix

Red Cedar

Chippewa

Lac Qui Parle

Crow

Ft. Snelling

Minnesota

Lake Pepin

Black

Blue Earth

Mississippi

0   50 miles

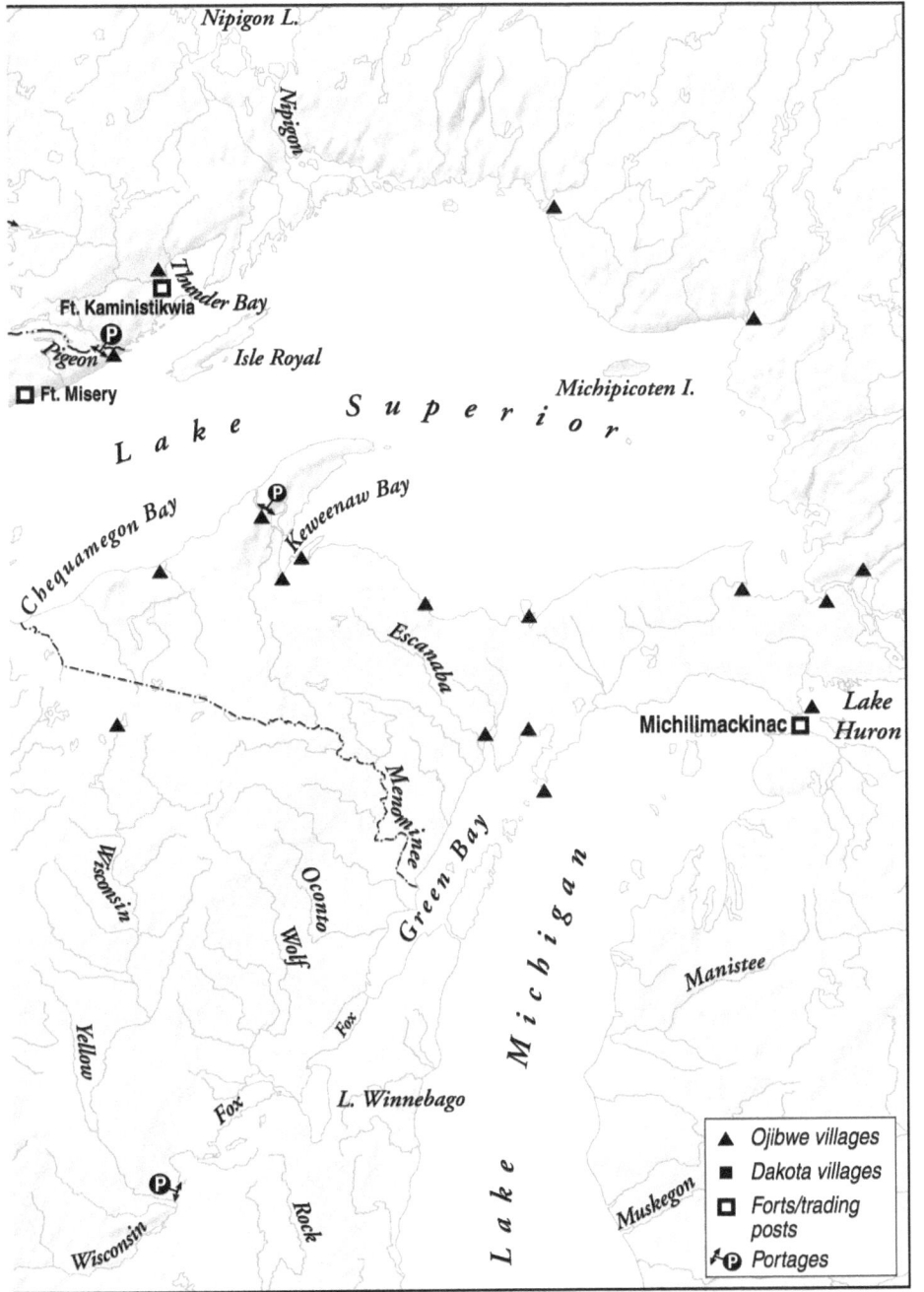

Nipigon L.

Nipigon

Ft. Kaministikwia

Thunder Bay

Pigeon

Ft. Misery

Isle Royal

L a k e   S u p e r i o r

Michipicoten I.

Chequamegon Bay

Keweenaw Bay

Escanaba

Michilimackinac

Lake
Huron

Wisconsin

Menominee

Oconto

Wolf

Fox

Green Bay

L a k e   M i c h i g a n

Manistee

Yellow

Fox

Rock

L. Winnebago

Muskegon

Wisconsin

▲	Ojibwe villages
■	Dakota villages
☐	Forts/trading posts
⚲Ⓟ	Portages

Preface

I began researching the material for this book in the early 1990s and like most research it opened many new avenues of exploration. The spark that ignited the flame that became this book was my love for the wilderness areas of northern Minnesota, Wisconsin, and neighboring Ontario, Canada. Since most of the country mentioned is a maze of interconnected waterways my mode of exploration became the canoe. Becoming infatuated with the land led me to a vast reservoir of literature about the history, geology, plant, and animal communities that the region gave rise to. Most of the written history of this region derives from the fur trade era and Native American life and culture. It is in the myriad of journals, treaties, legends, and others that I would get small anecdotes, peeks, and general references to a family called Bonga. My relationship with all this became more than an avocation, it became the core of my existence. The way I enter this wilderness is the same manner others have, and that is to seat myself in a canoe. No man-made vessel is more appropriate in its natural surroundings than the canoe country of the Northwoods.

Over nearly three decades I have struggled to complete and see this book become a reality and for much of that time, I felt not up to the task. I am woefully without any sheepskins or credentials to back up my endeavor as I am wholly self-educated. Not to mention, who would place any faith in some reclusive nut living totally off the grid, pumping all water need by hand, heating with his own wood, erecting a small solar system to power his lap top, gardening, foraging, hunting, and howling with the wolves?

No matter where I journey in my canoe, I sense the spirits of many who plied the same waterways I have. It is here that I become aware of the three generations of the Bongas who found freedom here in the wilds of the great Northwoods and prospered here and left their finger prints all over the *Le Beau Pays* (the beautiful land). Who they were and what they did here is plainly evident today yet their names and what they did have fallen through the cracks of history. Their deeds and works are still here though much is buried in the early history by the fact that they were not white-skinned people but were Blacks whose patriarch was a black slave who somehow escaped and found his "safe abode in the wilderness where all things are free."

I became mesmerized by the tidbits of information concerning the deeds and legends of the people named Bonga. For close to twenty years, I dropped out of modern society as best as I could and my wife, my dogs, and I lived off the grid in a remote and isolated wild setting where my neighbors were wolves, bears, winged creatures and the four-leggeds. This opened my mind to what truly is reality and the fact that the few remaining places on earth where one can experience this truest sense of freedom. When I hear a wolf howl it is the sound of freedom to me. Here, all things are free.

Although I am not professional writer, I have been an avid reader with a desire to express my feelings and opinions for the world we now live in. I have done my best to tell this story with clarity in a chronological order and with as much conciseness as possible. Any errors are entirely my fault and no one else's.

What you are about to read is a story that is, or should be, as American as any story ever told. It is my hope that it will further define who we are, "that this is nation conceived in Liberty, and dedicated to the proposition that all men are created equal."

My sincere hope is this book will make the name, Bonga, be regarded as one of the great names in my beloved state for which they did so much by their deeds to shape it for all people. Move over Paul Bunyan make room for George Bonga.

A Great *Mai* Pole

An Introduction

I have spent a good deal of my life canoeing the wilderness of the Canadian Shield, but I've always returned home to my beloved Mississippi Headwaters Country. I live here to experience the backcountry by canoe on the remote waterways in the glacial moraines of north central Minnesota. It is in this place on the infant Mississippi where I feel a deep abiding affection for the beauty, diversity, and wildness of the land. But there is something else I sense here. This "sense" comes to me when shooting through the narrow rocky riffles of the infant Mississippi River as its channel passes through high sandy banks forested with spruce and pine and then emerges into vast wetlands of *manoomin* (wild rice). It is in this wild and silent place that I sense the spirits of the many human beings who preceded me and made this land their home.

In these wild and silent places I feel the presence of a man's spirit—a man that has captivated me. I have been on the trail of this man's spirit for decades and feel as though I know him intimately. His spirit lingers over the land from White Earth to the Namekagon River—from Basswood Lake to Fort Snelling. But it is here in the Headwaters Country, where he made his home, where his spirit is the strongest. Possibly, the presence I feel is his spirit urging me to tell his story. His story is what is best about America, but it has fallen through the cracks of history. The man is George Bonga. The story I'm about to tell you starts with his grandfather who was brought to the New World as a slave.

Though the story starts with an enslaved black man, it soon develops into the proud heritage of a family with its roots in Africa, now mixed with the blood of the Anishinaabeg. They lived in a time when the nation embraced slavery and when the highest court of the land ruled that Blacks were only 3/5ths of a human being. But the Bonga family found refuge from the racism prevalent in the civilized parts of America. They did not see the wilderness of northern Minnesota as something that required taming or settling; they saw it as freedom and as home. They saw the infinite waterways as a route to freedom and the northern forests as a land in which to make a home. The wilderness of the lakes and rivers of the Northwoods was the great equalizer for the Bongas.

The Bonga family was deeply imbedded in the culture and economy of the fur trade. In the vernacular of the fur trade a *Mai* or maypole (also called a "lob pine" or "lobstick") was a great and ancient old-growth white pine which voyageurs would climb with an axe lopping off all the lower limbs. This left only a tuft at the top of the tree rendering it recognizable from a distance as a landmark of importance. Sometimes the voyageurs did this to honor an important passenger, an important landmark, or simply to mark a portage. Whatever the purpose, it was a benchmark to be seen from a distance to safely guide and direct us on our journey. Today, the few scattered *Mai* remaining on the land are indeed rare. The Bonga family is a great *Mai* pole for Americans to sight our bearings on and guide us in the right direction in which we may be better people.

A Dark Cloud Approaching from the East

Minnesota's First Criminal Trial

No one could have predicted the events that would occur in 1836. The year started out as most do in the wilderness of the Northwoods, but a great change was coming from the east. The looming changes in Headwaters Country would impact not only the people that resided there, but would ripple all the way to the young nation's capital.

To understand the events of 1836, we must understand the historical context of the region. As early as the 1660s the demand for furs in Europe was the dominant economic engine in North America. The first white men were French-Canadians such as Radisson and Groseilliers who were lusting for wealth and adventure and traveled as far west as Lake Superior. They were, in turn, followed by La Verendrye and other Frenchmen like him. For these men the country was the *Pays d'en Haut*—the Upper Country. By the late 1700s, the domination of the fur trade shifted from France to England. The era of the fur trade was not just a moment in North American history, but rather it spanned two hundred years, beginning in the mid 1600s and continued until the 1840s.

Claims of ownership of what is now Minnesota by western civilization standards would result in a long list of entities, including four countries and five United States Territories. Minnesota Territory was created in 1849 and Minnesota became a state in 1858. The important thing to

15

remember is that before the arrival of *gichi mookomaanag* (white people), this land was entirely Indian Country or the *Pays Sauvage*.

A major change occurred in 1825 with the Treaty of Prairie du Chien which was facilitated by the whites to pacify relations between the Ojibwe, who dominated the northern forest, and the Dakota who resided in the southern half of the state. For a hundred years the Ojibwe and Dakota had vacillated between peace and war. The warring had disrupted the fur trade thus making peace between these two Indian Nations advantageous for the white man's business as fur traders. If you were a white man in this region, you were either in the fur trade, a soldier, or one of a very few missionaries.

There were a number of Ojibwe Bands throughout northern Minnesota, but arguably the most *ogichidaa* (warrior-like) of them was the Leech Lake Band of Ojibwe. They were referred to as the Pillagers—*Muk-im-dua-inini-wag, men who take by force*[1]—for their strength and independence in pushing into what was previously the land of the Dakota. As their name indicates, their stronghold was in the area surrounding Leech Lake—*Gaa-zagaskwaajimekaag*—the third largest lake in Minnesota. This region, controlled by the Leech Lakers, was essentially Mississippi Headwaters Country with Leech Lake roughly located within a great arch made by the clockwise flow of the great river resembling the crook on a shepherd's staff.

By 1806, aside from some fur traders and Zebulon Pike, few white men had ever reached Leech Lake. But when Pike arrived at the Leech Lake village on Ottertail Point on February 1, 1806, the first thing he did was shoot down the Union Jack and raise the "Stars and Stripes." This was his manner of emphasizing that the region was no longer British held land and that British traders should stay north of the Canadian border.[2]

With the exception of a small number of rugged Scotch/Irish fur traders, very few whites had penetrated the *Pays Sauvage* prior to 1832 when Henry Rowe Schoolcraft arrived. To assist him in navigating the Headwaters he was accompanied by physician, geologist, and botanist Douglass Houghton, Presbyterian missionary William T. Boutwell, John Johnston, Schoolcraft's brother-in-law and direct descendant of the great chief of northern Wisconsin and UP Michigan, White Fisher (*Waub-O-Jeeg*), Lt. James Allen with a ten man, hand-picked crew of soldiers, and a crew of twenty boatmen (voyageurs of French and French-Indian mix).

On the return trip Schoolcraft had several obligations which were in reality his primary reasons for the expedition. These included vaccinating the Leech Lake band for small pox, proposing peaceful relations with the Dakota, and determining the trading relations of the Leech Lakers with Canadian traders. The excursion to the "Headwaters" was not among the principal reasons for this trip in the eyes of the government. Going to the Headwaters was to be permitted only if the opportunity arose. But from the beginning finding the source of the Mississippi was first in Schoolcraft's mind.

Lt. Allen was chosen for this role due to his map making abilities, and he was also required to keep a journal. Throughout his journal he noted the strength of the Indians, their attitude towards the United States and to the fur traders. Allen makes some interesting observations about the geographic aspects of Leech Lake as well. According to Allen it was the largest of the lakes contributing to the Headwaters of the Mississippi and the numbers of Ojibwe residing on this great lake Allen estimated at 806. Allen also addressed the bountiful game and other resources of this great lake and the independence, pride, and deport of the Leech Lakers. He writes:

"Their country abounds in furred animals and game, and the lake affords abundance of fish; whitefish, herring, and tullibee, which they take in gill nets at all seasons. Deer and bears are the principle animals of the forest which are hunted for their meat; and beavers, otters, martens, and muskrats are the chief furred animals, which are taken in such great numbers as to make this one of the most valuable posts of the north for the American trade. About seven thousand dollars' worth of furs are annually sold to the American traders, and great quantities are taken from here across the lines to the British trader at Rainy lake, and sold there for whisky and some British goods. These Indians have a partiality for the British, which they take no pains to conceal, and, as far as is their power, they obtain their supplies from the British traders. Mr. Aitkin is of the opinion that four of five thousand dollars' worth of furs are annually traded by this band across the lines to the Hudson Bay Company. From their remoteness from white settlements, they still retain much of their native character. They have not been debased or enfeebled with whiskey, from the difficulty of obtaining it in great quantities; and, unlike most of their tribe, they are strong, athletic, muscular men, of large stature, and fine appearance, looking proud, haughty, and subdued; and carrying an independence and fearlessness with their manner, that indicates a full estimate of their own strength. They have sometimes robbed their traders of a part of their goods, and have hence acquired the name of "The Pillagers," or "the Robbers;" but, of late years, they have been less troublesome to the traders, and are not much complained of except for their impudence, and total disregard of, and disrespect for the power and Government of the United States. They are undoubtedly inimical to our Government and friendly to the British; and such is their ignorance and arrogance, that they have threatened to drive away the American trader, and bring a British one, whom they would maintain and protect among them.

The nature of their country protects them from inroads of their enemies to their villages; and they feel inaccessible and secure from any power whatever, even that of the United States. The traders have, in vain, to threaten with the power of the government to check their excesses; their reply is, that they have not yet seen that power, and that it cannot reach them

It is probable, however, that our visiting them with such apparent ease may have the effect of lowering their ideas of their inaccessible position.

They have several war chiefs who are much superior, in appearance, to Flat Mouth, and who have much better character for warlike qualities. But the latter is the great chief in council, where his oratory sustains his authority; and he is acknowledged, by all, their principle chief."[3]

In addition to the great and powerful civil chief of the Leech Lake Band, *Esh-ke-bug-e-koshe*, often referred to by the whites as "Flatmouth", there was another man, a white man, whose importance was paramount to all who resided in the territory. That was William Alexander Aitkin who, as head of the Fond du Lac Department of the American Fur Company (AFC), was arguably the most powerful and influential non-Indian man in the Fond du Lac Department which covered an area comprising the northern half of Minnesota and a portion of northwestern Wisconsin.

William Aitkin began his career in the fur trade in 1802 as a North West Company (NWC) man. Historian Larry Luukkonen says of Aitkin:

> "...perhaps the one who best symbolized the very essence of the headwaters trader in the old Fond du Lac Department was William Alexander Aitkin. In fact, no historical account of the fur trade in Northern Minnesota would be complete without a reference to him. One can also argue that Aitkin's career in the fur trade was the history of the American Fur Company in Minnesota, because he played such a large role in its operations, at least during the years 1829 to 1838."[4]

Once Schoolcraft's expedition reached the Headwaters, their return trip brought them to *Esh-ke-bug-e-coshe's* village on Ottertail Point of Leech Lake where Dr. Houghton vaccinated the Ojibwe for small pox and Schoolcraft urged peace between the Ojibwe and Dakota.

After Schoolcraft's visit in 1832 nothing very extraordinary happened until the year of 1836, when a single event on Upper Red Cedar Lake would not only impact

Anishinaabeg in the Leech Lake area but have repercussions with the 1837 Treaty at Fort St. Peters—which was the first land acquisition of Indian lands in the territory—and beyond.

The year of 1836 started out quiet enough. It was a bitterly cold winter which seemed to be the norm in this region of North America. Of that particular winter, the Reverend William Thurston Boutwell, who served on the Schoolcraft expedition, and who stayed on at Leech Lake as a missionary, wrote the following:

> "There has been nothing, so far as I have discovered, or been informed, like a disposition to go to war this spring... The past winter has been severe – the depth of snow greater, by far, than has fallen for several years. Feb. 1 the mercury fell to 40 deg. below zero. This is the extreme. Graduated on the scale I have – it fell nearly into the ball."[5]

Earlier, George Bonga, the legendary 'half Black-half Ojibwe' AFC trader for Aitkin at Leech Lake, had been asked by Aitkin to establish a permanent post on Ottertail Lake which is a many days' journey southwest of Leech Lake. More notably, it was located on the boundary or war zone between the Ojibwe and Dakota, a place thought by many to be far too dangerous for an Ojibwe to be anywhere near and open to attack by Dakota who had been at war with the Ojibwe for nearly 100 years. William Aitkin would not have selected George Bonga for this dangerous task if he had not been fully satisfied that George would pose such a powerful and authoritative image that would demand respect and awe by the Dakota.

Barry Babcock

Reverend Boutwell wrote Henry Schoolcraft in Sault Ste. Marie in June of 1836:

> "...There is, evidently, a growing desire on the part of required his two children to attend regularly to instruction; others occasionally. The Elder not a few, to cultivate gardens more exclusively and better. These are making gardens by the side of me...The Big Cloud has Brother has procured him a comfortable log house to be built – bought a horse and cow. I have bought a calf of Mr. A. for him.[6]
>
> I am making the experiment whether I can keep cattle here. They have wintered and passed the spring, and we are now favored with milk, which is a rarity and luxury here.
>
> Mr. Aitkin is establishing a permanent post of Otter Tail Lake. G. Bonga had gone with a small assortment of goods to build and pass the summer there. The Indians are divided in opinion and feeling with regard to the measure. Those who belong to this lake, or make gardens in this vicinity, are opposed to the measure. Those who pass the summer in the deer [waawaashkeshi] country and make rice towards the height of land, are in its favor. It is on the line dividing us from our enemies – some say, where we do not wish to go. Whether he has consulted the agent on the subject, I know not."[7]

Aside from the events already mentioned, on August 19, 1836, the French astronomer and mathematician Joseph N. Nicollet, arrived at the Ojibwe village of *Esh-ke-bug-e-koshe* on Ottertail Point. Nicollet was on his journey to verify Schoolcraft's citing the source of the Headwaters of the Mississippi River. Nicollet was guided there from Fort Snelling by Francois Brunette who was a six-foot four inch, mixed-blood guide hired for eighty to one-hundred dollars. Brunette turned out to be a wise choice. Nicollet described him as "a giant of great strength but, at the same time, full of the milk of human kindness, and, withal, an excellent geographer." Nicollet's arrival caused great excitement among the band while Chief Flatmouth was absent, and many of the men became quite agitated and hostile to Nicollet. Nicollet feared for his life. In his astronomical notebook for August 19 Nicollet wrote: "But, during the first three days of this week, the Chippeways of the lake greatly annoyed me; and, from mutual misunderstandings, even put my life in jeopardy, as my guide scarcely dared to side with me, for fear of exposing himself."[8]

Hostilities calmed down when Reverend Boutwell, who also resided on the big lake, received news of potential trouble, and hurried by canoe to Ottertail Point and pacified the agitated warriors. Soon, Nicollet became much liked by the Leech Lakers and was generously outfitted and guided by a Leech Lake elder, *Gay-gued-o-say,* who was said to know the source of the Headwaters so well that it was called "the grounds of *Gay-gued-o-say.*"[9]

On Nicollet's return trip from the source of the Headwaters, he again stopped on Leech Lake at Ottertail village where his expedition re-provisioned themselves for the 500-mile return trip to Fort Snelling. Nicollet wrote: "Our crew is manning two canoes. The large one that we are supposed to return to St. Peter [Fort Snelling] is twenty-four feet long. I am in it with Brunia [Brunette], Desire, and the mulatto Stephen [Bonga], a native half-breed."

Stephen Bonga is George Bonga's older brother.

The Momentous Event

In late autumn of 1836, William Aitkin's oldest and favorite son, Alfred, after years of tutoring by his father in the many tasks and responsibilities of operating a fur trading post, was placed in charge of the AFC post near the mouth of the Turtle River at the north end of Upper Red Cedar Lake—*Gaa-miskwaawaakokaag* (place of many red cedars).

Alfred Aitkin, a mixed-blood, was educated at Mackinac, Michigan. He was just twenty years old when his Father placed him in charge of the Upper Red Cedar Lake post. All information regarding young Alfred shows he was well liked by all. Alfred's mother, Striped Cloud (*Bay-ji-quod*), was a descendant of "Broken Tooth" a very powerful and important Ojibwe chief at Big Sandy Lake.

Alfred had just returned to the AFC post on Upper Red Cedar Lake after a business trip to Red Lake. It was at the AFC post on Upper Red Cedar Lake on December 6, 1836 when young Alfred was murdered. There are different versions of the circumstances of how the murder occurred but we can be certain that it happened because of a love affair. From all available information, I believe the correct version of events is that young Alfred was aware that a third party—who was known by two names, *Ghe-ga-wa-skung* (He who walks along the shore) and *Pashkwewozh* (Old Nighthawk) and believed to be a high-ranking medicine man—was having an affair with a married woman. Fearing *Ghe-ga-wa-skung* may do something drastic, Alfred Aitkin sent the married Ojibwe woman and her Ojibwe husband to Big Winnibigoshish Lake, nine miles downstream on the Mississippi River from Upper Red Cedar Lake. On the night of December 6 Alfred was awoken from his sleep by a voyageur informing him that *Ghe-ga-wa-skung* was trying to tear down one of the storehouses at his post.

Bonga

Reverend Boutwell, who had a mission nearby on Leech Lake and likely had more contact and history with the deceased and events that night, has his version of the murder printed in the book *Minnesota in Three Centuries* which includes passages from his diary.

"The circumstances, [of Alfred Aitkins murder] as Rev. Boutwell says as they were given to him, were as follows: A Red Cedar Indian had a wife of ill repute. Another Indian of the band named Ghe-ga-wa-skung had become involved with her and was much attached to her, to the extent that he planned to kill her husband. Alfred Aitkin, the young trader was fully informed of all the facts and attempted to stop the scandal. He and some of his men had returned from Red Lake December 5. The Indian with the Faithless wife was one of his employees. The young trader directed a squad of his men to go to 'Lake Winipeck,' [Lake Winnebigoshish] for him and ordered that the disgraced husband and his disgraceful wife accompany the party. The woman had said to her husband, concerning her lover: 'He is always after me;' and so the husband was very willing to take her with him to Winipeck... 'to get her out of the way,' as Boutwell tells us.

The party set out early. Ghe-ga-wa-skung soon discovered that his inamorata had gone and he was furious. He knew that young Aitkin was in part responsible and he was greatly incensed against him. Boutwell relates what followed: 'Alfred remained with one man and a lad of sixteen. In the morning the man came in and told Alfred that an Indian was cutting his store down with an axe. Alfred opened the door and told the Indian [Ghe ga wa skung] to desist; but he paid no attention. Alfred went and took the axe from him; the Indian, took his gun, which he had hid, and committed the horrible deed. The Indian supposed Alfred was the cause of sending away the man's wife. He had loaded his gun with the determination of killing the woman." [10]

We may never know the complexities of a murder committed over 187 years ago but love affairs often involve extenuating circumstances and operate in secrecy that we may never know today and can only speculate the causes. One thing that we do know is that *Ghe-ga-wa-skung* was a "healer" or medicine man as some may refer to him. Being a healer gave him a degree of stature, powers, alliances with other band members and influence which will become apparent.

Though the murder occurred on December 6, 1836 on Upper Red Cedar Lake, word of Alfred's death did not reach William Aitkin until nearly a month later. This was because of William's absence from his headquarters on Big Sandy while tending to business at Lapointe, an island on Lake Superior, nearly 190 miles away by overland trails. No attempt to arrest the murderer was made until Aitkin returned. As far as we know during this period from Alfred's death to William Atkin's learning of the event, *Ghe-ga-wa-skung* was on Upper Red Cedar Lake.

In a letter written to Ramsay Crooks, dated January 4, 1837, William Aitkin wrote: "Dear Sir; I write but alas what have I got to say, to tell of the murder of my poor boy Alfred...at Upper Red Cedar Lake about a month ago..."[11] Sometime after this letter was written, Aitkin and three other stout and resolute men set out on the long overland journey by dog sled from Sandy Lake to Leech Lake. But before Aitkin departed Sandy Lake, he "...sent word to all the different posts in this region that no man is to get a charge of ammunition or a pipe of tobacco until the accomplish is secured." William Aitkin, as head of the Fond du Lac Department of the American Fur Company, halted all trade—not one ounce of gun powder, nor one musket ball or a pipe of tobacco was to be traded until the killer of his son was apprehended or killed. [12]

It is easy to imagine the strained faces of the men from Big Sandy as they urged their dogs on through the snow clad and frozen wilderness of the Northwoods, eager to extract revenge and pondering what the future held for them. Grief enveloped Aitkin and anxiety for vengeance gripped his soul. The men would be straining their dog teams to reach their destination 150 miles from Aitkin's headquarters on Big Sandy Lake, not knowing where the alleged killer would be a month after the killing.

Upon arriving at Leech Lake, Aitkin and his sub-traders sent out word for re-enforcements. The posse was enlarged to twenty men. When the men arrived at one of Aitkin's posts on Leech Lake, they learned that *Ghe-ga-wa-skung* or *Pashkwewozh,* was known to be encamped with family and friends at the Ojibwe village on Great Island—*Gichi Minising* (now known as Star Island)—on Upper Red Cedar Lake. This group of well-armed men set off for Upper Red Cedar Lake by dog team under the cover of darkness and under the "full moon of the wolf." Arriving at Upper Red Cedar, the posse waited in the moonlight among the ancient red pines about the shores of the lake eager to capture the killer of young and beloved Alfred Aitkin.

Rev. Boutwell joined the posse. Regarding Rev. Boutwell, William Aitkin wrote: "Our mutual friend, Mr. Boutwell, joined the party, with his musket on his shoulder, as a man and a Christian, for he knew it was a righteous cause, and that the arm of God was with him."[13]

Rev. Boutwell wrote in his diary on Friday, January 13, 1837:

> "About 10 o'clock Sabbath evening, Mr. Aitkin arrived with three or four men from Sandy Lake. He immediately sent to Lac Winipeck for men to join his party here (Leech Lake). On Wednesday I started with him for Red Cedar Lake to apprehend the murderer, accompanied by ten half-breeds, six Frenchmen, the clerk of the post, Mr. [Allan] Morrison, and Big Cloud. We encamped near the borders of Red Cedar Lake. Left at midnight and proceeded to Grand Island where we left our dog trains, and reached the Indian encampment an hour before day. Secreted ourselves until daylight, when we sallied forth and came upon the Indians while they were yet asleep. Secured first the axes, guns, and knives; and then took the murderer without resistance and brought him to Leech Lake.
>
> Sunday, 14th. – As Indians are arriving, we thought best to send the criminal on to Sandy Lake, while Mr. Aitkin remained to see the Chief, for whom he had sent, and to whom he wished to make some communications. Yesterday morning five armed men started with him [the accused], but, strange as it may seem, at midday, and on the open lake [Leech Lake] he made his escape."[14]

Ghe-ge-wa-skung was a captive and a sense of relief pervaded the men of the posse but for some inexplicable reason, while the posse transported their captive across the vast expanse of a frozen Leech Lake under a bright sunny and bitter cold day, *Ghe-ga-wa-skung* escaped. The white man's history does not record how this escape was accomplished. It may be partially or totally due to the intervention of *Ghe-ga-wa-skung's* brothers or relatives, or there may have been another, more incredible answer that has not been revealed.

A possible missing piece of the puzzle concerning the escape of *Ghe-ga-wa-skung* is found in *The Journals of Joseph Nicollet*. In Nicollet's interactions with Anishinaabe he learned of "ceremonies," one which he describes is *Manidookaazo*, in which statuettes are used in a prescribed protocol of ceremony to attract game for food to stave off starvation or for other critical uses. Nicollet states that a "healer" with extraordinary spiritual powers may appeal for similar results without the use of statuettes and in fact, the ceremony has been used to free one's self from bondage. Nicollet suggests that Aitkin's murderer may have escaped in this manner.

> "A chained prisoner will perform an identical
> ceremony. He will ask his manito to give him
> the power to detach his bonds and be free. It is
> surprising how often such prisoners succeed
> in doing this – for example, Pashkwewozh, the
> murderer of Aitkin's son. Of course, in such
> cases there are no banquets, no instruments,
> and no statuettes. Under the circumstances, the
> prisoners say they perform the ceremony using
> their own power, and when they succeed, they
> are recognized as great men."[15]

Not only were these ceremonies viewed with respect

and validity by Anishinaabeg, they were also seen by some white fur traders as useful solutions for life's basic needs. The NWC fur trader of the Yellow River country in north-western Wisconsin, George Nelson, often appealed to native people to perform ceremonies when he and his men were in dire need of food.

Contemplating the mystical powers of the ceremony Nelson wrote:

> "But how is it possible that such things can be? Do you really think that an insignificant root of no apparent power or virtue whatever can affect such things?" Thus I would frequently question and their answers with little variation were universally the same.

> Yes, most certainly, it is not the root alone, but with the assistance of that one of his Dreamed that is most powerful, and most fond of him: he! You white people, you know not; you are consummately ignorant of the Power of our Great Medicine Men. Many things might I tell you much more surprising – but you do not believe these trifles, how much less, then, those you do not know? What then is to be done! how do with, what say, to a people so blind, so infatuated!"[16]

It would be fascinating and useful to know the specific details of the escape and more facts concerning the life of *Ghe-ga-wa-skung/Pashkwewozh* but that is, unfortunately, lost to the winds of history. If more were known of him, we may find reasoning to be sympathetic to him.

After the escape, a second posse was formed under the leadership of the gigantic and powerful Francois Brunette who had guided and acted as interpreter for the French geographer, Joseph Nicollet in the summer of 1836. One of the men picked by Brunette to find *Ghe-ga-wa-skung* (or *Pashkwewozh*) was his close friend and associate, George Bonga, the mixed-blood trader, and son of Pierre Bonga. George Bonga, like Brunette, was an enormous man; well over six feet tall and had an extraordinary powerful build. His reputation as a canoe man, his extraordinary feats of physical strength and his keenness of mind was incomparable as he had an education exceeding most white men of his day. Bonga's reputation was as being a rugged and capable man of the wilderness and a man to be reckoned with. As events were to unfold, George Bonga would become respected by the men of his day as the biggest, strongest, and smartest man in the Northwoods. Brunette selecting George Bonga proved to be the correct decision as George succeeded in capturing the fugitive. Historian Lucius Frederick Hubbard describes the capture:

> "The chief agent in running down the murder was George Bonga, the mixed-blood Indian and negro, sub-trader under Aitkin. He followed him day and night for the entire six days, in bitter sub-zero temperatures before catching the murderer and his brothers on Jan. 20th, 1837. William L. Quinn says Bonga's unrelenting pursuit was long a matter of comment in early days...The murderer was lashed to a dogsled, which was pulled by three dogs and taken to Fort Snelling [the party arrived at Fort Snelling on February 20th, 1837]. William L. Quinn, then a lad of nine years, remembers that when the party reached the Fort the Indian had a perfect network of ropes and cords about him..."[17]

When the determined tracker caught up with the fleeing Indian and his brothers, *Ghe-ga-wa-skung* was too weak to stand, his feet were frozen, and he had to be carried by his brothers. Bonga's dogged pursuit became a major news event in the region and became a legend in the territory during this period. Big George would make sure there would be no second escape by tying the fugitive in a "perfect network of ropes and cords about him..."[18]

No records exist of the events indicating where and how Bonga pursued the accused murderer. But living and spending so much time in the same locations where these events unfolded have caused me to often theorize as to what was the escape route taken by *Ghe-ga-wa-skung* and his brothers had taken.

Considering the route taken by the original posse (before the escape) to get from Upper Red Cedar Lake to Leech Lake, the shortest, easiest, and quickest way was by the ancient route commonly used by Native Americans for centuries which today is called the Pike Bay Connection. It is the route that Leech Lakers traditionally used in travel from Leech to Upper Red Cedar in 1805. This was and has remained the favored route between Leech Lake and Upper Red Cedar for those who travel year-round between the two great lakes.

After leaving Star Island, the posse with their captive would have crossed Upper Red Cedar Lake by dog sled in a direct southern course, through the channel that connects Upper Red Cedar Lake to Lower Red Cedar, now known as Pike Bay. At the south end of the lake, they would have crossed two short portages through Ten Section Lake into Upper Moss Lake where a long portage at the south end of Moss Lake would take them into Little Portage Lake. At the west end of this small lake is Portage Creek that flows south into the Steamboat River which flows south into Steamboat Bay on the northwest corner of Leech Lake.

Turtle River Lake

Turtle R.

Big Rice Lake

Big Lake

Kitchi Lake

Kenogama Lake

American Fur Co. Post

Andrusia Lake

Sugar Lake

Mississippi R.

Lake Winnibigoshih

Star Island

Cass Lake

Wolf Lake

Cass Lake ▫

Pike Bay

Sucker Lakes

Portage Lake

Sixmile Lake

Moss Lake

Pike Bay Connection Portage

Lake Thirteen

Steamboat Lake

Portage Lake

Leech Lake R.

Crooked Lake

Sucker Bay

Swamp Lake

Back Bay

Boy River

Leech Lake

Trader Bay

Boy Bay

Walker Bay

Oak Lake

Townline Lake

0   5 miles

Tenmile Lake

The long portage connecting Moss and Little Portage was described by Schoolcraft in his 1832 journal:

> "The portage from Pike's Bay, (where we arrived at twelve o'clock in the morning, after a two hour's journey from the island [Star Island]) commences on the edge of an open pine forest, interspersed with shrub oak. The path is deeply worn, and looks as if it might have been used by Indians, for centuries... Markings and hieroglyphic characters were pointed out to us on the pines, some of which were said to be so ancient as to have been made by the people who occupied the country before the Ojibwais. Of the truth of this assertion there did not appear to be any means of judging. A blaze on pinus resinosa [red pine], if made upon a matured tree, may be considered as comparatively permanent, from the fact that the outer bark is not apt to close over it, while the gum that exudes over the wounded surface has some of the properties of a varnish. How long the rude drawings of birds and animals made with charcoal would thus be preserved is a mere matter of conjecture, and must depend upon observations which we had no means of making."[19]

It would be safe to assume both the fugitive and the trackers were on *aagimag* (snowshoes) unless the fugitives escape was so hastily accomplished as to not be outfitted with snowshoes or the snow was not deep enough to require them.

As it was, once on the vastness of Leech Lake, where the escape occurred, I would suspect the most likely and logical direction they fled would be west. I doubt they went east as they would be more likely seen on the big open lake and south would be less plausible as it would probably be taking them into less well-known territory making travel more questionable. Going north would be taking them towards Upper Red Cedar Lake where they had come from. So having thought about this escape route, I would conjecture they went west. Going west would get them off the big lake faster. I would suspect they traveled on frozen river surfaces; perhaps the Kabekona River which enters Leech at Kabekona Bay which would take them westerly via river and lake ice to the Gulch region; an area of rugged terminal moraines. From these moraines, they may have gotten on the Schoolcraft River or upper portions of the Mississippi, or they may have gone up *Kabak Saghidawag* (Steamboat Lake) into the Necktie River which by traveling westerly and upstream, the river turns to the north where they could reach *Bemijigamaag* (Lake Bemidji) and the Mississippi River. Either way the travel over land and frozen water surfaces by snowshoes in bitter subzero temperatures, the distance covered in six days and six nights would be substantial. The land being covered by a blanket of snow would have made tracking easy unless a stiff wind came up erasing their tracks from the trail. I doubt if the tracks would have been covered by falling snow as it was told that it was bitterly cold; it rarely snows in such cold weather.

Another possible route and one, like the previous two was often used by Leech Lakers, would be to depart Leech Lake on the west shores near where the town of Walker exists today. Here there are a chain of small lakes, creeks and portages that would get them into what Schoolcraft called "The Long Lake" or the "Eleventh Lake" in his journals. This lake today is "Eleventh Crow Wing" and is the

source of the Crow Wing River. However, it would be unlikely that they had any intentions to travel this route as it
gave them two options: down the Mississippi to the central
and southern region of the future state or west to the White
Earth area; both of which would be too near the territory
of the Dakota.

I have also considered the possibility that the fugitives
fled east across the widest open body of Leech Lake towards Bear Island or the Boy River on the far eastern shore
but this causes me to believe the formation of dangerous
and difficult pressure ridges that form on the lake would
discourage them from doing so under the circumstances.

Another possible escape route would be to the south of
Walker or Shingobee Bay. Here they would pick up the Old
Crow Wing Trail that was then a primitive foot trail. From
that point they could travel towards the Pine River where
they would find aid with the Mississippi Pillagers.

Living here and being familiar with the land and weather conditions in winter, it is easy to visualize the scene as
Bonga made his way through the *Le Beau Pays* (the beautiful land). He would have seen the ancient white and red
pines lining stretches of the river valleys, their boughs
covered with a hoar frost in the mornings, water vapor
rising from an opening in the ice on the river where the
current wore through, the starkness of the naked limbs of
tamaracks devoid of their needles or the densely foliated
white cedars. Likely, he would have followed the *Miikana
Ma'iingan,* (the trail of wolves) on the river ice directing him
away from thin ice and he may have interrupted a moose
browsing on shoreline cedars. If the night was moonlit,
he may have traveled all night under or if a new moon he
would be under the milky-way or the northern lights, but
wherever the tracking took place, he was on land that he
knew well.

Bonga

Whether George Bonga was alone or had travel companions is uncertain, but George was thirty-four years old then and knew the lay of the land as well as anyone. In fact, George and his brother Stephen both stated that they had been to the Headwaters before Schoolcraft. I believe George's knowledge of the land and his intimacy with the Anishinaabeg likely gave him a good guess at where the fugitives would go and very well may have anticipated their selected route and destination and got ahead of them by a different route, cutting them off to intercept them. I assume that when George finally caught up with *Ghe-ga-wa-skung* and his brothers, they were so worn down and cold that they were ready to give up and be done with the ordeal.[20]

Being well acquainted with the land and its bitter cold winters leaves me in awe of the dogged pursuit made by George Bonga. No wonder the story of Alfred Aitkin's murder and subsequent circumstances catapulted George Bonga into fame and attention in the young territory of what would become Minnesota.

Minnesota's First Criminal Trial

When *Che-ga-wa-skung* was turned over to authorities at Fort Snelling, they were told that the trial would not be held until the following May in Prairie du Chien, Wisconsin. That's because, as the county seat of Crawford County, Prairie du Chien had the nearest courthouse within the jurisdiction of the territory.

In a letter nearly two months after the murder, William Aitkin wrote from Sandy Lake to Henry Schoolcraft in Sault Ste. Marie, now Indian agent overseeing the region. Being two months after the murder of Alfred, William Aitkin's thoughts are presumably more objective in recalling the events.

Barry Babcock

"Since I left you at St. Peter's I have had a
severe trial to go through. I came up by Swan
River, but heard nothing there of the melan-
choly event which had taken place during my
absence at Upper Red Cedar Lake. My eldest
son had been placed at that place last fall,
in charge of that post. You saw him I believe,
last summer; he was in charge of Leech Lake
when you were at that place. He was a young
man of twenty-two years of age, of very amia-
ble temper, humane and brave, possessed of
the most unbounded obedience to my will, and
of the most filial affection for my person. This,
my son, was murdered in the most atrocious
manner by a bloody monster of an Indian. My
poor boy had arrived the evening previous to the
bloody act, from a voyage to Red Lake. Early the
next morning he sent off all the men he had to
Lake Winnipeck, excepting one Frenchman, to
bring up some things which he had left there
in the fall. A short time after his men had gone,
he sent the remaining man to bring some water
from the river; the man returned into the house
immediately, and told him that an Indian had
broken open the store, and was in it. He went
very deliberately to the store, took hold of the
villain, who tried to strike him with his tomahawk, dragged him out of the store and disarmed him of his axe, threw him on the ground,
and then let him go – and was turned round
in the act of locking the store-door. The villain
stepped behind the door, where he had hid
his gun, came on him unawares and shot him
dead, without the least previous provocation

whatever on the part of my poor lost boy. When arrived, I found the feelings of every one prepared for vengeance. I immediately, without one moment's loss of time, proceeded to Leech Lake. In a moment there were twenty half-breeds gathered round, with Francis Brunette at their head, full-armed, ready to execute any commands that I should give them. We went immediately to the camp where the villain was beyond Red Cedar Lake, determined to cut off the whole band if they should raise a finger in his defence. Our mutual friend, Mr. Boutwell, joined the party, with his musket on his shoulder, as a man and a Christian, for he knew it was a righteous cause, and that the arm of God was with him. We arrived on the wretches unawares, disarmed the band, and dragged the monster from his lodge. I would have put the villain to death in the midst of his relations, but Mr. Boutwell advised it would be better to take him where he might be made an example of. The monster escaped from us two days after we had taken him, but my half-breeds pursued him for six days and brought him back, and he is now on his way to St. Peter's in irons, under a strong guard. My dear friend, I cannot express to you the anguish of my heart at this present moment."[21]

One month earlier, Aitkin made the following statements in a letter to Henry Hastings Sibley:

"I have got the monster into my hands, and it is only the power of an Almighty God which

has withheld me from cutting him into pieces...
As soon as I can get him safely on his way to
St. Peter's that he may be confined safety until
he is brought to trial, I will go in pursuit of
the other monster, and I will have him dead or
alive. I will show these Indians that they cannot
murder us with impunity.

They are generally disaffected to our
Government, and they say that the Government
are afraid of them; or otherwise they would not
have not made so any promises to them and
told so many lies. If the Government do not
take it in hand immediately and stop these high
pretensions of the Indians, they will eventually
have to make war upon them.

During my absence at Leech Lake, they used
our people very ill. They did not murder them,
but that was all; they compelled them to give
them all the goods they had on credit – never to
be paid – and if they had disconcerted all their
plans; for neither ammunition one load, nor
tobacco one pipe, shall they have from me until
I have ample satisfaction for all their outrageous
conduct since last fall."[22]

Aitkin's statement is erroneous in many ways. There
is no mention anywhere in the written record or in oral
history of an accomplice. There is mention of his brothers
aiding him in the escape but they were not implicated in
the murder. Aitkin mentions that "only the power of an
Almighty God" prevented him from cutting the murderer
into pieces is also incorrect. Aitkin stated in his letter to
Henry Schoolcraft; "I would have put the villain to death in
the midst of his relations, but Mr. Boutwell advised it would

be better to take him where he might be made an example of." And the statement that, "the whole country has been in a very unsettled state" and was nearing a state of war must be taken as one side of the story. The Ojibwe of Minnesota had never made war upon the whites and their record of violence against the Americans is almost completely absent. During the war of 1812, the British sought the aid of Flatmouth in waging war on the Americans. Presents and wampum belts were presented to *Esh-ke-bug-e-koshe* in enlisting his warriors to fight the Great Knives. The chief sent back the gifts with the blunt reply, "When I go war against my enemies, I do not call on the whites to join my warriors. The white people have quarreled amongst themselves, and I do not wish to meddle in their quarrels, nor do I intend ever, even to be guilty of breaking the window glass of a white man's dwelling."[23]

Aitkin's rants of payments due, extended credit and "never to be paid" are gross mischaracterizations of the fur trade. In fact, the reverse is true.

The other side of this story is that the fur trade often exploited the Indian for monetary gain. Huge interest rates were applied to goods received and, in many respects, Native people became indentured servants. We must remember that the Leech Lake Band of Ojibwe were not a docile band of Indians cow-towing to white traders, but had the reputation as a proud and independent people not yet tainted by the material needs and trading practices of the whites. They were not a people who would be pushed around. But it is easy to understand the grief and sorrow of Aitkin and this may account for his state of mind. He did shut down trade and did have the authority to consolidate his trading regime. But when considering written history as it regards the Indians, we must always remember that, as stated by Yellow Wolf of the Nez Perce, "...only his best deeds, only the worst deeds of the Indians, has the white man told."

The trial became a long, drawn-out process and the stunning decision was not rendered until 1838 when *Ghe-ga-wa-skung* was set free. Such a decision was rendered due to the fact that Alfred, although a mixed-blood, was viewed by the court as an Indian. The fact that he was seen as an Indian and that *Ghe-ga-wa-skung* was an Indian, the jury erroneously believed the court had no jurisdiction. If Alfred Aitkin was a full-blooded white, *Ghe-ga-wa-skung* would have been found guilty. In other words, the court held no jurisdiction over an Indian who committed a crime against another Indian and that is what the jury saw: Alfred as an Indian.[24] In a letter from Thomas Pendleton Burnett, the District Attorney, who prosecuted *Che-ga-wa-skung*, to William Aitkin, Burnett explained the facts and result of the trial:

> "The trial of the Chippewa Indian at this place, ended on Friday last; and you will be disappointed in learning that he was acquitted. The facts of his guilt were all satisfactorily established, although we were unable to introduce the black halfbreed as a witness on account of his ignorance of the obligation of an oath and a state of [?] existence. The point upon which the verdict of the jury was given was, as I understand, whether the deceased was an Indian or a white man. The law of Congress extending the laws of the United States in criminal cases over Indian Country excepts offenses committed by one Indian, against the person or property of another Indian. The judge decided that the first rule of law was that the character and name of children followed that of the mother; but that

rule was superseded by another – upon proof of marriage and legitimacy, upon which proof the law would give to the children the character and condition of the father; and to do this it was not necessary to prove an actual marriage by certificate and the production of a license, etc., but the fact might be established by general reputation in the country and by the acknowledgment of the parents, etc.

It was proven upon the trial that the parents of the deceased were generally reputed, where they were known, to be husband and wife, that the deceased was acknowledged by them to be their legitimate child, and that he was brought up and educated as a white man and pursued the business and habits of white men. According to the repeated instructions of the courts, this gave him the character and rights of a white man, yet the jury decided that he was not such. Both the law and the evidence were against the decision.

The Indian [Ghe ga wa skung] since his discharge has gone down to Du Buque. He says that he is afraid to return to his own country. He states that he is not afraid of the Indians but of you; that you have said that if he should ever return you would kill him. I have heard it spoken of here that you or some of your family would undertake to avenge the death of your son and the assertion made that if you should do so, every legal step would be taken to have you prosecuted. I have stated that I do not believe you would do anything of the kind and

I would advise you as counsel and friend to let
the matter rest. You have appealed to the legal
authorities, and however erroneous the decision
may have been, the public voice will say that
all ought to abide by it. A contrary course may
create for yourself great difficulties and trouble
without any corresponding benefit.

I made every exertion in the management of
the case of which I was capable in which I was
greatly advised by your brother who was present. I believe that he is satisfied that nothing
was left undone by the counsel for the prose-
cution. He will probably write to you more fully
upon the subject. I am very respectfully your
friend. T. P. Burnett"[25]

Back at Leech Lake, while the trial was in progress,
many Leech Lake Ojibwe with loyalties to *Ghe-ga-wa-skung*
were angered over the case. They had threatened Boutwell
and other missionaries. *Ghe-ga-wa-skung's* family and
friends had threatened George Bonga. In a letter to Rev.
Boutwell, George Bonga related the tense situation in
Headwaters Country: "Another thing, Sir, I must notify you
of the talk of some of the Indians here. It is they who say
if Ghe-ga-wa-skung is hung, they will set fire to my stores
and break my canoes. For my part I don't think they are
really in earnest in these words."[26]

The precedents of the jury verdict in *Ghe-ga-wa-skung's*
trial were broad and far reaching. As reported in *Minnesota
in Three Centuries,* it "was the first criminal case for an
offense committed in what is now Minnesota. It was also,
the first murder case under the code of Wisconsin territory.
The precedent of his acquittal, when he was clearly guilty
within the law, was a bad one, since it has frequently been

followed in similar cases, to the great outrage of justice."[27]

Another significant fact of this 1838 trial was that it was held twelve years before Minnesota became a territory and twenty-one years before it would become a state.

How remarkable, too, that George Bonga's key role in apprehending the killer was far from the end of George in this story as his involvement would continue to reach a higher level of importance that would eventually impact the United States Government and their access to the vast regions of virgin pine forests.

Impacts of the Case

Looming over these historical precedents was the impact this decision threatened to have with the mixed-bloods in the territory that was soon to become Minnesota. Before considering the threat to the mixed-blood population, one may wish to consider the words of the historian William Whipple Warren who wrote in 1852, "Of French and American extraction, the Ojibways number about five thousand persons of mixed-blood, who scatter throughout Canada, Michigan, Wisconsin, Minnesota, and the British possessions. Many of the Ojibway mixed-bloods are men of good education and high standing within their respective communities." The implications of *Ghe-ga-wa-skung's* court decision to the mixed-blood population of Minnesota were many: Were they still seen by the government as citizens? Could they vote? What were their rights? Were their children citizens? All the existing rights as citizens of the United States they thought they had were now in question. The jury's verdict set the mixed-bloods into turmoil. Besides their threats to avenge the murder of young Alfred Aitkin, the mixed-bloods threatened to use their influence to dispute or disrupt the Treaty of 1837, which was being negotiated as the trial took place.

In this very important treaty, the Ojibwe of Minnesota and Wisconsin ceded a large portion of east central Minnesota and a larger portion of central Wisconsin to the whites. It was the first major land acquisition treaty in the region that would become Minnesota and set a precedent for subsequent treaties as the Ojibwe chiefs negotiating insisted on retaining all their rights to hunt, fish and gather on all ceded lands. They also stressed that land and waters on these ceded lands must be protected from pollution not only for their sustenance but for their culture as it was the land that gave definition of who they are as a people. The intent of the whites in having this treaty was for access to the great stands of immense virgin white pines that were in Indian Country. In fact, many called the 1837 treaty the "White Pine Treaty" as the timber harvested here was used to build the great cities of Chicago, St. Louis and more.

The disgruntled condition among the mixed-bloods and their threats towards *Ghe-ga-wa-skung* gained the attention and concern of the government. In a letter sent to the Commissioner of Indian Affairs T. Hartley Crawford, Wisconsin Territorial Governor Henry Dodge stated:

"I enclose to your Department in October last a talk of the half-breed Chippewas held at Lapointe last season. On that occasion they complained that the Indian who murdered young Aitken, a half-breed Chippewa, had been acquitted by the U.S. District Court, upon the grounds that his mother was an Indian woman, and that the half breeds, in a legal point of view, were placed upon the same footing that one Indian would be for killing another. Satisfactory explanations should be made them on that subject. The half-breeds always exercise a

great degree of influence over the minds of the
Indians, and I consider them as a connecting
link between the whites and the Indians; and,
should they instigate the Indians to mischief on
that exposed frontier, it might be attended with
the most fatal consequences to our settlements
on that remote border."[28]

The mixed-blood people from Leech Lake had gotten
the attention of the United States Government.

The government's reaction to the overt intentions of the
mixed-bloods, who wanted revenge for the murder of young
Alfred, was to threaten them by withholding the payment
of $100,000, known as the "Half-breed script," due them
from the Treaty of 1837. In a letter dated July 16, 1839,
former U.S. Senator to Michigan, Lucius Lyon, who was
now commissioned to distribute the money to Chippewa
half-breeds under the Treaty of 1837, wrote the following to
Commissioner Crawford:

"Sir, In my letter of yesterday I promised to
write to you in relation to the murder of Alfred
Aitken. I have had several conversations with
persons well acquainted with the half-breed
Indians with whom I am commissioned to treat;
and I much fear that I cannot prevent them
from carrying their threat of revenging the
murder of Alfred Aitken into effect by threaten-
ing to withhold from them the payment of the
money due by the United States as is intimated
to me in my instructions.

They are a proud, sensitive people who are
anxious to be recognized by the Government
as citizens of the United States and to receive

protection from its laws. This they evinced by delivering up the murderer of Alfred Aitken to the civil authorities instead of punishing him according to Indian customs by taking his life themselves. Having failed (as they suppose) in receiving justice from that source. I very much fear an attempt on my part to make the payment of the $100,000 conditional upon their relinquishment of the design to revenge the murder of one of their friends would only tend to exasperate them, and precipitate the commission of the very act which it is part of my mission to prevent.

As it is a matter of deep interest with the Government to retain the good feelings of these Indians; and to prevent them from resorting to the act of violence which they meditate at present, I would, suggest as the only probable means by which this may be accomplished, that I be authorized to engage the services of Col H. A. Levake [Henry Levake was a long time resident of Sault Ste. Marie and was politically active and served as a constable and justice of peace during Michigan's territorial period] to use his influence with them. He commands a regiment of half-breeds...and has more influence then any other person I know of, with the half-breeds that I am commissioned to treat with in this matter. His services may be secured for $5. or $6. per day and when the results to be accomplished are of such great importance I feel confident that I will be justified in using such means as will in my best judgment tend to its attainment.

Bonga

As the appropriations for carrying into effect
the stipulations of the treaty under which I am
acting is small [,] I fear it will not be sufficient
for this unforeseen additional expense. But if
there is any other appropriation out of which it
could be defrayed I deem it very important that
the services of Col. Levake be secured.

Very respectfully Yrs. &c
Lucius Lyon[29]

With the questions of mixed-blood citizenship, treaty rights, and withholding treaty annuities unanswered, the mixed-bloods from the Leech Lake region pulled together. I believe it was George Bonga who acted as composer and scribe for the brilliant correspondence to the government representatives. I have read many of the letters George wrote throughout his life and the following letter from the mixed-bloods to Sub-Indian agent D.P. Bushnell smacks of George's style and spelling. There are six names of mixed-bloods having signed the letter including George Bonga. Because George was sent to Montreal by his Father to get an education, could speak English, French, and Ojibwe fluently, he proved to be a prolific letter writer in the style of his day. It may be possible that one or more of the signees were also literate, but it is unlikely that any were superior to George in literary skills and they would have wanted George to undertake this important task as spokesperson.

It is easy to visualize George putting pen to paper as the principal mixed-bloods were present and advising George as he spelled out his and their concerns. It is here that we see the intelligence and understanding of justice, equality, and rights that these mix-bloods assumed they had but were in limbo. It also becomes evident that this gigantic figure of a man had a firm grasp of the meaning of freedom and what this trial could have on him and his people's rights.

"Lapointe July 24th 1839

D.P. Bushnell Esqr Sub-Indian Agent, Sir The undersigned appointed at a council of the Half Breeds, held on the 21st day of July inst for the purpose taking into consideration the matter of your Adress to us on the 20th with the approbation of all the half Breeds of the Chippewa Nation here assembled submit to you the following reply with the request that you will forward it to the authorities under which you act.

The result of our Appeal to the Government of the United States for the protection & redress has not surprised us – though under all the Circumstances of the case we had some right to Expect a different issue – The position which that address has assigned us is truly anamalous, and judging from the past, entirely consistent with the genius and policy of the Government towards the unprotected – Were we acquainted with our true position, we should then have no hesitation in the course we pursued – But of this relation we are ignorant[.] Government at one time affixing to us a position which at another it would deny, being governed it would seem by its own interest or Conveniency, with the Semblance of Justice or reason; We are regarded as Indians or white men, to suit the exigencies of the Case. These being the facts, then, can it be a matter of wonder that we have taken the course, and asked the redress we have in a matter which at once involves our liberty our property and our lives? That our situation is one of doubt and anxiety will not be denied – At one time we have the decision of a "Competent tribunal" giving to us the privileges and immunities of free White Citizens of the United States – the right of Suffrage, as instances in the decision of the House of Representatives in the contest for the delegate's seat from the Territory of Michigan in 1828 – which right has never been extended to the Indian tribes – At another time we have the decision of a "Competent Tribunal" "That Half Breeds are Indians and Consequently come within the perview of the Act of Congress, which declares that the Jurisdiction of the United States shall not extend to crimes committed by one Indian against the person or property of an other Indian in the Indian Country, as instanced in the decision of Judge Dunn in the case which has given rise to our dissatisfaction – And again – but a short time after this decision, a half Breed one of our number was removed from this part of the Country for an alleged violation of the Laws of the United States!! Is this consistency? It may be policy, but not Justice – It is told us that the decision of Judge Dunn must be considered as the Law – Is not the decision of the House of Representatives alluded to Equally the Law? If so we know not to what Subterfuge our self willed guardians will resort to reconcile the variance – or whether in the pride of their might they will deign to bestow upon us any other than the language of menace

Your offer of pecuniary satisfaction or the life
of a valued friend, to be wrung from the scanty
pittance of the poor Indian we reject – The Band
to which the Murderer belongs is not Entitled
to any part of the annuity; and therefore we
cannot consent to or abett in the Commission
of so great an act of injustice, as your proposition would suggest. The proposition itself shows
our character & motives have been Entirely
Misunderstood.

The menace contained in your address that the
$100,000 due us would be withheld until this
difficulty is peaceably adjusted, did it Effect
the undersigned alone would have little weight
to deter us from our purpose though we know
full well from the experience of the past that
it would be carried into Execution – From the
sense of Justice, or good faith of our Self-Styled
Guardians we Expect nothing. Every act of
theirs towards this Tribe of Indians and indeed
towards every other tribe has been marked by
injustice & bad faith – The $100,000 which we
now claim as right, has already been withheld
from us one year under some trifling pretext.
The damage to us by this delay has been great,
and if paid this year will barely Compensate the
recipients for the time and money Expended in
being twice Compelled to travel a great distance
to receive it.

However as in the interest of the greater part
of the tribe are involved we have Concluded in
Consequence to give you the pledge you require,
and we do accordingly promise to bury the

hatchet – and that none of us will seek the life of Aitken's murderer. This pledge will be rigidly adhered to.

This Sir, is our answer and is we have manifested an improper degree of warmth, it cannot be denied that we have ample cause Permit us in Conclusion however to disclaim any intention to give offence to yourself personally. And to express the high sentiments of respect and Esteem which your deportment to ourselves and the other Indians, since you have been among us, merits Very Respectfully your Obdt Servants—

Joseph Muchard
Michal Cadott[e]
George Bongar [Bonga]
Vincent Le Roy Jr [Roy]
Joseph Gauthier
Francis Brunts [Brunette][30]

Note George Bonga's name as one of the "half-breed" appellants at the bottom of the letter.

As for *Ghe-ga-wa-skung*, he was set free and never returned to northern Minnesota for fear of being killed by Aitkin or the mixed-blood people and lived out the remainder of his life in Dubuque, Iowa.

Final Thoughts

The murder of Alfred Aitkin, the trial of *Ghe-ga-wa-skung*, the role of George Bonga, and the repercussions of the trial were a major news item not only in the region but the nation. These events apparently have been forgotten, ignored due to race, or have simply fallen through the cracks of history. It is difficult for us to relate to the impact this murder, the subsequent trial, and the potential effects on the 1837 Treaty had not only the mixed-blood population but on the entire general population of the young territory that was to become Minnesota. "There were, in fact, probably five times as many Indians as whites in the territory in 1849." And in the 1850 census, "People of mixed Indian and white parentage may have accounted for as much as a third or even half of the territory's 1850 population..."[31] These population numbers from 1849 and 1850 can be somewhat misleading in trying to grasp the much higher ratio of Indians and mixed-bloods to whites in 1836. The non-white population in the late thirties would be much more significant than they were in 1850.

In examining the events, verdict of the trial, and the attention paid to the outrage and protestations by the mixed-blood people in the territory, the final outcome reinforced their status as franchised citizens. Whether this was due to the threats of mixed-bloods looming over treaties, their reputed influence with tribes, or threatened acts of revenge, can only be speculated, but the evidence seems to say that the outrage over the jury verdict swung things in favor of the mixed-blood people. They were seen by the government as having too much clout to ignore.

The murder of Alfred Aitkin and the verdict of the jury was an event of paramount importance to the liberties of a huge block of the population in what was to become Minnesota. The mixed-blood people, with George Bonga apparently standing foremost among the leaders, made waves that were felt at the highest levels of state and territorial government. The results were that the verdict was ostensibly ignored, at least as it applied to the rights of mixed-blood people in the territory. The scenario of events shows that this man, George Bonga, a Black/Ojibwe, was a man of influence, commitment, respect, and principle and found himself in the vortex of this historical event in a time when many in the rest of the country were slave holders or legitimized slavery.

Understanding the prominence of George Bonga in this specific occurrence one must ask, why do we not know more about this man and his family? The remainder of this book will do its best to put the Bongas back into their deserved and proper place in history and the first place to start is with Jean, the Black slave.

Bongo from the Congo

Jean Bonga

The true origin of the Bonga family begins in Africa with Jean whose story most likely began in the mid-seventeen-fifties when a free, independent black man was swept up in the slave trade. The means by which his freedom was taken from him can only be speculated. Hints of what was his ancestral home may have clues in what is behind the name, "Bonga."

One historian, Carl Zappfe, suggests that the name Bonga is derived from a tribe by that name in Eastern Sudan. Zappfe also notes a variation of the spelling "bongo" is Spanish for a native dugout or canoe, and also cites Bongo in reference to several large antelope in Africa. The spelling "bonga," in the Tagalong language of the Philippine Islands, is the betel palm or nut.[32]

My research has shown that there is a province or town named Bonga Camp in eastern Ethiopia, near the town Gambella where Sudanese refugees found sanctuary during the recent civil war in Sudan.

I have heard the Ojibwe of the Leech Lake Reservation in northern Minnesota say "Bongo of the Congo." This may be a more plausible explanation as there is a substantial group of people called Bonga in the Congo. Of Congo's current population of over four million people, most are of the group Bantu, a name that refers to people living in Central, Eastern, and Southern Africa. The Bantu originated from Nigeria and Cameroon and migrated to Southern Africa about two thousand years ago. In present day Congo, non-Bantu tribes account for only three percent of the population. The Bantu comprise many different ethnic groups such as the Kongo, Teke, Sangha, and the Mbochi. The Mbochi includes the sub-groups; Kouyou, Makoua, Bobangi, Moye, Ngare, Mboko, and Bonga. These people are noted to live along navigable rivers such as the Kouyou, Alima, Sangha, and Likouala that are teeming with fish. They raise poultry, sheep, goats, and catch fish in the rivers. They are also well known for being farmers who grow coffee, cocoa, tobacco, and rice.[33]

The man who became Jean Bonga was most likely living in Congo when his life as a free man ended dramatically, in what I believe to have been in the 1750s, and became the worst possible nightmare imaginable. I believe the only thing he brought with him across the Atlantic, and that he clung to so dearly, was the name of his home and people: "Bonga."

The Bonga history begins in Africa. However, for the Bongas in North America, it begins in the early 1780s where the Straits of Mackinac connect Lake Michigan to Lake Huron. Mackinac, then known as Michilimackinac, was of vital importance to the burgeoning fur trade and to Native Americans because of its location. Mackinac was an important depot that provided provisions to fuel the stomachs of the voyageurs who were the muscle of the fur brigades.

The name Michilimackinac refers to the island on which Fort Mackinac was re-constructed shortly after the attack on British troops at its former site on the south side of the Straits of Mackinac. There, approximately seventy British soldiers were killed by Ojibwe using a lacrosse game as a ploy to gain entry into the walled fort during Pontiac's Uprising in 1763. The name itself is probably a corrupted pronunciation and spelling of the Ottawa and Ojibwe word for "Great Turtle" due to the shape of the island. The name references the snapping turtle or "*Mikinaak*" who is one of the Seven Grandfathers and represents "truth." The turtle has profound importance in Ojibwe culture and spiritual beliefs as he is Turtle Island/North America, the ancestral home of the Anishinaabe.

As Mackinac is important for supply and entry to Lake Michigan, Sault Ste. Marie is equally important as an entry point to Lake Superior and an important fishery for Native Americans. Both sites were also important for their strategic military locations that were vital to the British and the expansion of white America.

Sault Ste. Marie is historically and spiritually important to the Anishinaabe Ojibwe. During their westward migration, the Ojibwe arrived at the area about the Sault or 'rapids' of the Saint Mary's River which had been foretold as the "fifth stopping place" of the Seven Fires Prophecy of the Anishinaabe Ojibwe. The prophesy, told centuries ago by Ojibwe spiritual leaders, warned of a light-skinned race coming and advised that many of the Anishinaabe people start a westward migration in case the light-skinned people were coming with bad intentions. At this spot, the Ojibwe and the rapids became synonymous with each other. It was at this time that the Ojibwe became known to the French as the *Saulteurs* (cascaders) and *Saulteaux* (cascades) and to the Dakota people as *Iyo-hahantonwan* (cascading water people).

It was at the Rapids of the Saint Mary's River that the Ojibwe found an abundant supply of whitefish—*adikameg*—which became very important, both culturally and as a food source to their people. The flavor and delicacy of the Lake Superior whitefish, netted at Saint Mary's River, is said to be unrivaled.

Bonga

Though Jean Bonga ended up at Michilimackinac, where this enslaved man who would become Bonga first came to be in North America is up for speculation. Historians do not have much information concerning Bonga's first home in the new world. The written history of this man is scant at best. George Bonga, the Grandson of Jean, wrote in 1872:

> "I have always been sorry, that I did not ask
> my father while living, if he knew where he
> immigrate from. I am now inclined to think,
> that they must have come, from the new State
> of Missouri, as he did not Speak anything but
> french. I presume at that time, Very few in-
> habited that out Skirts State, Iowa, Illinois &
> Michigan except those connected with the fur
> trade...My grand father [Jean] & family of 5 or
> 6 children, might have been taken Prisoners
> by the Ind.s & sold to the Indn traders. That is
> the only way I can guess at it. I understood my
> father to say, that all his father's family came
> to Mackinac, this I am certain of, for I had one
> Uncle & 2 Aunts, who went to Montreal with the
> Ind traders."[34]

From George's words, it appears that those early years in his Grandfather's history were not passed down in any detail nor does there appear to be much family interest of their Grandfather's origins. Stephen Bonga, George's older brother, in an essay titled, *Head of the Lake*, referring to his Grandfather or Father states, "when a mere child, he had been taken captive from his southern home by a band of marauding Indians, who afterward sold him to the Chippewas." Stephen may be confusing his Grandfather and Father.

Barry Babcock

There have been a number of interesting anecdotes about Jean Bonga's origins; some noteworthy and others simply wrong. One historian in trying to fill the holes in our knowledge of Bonga's past has an interesting hypothesis involving the aristocratic French Dandonneau family, also known as "Au Sable" or "Point au Sable," who owned and operated a French plantation on Martinique, an island of the Lesser Antilles in the Caribbean Sea. It is here that this historian believes Jean Bonga made his first stay in the New World.

Au Sable is French for 'sand' or 'sandy'. The French master, Dandonneau, gave the new slave the name "Jean Baptiste Point au Sable" or "Jean-Baptiste of Sandy Point" and here, Jean learned French. The supposition is made that Dandonneau so liked "Jean Baptiste" that a marriage was arranged with a favorite female slave named Jeanne. At or around 1776, these two had a son named Pierre and as a result of the naval engagements between the English and French during the American Revolution, Jean and family were apparently set free on the mainland to find their own way. The first thing they did was to get out of the slave belt and find their way to a settlement in Missouri. The presumption is that the Bongas' origins have them leaving Missouri in 1779 and settling at the bottom of Lake Michigan and opening a trading post where Chicago would later arise. At this time, Jean changed the family's name from Au Sable to Bonga. This was around the time of the Treaty of Paris in 1783 which left unclear who was to control Fort Mackinac and the island of its location. In 1782, the English put a new commandant in charge of Mackinac by the name of Col. Daniel Robertson. At about this time the Bongas were declared escaped slaves and were taken and sold to Col. Robertson whereby Mackinac became their home.[35]

Bonga

Another study finds that the Jean Baptiste Pointe du Sable is an entirely different man from Jean Bonga who as a slave was owned by Col. Robertson. There are indeed interesting and fascinating similarities, such as they were both former slaves, had similar names, spoke French, found in the same parts of the country, said to be large, strong, and good looking, but the dates and other evidence in these two accounts do not agree. In an essay by Thomas A. Meehan, entitled "Jean Baptiste Point du Sable, The First Chicagoan," he discusses several different possibilities of who this man really is. Meehan notes that until 1933, it was generally accepted that Point du Sable was a free Santo Domingo (now Dominican Republic) black or mulatto. Meehan cites the historian Milo Milton Quaife who makes the supposition that du Sable was not a Santo Domingan but a base-born descendant of the famous Dandonneau family, originally from Bourges, France. Soon after 1627 Jacques Dandonneau, together with his wife Isabella and their son, Pierre, migrated to Three Rivers and later to Champlain in Canada. This son, Pierre, acquired the title "Sieur du Sable." His descendants became known by both names, Dandonneau and Du Sable. In the course of time the family spread to Montreal, Mackinac, and St. Joseph, and many of its members were engaged in the fur trade. Quaife concludes that "Jean Baptiste Point du Sable was the offspring of a Negro woman and one of the numerous male descendants of Angelique du Sable (wife of Charles Chaboillez and, after his death, Ignace Jean), many of whom were involved in the fur trade." As both Meehan and Quaife point out, this is a mere "supposition" and until something concrete comes up, this theory does not outweigh the belief that Du Sable came from Santo Domingo.[36]

Meehan makes an interesting point regarding language, culture, origin, and other possibilities which applies to both Point du Sable and to Jean Bonga:

"...By the Treaty of Ryswick in 1697 the Spanish ceded the western part of Haiti to the French, who had come there as early as 1638 and had had definite settlements since 1659. Negroes had been imported into Haiti and Santo Domingo [Spanish east Haiti] since the year 1517, and mixed-bloods were common. Under the French regime many of the Negroes were cultured, well-educated and became landowners of wealth. Many of them, because of the kind treatment of the French, migrated to Louisiana and thence up the Mississippi to various other French possessions."[37]

When reading about Jean Baptiste, a man who seems so gifted and talented, one hopes that the dates and records correspond to Jean Bonga, but unfortunately, that is not the case. What we do know is that Baptiste was born before 1750 and died in 1818. In 1779 he fled his home on the site which would become Chicago to Michigan City, Indiana where he was arrested by the British for being a spy and American sympathizer. As a prisoner he may have been sent to Mackinac. It appears he was not held long and made a favorable impression on Lieutenant Governor Patrick Sinclair and was hired by Sinclair to do several different tasks. In 1790, another English official, who kept a diary, noted that he stayed at Jean Baptiste's establishment in Chicago. In the 1770s Baptiste took a Potawatomi wife and in 1778 the marriage was solemnized in Cahokia, Illinois by a Catholic priest. By this wife he had a son, Jean Jr. and a daughter, Suzanne. In 1800, he left Chicago for St. Joseph, Missouri where he lived out the remainder of his life till his death on August 28, 1818. Jean Baptiste Point du Sable is now widely regarded as the first permanent resident of Chicago. The dates of Jean Baptiste and Jean Bonga, unfortunately do not coincide. What is valuable in this research is to find that this talented Black man, Jean Baptiste Point du Sable is the first Chicagoan.

Even though Jean Baptiste Point du Sable is clearly not Jean Bonga, these insights into Point du Sable give us some hints and possibilities into what and how Jean Bonga found his way up the Mississippi River and into the region of the Great Lakes and the north woods.

More definitive historical evidence of Bonga's journey can be found in the life of Col. Daniel Robertson of the British Army. As mentioned previously, Thomas Meehan notes that during the period when Point du Sable was arrested in 1779 for being an American sympathizer or spy, it is apparent that he was not held long as his name is found in account books in Detroit in 1782-83. It is during this time frame that the Lieutenant-Governor of Mackinac, Patrick Sinclair, was so impressed with Jean Baptiste's abilities that he placed him in charge of his "Pinery," a few miles from Port Huron, Michigan. I note Sinclair here because it was Sinclair who was re-placed as Lieutenant-Governor at Michilimackinac (Mackinac Island.) by Col. Robertson. Col. Daniel Robertson becomes a pivotal person in the story of Jean Bonga.

Daniel Robertson was born in Dunkeld, Scotland in 1733. When Robertson was twenty-one years old, he enlisted in the British army and must have had some medical training prior to his enlistment as he was appointed a surgeon's mate. In June of 1756, his regiment was shipped to Albany, New York. In July of 1756 he was promoted with an ensigncy, and in 1760 he participated in the capture of Montreal during the French-Indian War. About this time, he married a young widow, Marie-Louise Reaume, which gave him an avenue to the connected and established Canadian families of the colony. Being at war with the French, and a soldier, he was shipped to the West Indies where he participated in the capture of Martinique in April 1762 and gained rank of lieutenant. Shortly after Martinique, he was part of the capture of Havana, and then was shipped back to North America where he found himself in western Pennsylvania where he participated in efforts to quell Pontiac's Rebellion. With the Treaty of Paris and the end of the French-Indian War, the army was reduced in size and Robertson found himself back in Montreal.

Between 1763 and 1773, Robertson became active in civic duties, had six children, two dying in infancy and in 1773 he lost his wife, Marie-Louise. When the American Revolution began, Robertson was appointed a major in the Montreal militia and in 1775 captain-lieutenant of the first battalion of the Royal Highland Emigrants whence he was ordered to defend Fort St. Johns (*Saint-Jean-sur-Richelieu*) against General Montgomery and the Americans. The fort was besieged and with its surrender, Robertson was taken prisoner. He was exchanged and returned to his regiment in 1777.

In September 1779, Robertson was appointed commandant of a small post at Oswegatchie (Ogdensburg, N.Y.). From this post he supervised raids on Americans in the Mohawk Valley. Some of these raids, he personally led. As a result of his successes in the Mohawk Valley, he obtained a commission for his son as ensign to serve as his aide. Next in Robertson's rise in the British Army, he was appointed to take over the troubled post at Michilimackinac (Mackinac Island) on September 18, 1782, where a fellow Scotsman, Lieutenant-Governor Patrick Sinclair was having serious problems, mostly of a financial nature.[38]

It was at this time, when Robertson was transitioning command from Sinclair to himself, that Robertson found himself in possession of three slaves that formerly belonged to Patrick Sinclair – and Robertson wondered what to do with these Blacks left behind by Sinclair. Sinclair had captured, "an Old Man & Woman and a young woman" during an unsuccessful attack on the Spanish in St. Louis in 1780. Even though a second daughter and a son were not mentioned, the evidence that this was Jean is compelling. Sinclair suggested Robertson could "return them back to their masters at the peace." Col. Robertson was repelled at this notion, saying their masters were "a sett of Spanish rascalls" and that he and Sinclair had a better right to them.[39]

It is very probable that two of these Blacks were Jean and Jeanne Bonga. How these slaves got to St. Louis may be based on the previous information stated about French owned slaves on French possessions in the West Indies who were dropped off by the French or found their way to the mainland. They then made their way to Louisiana and worked their way up the Mississippi River, out of slave territory to Missouri where Sinclair rescued them from the Spanish. As George Bonga stated, "I have always been sorry, that I did not ask my father while living, if he knew where he immigrate from. I am now inclined to think, that they must have come, from the new State of Missouri...I understood my father to say, that all his fathers family came to Mackinac, this I am certain of."[40]

Jean and Jeanne had three children; Rosalie, Charlotte and Pierre. It is likely that Jean and his wife were middle aged or older and their children were in their teens or were young adults by the time they came to Mackinac. How they came to Mackinac we cannot be completely sure, but the presumptions made earlier about French-speaking black slaves making their way north has particular interest in that Jean and family traveled up the Mississippi River to their ultimate freedom. The fact is, we may never have a fuller and more detailed story of how Jean Bonga came to be in the great Northwoods and have progeny, living in the vortex of the North American fur trade, who were destined to have an impact on the people and land they touched. But what we do know is a plausible start.

To understand more, we must go back to Col. Robertson. His work at the fort was mainly to discourage inter-tribal hostilities and help facilitate the fur trade. When news that the American Revolutionary War ended in 1783 and word arrived that Mackinac Island was to be included within the United States, Robertson became concerned. He would have to evacuate the fort. Immediately, he began to inspect the north shore of Superior for a new fort location and chose the present site of Thessalon, Ontario. It was during this time that Robertson became associated with men like James Grant, Joseph Frobisher, and Simon McTavish, who were the founders and partners of the North West Company (NWC)—men who ruled the day when it came to the fur trade and pushed the Hudson Bay Company (HBC) to the edge.[41]

Around 1785, the British government decided not to abandon Mackinac Island. Now that Col. Robertson no longer had to concern himself with overseeing an enterprise as demanding as moving Fort Michilimackinac, he settled down to tasks such as acquiring land grants for several of his daughters and his cronies in the NWC. Although he used his influence to improve his own family's economic status, he appears to have been an efficient officer and well-liked by the Native Americans. During this period in Robertson's tenure on Mackinac Island, he built a summer home on a rock outcrop at the southeast corner of the island. A number of sordid tales are attached to this site, known as "Robinson's Folly," which is a corruption of

Bonga

Robertson name. One legend has it that Robertson jumped from this rock outcrop in 1787 due to "a mad infatuation over a beautiful but phantom maiden" and died. This is entirely false as it is known that he died in Montreal in 1810. By 1787, Col. Daniel Robertson had attained an appreciable amount of wealth along with name importance. This and his connections to the fur trade got him a membership in the North West Company's prestigious Beaver Club of Montreal.[42]

In the summer of 1787, Robertson was relieved of his post and he returned to Montreal. Before he left Robertson freed his slaves, Jean and Jeanne Marie Bonga and children. It is believed that in Robertson's will, he would have freed his slaves upon his demise but upon learning of his termination at Mackinac Island, he manumitted the Bongas.[43]

Thus, on May 10, 1787 Jean Bonga, Jeanne Marie Bonga, and their children, Pierre, Rosalie, and Charlotte, became free people. It is more than imaginable; it is most probable, that Jean, his wife, his two daughters and his son Pierre, went outside at dusk in the cool spring air of Lake Huron on Mackinac Island and took a deep breath. They all knew they were breathing air the first time as free people. It had been a long odyssey for Jean, taken from his home and life in Africa with nothing but the name of his tribe, with all the inhumanities and injustices in the journey they had taken, yet clinging to life and hope that one day he might again find freedom. Now, here he is looking at these great lakes and the vast wilderness beyond them and knowing that he is free. His family has arrived in this safe abode in the wilderness with the content of their character intact. The Bonga family found their salvation in the vastness of wilderness they gazed upon where all things are free. The future of the Bongas was limitless.

Writing years later, Henry Rowe Schoolcraft would remark of the Bongas:

> "...Mrs. La Fromboise, an aged Metif lady ... She also says that Captain Robinson [Capt. Robertson], while commanding at Mackinack, discharged a negro servant named Bonga, who afterwards, with his wife, purchased the house and lot in which Mr. Wendell now lives (the old red house next to Dousman's south), where he kept a tavern, and maintained a respectable character. He afterwards sold out and went to Detroit and lived with Mr. Meldrum.
>
> She adds: 'The son of this Bonga was the late [Pierre] Bonga, who died as a comme, at Lake Winnepec [Lake Winnibigoshish,] of the Fond du Lac Department. The present Stephen Bonga of Folleavoine, a trustworthy trader, is the grandson of this Bonga – Robinson's freed slave. His connections are Chippewas, and all speak the Chippewa language fluently.'
>
> Having seen and known this Bonga, the grandson, I was led to remark that climate and intermarriage have had little or no appreciable effect on the color of the skin."[44]

It is likely that during Jean Bonga's life on Lake Huron, he would have seen a steady flow of large birch bark canoes, loaded with trade goods, manned by French-Canadian Voyageurs and their accompanying English, Scotch, and Irish clerks, *commis* (clerks in training to become a bourgeois), and *Bourgeois* (proprietors in the business). This, I believe, would have a great influence on where the Bongas would go next.

Bonga

Prior to arrival at Michilimackinac, the canoe brigades ate peas which they consumed since departure from Montreal, but at Michilimackinac they were refurbished with Indian corn and lard. Mackinac was the great crossroads of the fur brigades. From the "great turtle" some brigades went south into Lake Michigan and on to Illinois and Wisconsin and many entered Green Bay and portaged into the Chippewa and Wisconsin Rivers which enabled them access to the Mississippi in southern Minnesota. However, for those headed to the *Pays d'en Haut*, the country north and west of Lake Superior, they had to do the difficult portage around the St. Mary's Rapids into the far eastern part of Lake Superior, the largest surface area of fresh water in the world.

While at either Mackinac or Sault Ste. Marie, voyageurs traveling this way had a layover while the Commis and clerks took care of business. Here the voyageurs drank, ate, womanized, and generally acted up. This would certainly have been behavior that Jean Bonga was accustomed to seeing in the fur trade. Living in this distant outpost in the wilds of North America, Jean Bonga would have had his education and outlook shaped by the culture of the fur trade and Native Americans. Jean and his family would also have been exposed to different languages—Ojibwe, French and English—though they spoke fluent French from their years as slaves in the French-West Indies. It would have been nearly impossible to function here without being able to speak all three languages. This was a heterogeneous country of all the above. With the knowledge of these three languages came an understanding of the ways of life of the three cultures—skills that would be invaluable in the future for Bonga generations.

The stories French-Canadian voyageurs told at Mackinac of the vast wilderness of roaring rapids, great rivers, endless forests rich in fur bearers, country wives, and the colorful lives they led in the *Pays d'en Haut* undoubtedly fell upon the ears of the Bongas. It is interesting to imagine Jean and his son Pierre pondering the exciting lives of these romantic and adventurous voyageurs. These visions of voyaging in the *Pays d'en Haut* were incubating in the mind of Pierre and sometime in the 1790s, Pierre made the leap into the fur trade.

Jeanne Marie died in 1794 and Jean did not last long after his wife's passing, dying on January 20, 1795. Whatever the cause of death may be, Jean certainly was cognizant of the fact that he was of slave origins and by fate and circumstance made the best out of the worst of conditions. He knew what bondage was and he knew freedom. Jean's memory would be of the brutalities of slavery yet he escaped this bondage and found his way into the wilds about Michilimackinac. He, with his wife, lived a relatively comfortable life "and maintained a respectable character" as a free man and a respected inn keeper. What a life this old man must have seen and experienced: forests and savannas of Africa with the multitude of wildlife, the rivers of Congo with alligators and hippos, the Atlantic Ocean and likely the French-West Indies, the great Mississippi River, and finally the Great Lakes and the Northwoods.

This "respectable character" would be a trait passed on to their children who would spread over the land and leave behind a legacy that would have made old Jean and Jeanne Marie proud.

Where All Things Are Free

Pierre Bonga

The history of the fur trade in North America spans nearly two-hundred years and its participants include some of the most colorful and daring entrepreneurs in our history. The fur trade story in North America was dependent on four groups of people. First, Native Americans who provided the procurement component of the business and were also the source of sustenance for the traders, providing the food (mainly wild rice and game) that kept the traders alive in the harsh winters of the north. Second, the *bourgeois* at the management end of the trade who were the partners that ran the business. This includes men like Alexander Mackenzie, Alexander Henry the Elder, Alexander Henry the Younger, and the irascible Peter Pond. Third, The *commis,* the clerks, who managed the affairs at trading posts while training to become *bourgeois*. And fourth were the *voyageurs*, the muscle of the fur trade, without whom the fur trade would be as interesting as a stick in the mud for they gave it the romance and color that forever links them to the culture of lake country in the Northwoods.

Furs became the most sought-after resource in North America in the seventeenth, eighteenth, and into the nineteenth centuries. Fortunes were made in the fur trade as it was one of the most lucrative enterprises of its time. It was as early as the mid-1660s when ambitious and daring men known as the *coureurs de bois* or "woods-runners" intercepted fur pelts carried by Native Americans in route to Quebec and Montreal. It was at this time that the

71

"voyageur" originated and became one of the most colorful and interesting figures in North American history. But it was not until English rule from 1763 to the 1820s that the voyageur reached the zenith of his cultural definition and character.

There was a high degree of bravado, swagger, and ostentation among the voyageurs. One moment, he could be a drunken brawling beast—the next he could be a chivalrous gentleman, plucking a water lily for an infrequent lady passenger. They took great personal pride in their ability as the greatest canoe men in world history and took equal pride in the strength and stamina they displayed in carrying unbelievably heavy loads across long portages. The life expectancy of the voyageur was not long—strangulated hernia was not an uncommon cause of death along with drowning.

Most voyageurs were of Norman descent from small hamlets in Quebec. The future held little for these men laboring on their small farms. The notion of living their lives on the lakes and rivers of the Northwoods, shooting the rapids, or mushing a dog team under the northern lights was a much more attractable existence than spending their day with little to look at other than the backside of a team of oxen. They were as tough as nails, paddling a rigorous cadence of fifty to sixty strokes a minute for fifteen to eighteen hours a day and portaging loads weighing 180 pounds and more. In 1826, Thomas L. McKenney, traveling with a brigade of voyageurs, asked his voyageurs at seven o'clock in the evening if they wished to put ashore, he wrote: "They answered they were fresh yet...they had been almost constantly paddling since 3:00 this morning...57,600 strokes with the paddle, and fresh yet! No human being, except the Canadian French could stand this. Encamped...at half past nine o'clock, having come 79 miles."[45] And to make

Bonga

McKenney's observation even more remarkable, this happened on Lake Superior, the largest surface area of fresh water in the world.

Living in the Northwoods during the height, and then decline, of the fur trade, the Bongas would have been intertwined in the story of the voyageurs. In Grace Lee Nute's book, *The Voyageur*, the author makes reference to a man named Bonga as he arrives at the Grand Portage of Lake Superior which is nine miles in length. Each voyageur is required to carry a minimum of two ninety-pound packages of such goods and provisions as are necessary for the interior country. Nute states, "A member of the famous Negro-Indian family of voyageurs, the Bongas, is said to have had the strength that he could carry five."[46] Five 90-pound pieces totals 450 pounds. The Bonga that Grace Lee Nute speaks of is Pierre. The physical strength of the Bongas would remain legendary in the fur trade.

During the height of the fur trade, the *Pays d'en Haut* was not a system of unvisited waterways but a busy place of 'comers' and 'goers.' In the year 1777, 2,431 licensed engages are recorded in Montreal and Detroit.[47] During the height of the fur trade era, at least 125 important fur trading posts existed in what is now Minnesota.[48]

So much of this colorful and interesting history would be lost if it had not been for the *commis* keeping detailed records and journals of the everyday affairs of the fur trade. It was when reading one of these historical accounts that I came across a minor episode in the life of a Hudson Bay Company man by the name of John McKay, who was assigned the task of building a HBC post near the rival NWC post in 1793. The site selected by McKay was just a few miles below the falls which is today the site of International Falls, Minnesota. This HBC post was manned only until 1797. Of all the notes, diaries, and journals written by

McKay and his successors at this post, only one remains; the one penned in 1793.

Normally, these two rival fur trading Companies were bitter enemies but the "factors" of these two posts, McKay of the HBC and Charles Boyer of the NWC, got along splendidly. The men from these two competing companies would get together to sing, dance, play football, and celebrate Christmas and New Year's.

One particular instance caught my attention in this historical description from McKay's 1793 diary:

> "The fiddler for the numerous dances held at
> these two new posts was, according to McKay,
> one of the 'ordinariest negroes' he had ever
> seen, Robertson by name. As the well-known
> Bonga family of half Negro and half Indian blood
> originated in the Minnesota country with a slave
> whose master's name was Robertson, it is more
> likely that the escaped slave found his way
> to this safe abode in the wilderness where all
> things are free."[49]

The phrase, "...the escaped slave found his way to this safe abode in the wilderness where all things were free" captivated me. This black fiddler was, of course, Pierre Bonga, son of Jean Bonga of Mackinac.

When Pierre Bonga, one of the "ordinariest negroes" John McKay had ever seen, shows up playing the fiddle at the two fur posts on the Rainy River in the 1790s, he is already a *homes du nord*— a north man—one of those tough voyageurs who were also called *hivernants* or winterers, seasoned canoe men, spending the winter in the frozen wilderness of the *Pays d'en Haut*. His father, Jean, would be dead in two years and Pierre, by this time, was among the elite ranks of the voyageurs—a *hommes du nord.*

What is the chronological history of Pierre Bonga; who did he work with and where did he work? To answer these questions, a brief survey of the life of trader John Sayer will be helpful.

John Sayer

John Sayer was an early and daring adventurer in the fur trade. When Sayer first entered the fur trade, he was an unlicensed trader working out of Michilimackinac and Detroit. With the start-up of the NWC, Sayer entered into an agreement organizing the General Company of Lake Superior and the South Company (1785-1787). Two of those entering into this agreement were Jean Charles Chaboillez and Etienne Campion. After the American Revolution, the number of traders around Michilimackinac had grown so rapidly that Sayer formed a committee to regulate the trade.[50]

When the General Company of Lake Superior dissolved in 1787, Sayer, along with Jean Baptiste Cadotte, Jean Baptiste Perrault, and others formed the Sandy Lake Company (1788-1790). Sayer built Fort St. Louis or Fond du Lac on the St. Louis River. During the winter of 1789-90, Sayer was on Upper Red Lake while a number of his partners were on Leech Lake. Assuming Pierre began his career with Sayer, he would have had a great deal of exposure to the Fond du Lac Department which would be his world for the rest of his life.[51]

In 1791, Sayer went on his own forming, John Sayer & Company, thus becoming a *coureurs de bois* (woods runner) for the second time. From here he went west trading at Leech Lake and operating out of a supplier in Sault Ste Marie. During an absence from his Leech Lake post, his warehouse burned at a total loss. This put an end to Sayer & Company and he joined the North West Company. From 1791-92, Sayer dealt with many personal problems—his wife left him and his influential Ojibwe Father-in-law died.[52]

From 1793 to 1797, Sayer operated Fort Fond du Lac at the head of Lake Superior for the NWC as headman of the large Fond du Lac District. The Fond du Lac District includes parts of northwest Wisconsin and the northern half of Minnesota. These were tough times for the aging trader and intense competition required Sayer to spend greater amounts of his time traveling in the large Fond du Lac Department. Over the next few years Sayer is found wintering at Leech Lake, White Oak Point, Upper Red Cedar Lake, Yellow River and the Snake River. There is substantial evidence that Pierre was with Sayer of the NWC in 1795 as he is listed an employee "of JS & Co. [John Sayer & Co.] at Fond du Lac for the 1795 outfit at 900 *l*.[livres].[53]

With Pierre likely working for Sayer and the NWC prior to 1799, we begin to get a clearer picture of Pierre's chronological whereabouts in his career. Between 1799 and 1806, Pierre worked for Alexander Henry the Younger at Henry's Red River Post in Pembina. When Pierre departed the Red River country in 1806, he was back in the Fond du Lac Department until 1822, with the exception of the year of 1816 when he is said to have been at NWC post at Fort William when Lord Selkirk of HBC captured it.[54] Other than this brief hiatus at Fort William he was working in the large Fond du Lac district of northern Minnesota and could likely be found at important and productive fur trading posts at Leech Lake, Upper Red Cedar, White Oak Point, Big Winnibigoshish, and Big Sandy Lake. He may even have visited the upper parts of the Headwaters of the Mississippi River.

Bonga

Bonga is listed by the NWC in 1805 as an interpreter in the Lower Red R. department at 750 *l.* Charged for "sundries" [miscellaneous things] in the NWC's Fond du Lac department account books in 1812 and 1816 and credited with wages of 500 *l.* (NW) in 1812 and 600 *l.* (NW) in 1816. In 1817 he is listed as employed by the South West Company (SWC).

Finally, Pierre is employed by the American Fur Company (AFC) as a boatman in the Fond du Lac Department 1818, 1819, and 1822 outfits at $200. With Sayer having to spend greater amounts of his time traveling, it is very possible that he was also at Folle Avoine (in present day Wisconsin) with Pierre in his company sometime between 1795 and 97.[55]

Alexander Henry the Younger

The two bitter rivals, the HBC and the NWC, after decades of hostility and bloodshed merged in 1821. Border negotiations between Britain and the United States determining the US/Canadian border excluded British trading in the United States and enabled the trade south of the border to be controlled by the AFC.

It is well documented that from 1799 to 1806 Pierre Bonga was an engage' of the bold and daring Alexander Henry the Younger, the famed and renowned partner in the NWC. The important Red River Trading Post at Pembina was established by Henry in 1799 and operated by him until 1808 when Henry departed for the Saskatchewan River. There Henry managed fur operations before moving to the mouth of the Columbia River where his life ended by drowning in 1814. He chronicled his short and eventful career in his journal where we can find glimpses into Pierre's life during one of the most interesting and exciting times of the fur trade. Pierre would have been aware of all the contemporary Nor'Westers. Besides Alexander Henry, there was David Thompson—"*koo-koo-sint*" (man who stares at stars), Alexander Mackenzie who reached the Arctic Ocean in 1789 and the Pacific in 1793 twelve years before Lewis and Clark, and the daring Simon Fraser who descended the treacherous river named after him in British Columbia.

Henry the Younger's 1,600-page journal ended abruptly the day before he drowned in the mouth of the Columbia River in 1814. Elliott Coues edited Henry's prodigious journal and titled it, *New Light on the Early History of the Greater Northwest: The Manuscript Journals of Alexander Henry, Fur Trader of the North West Company and of David Thompson, Official Explorer of the same Company.* The first volume is exclusively of Henry's eight plus years on the Red River of the North for which Pierre Bonga was present everyday till June 10, 1806, and is seen as an important cog in the operation of the fur post.

Alexander Henry the Younger's journal begins in 1799 when he departs from Grand Portage on a journey to establish a trading post on the Red River of the North with a brigade of four north canoes. Henry gives the names and rank of the occupants in each canoe. The first canoe is occupied by Alexander Henry the Younger and his most skilled voyageurs. He notes the names and rank of each voyageur: "First Canoe.-1. Alexander Henry: Bourgeois, in charge of the brigade. 2. Jacques Barbe: Voyageur, conductor or bowman (ducent). Etienne Charbonneau: Voyageur, steerer, or helmsman (guide). 4. Joseph Dubois: Voyageur, steerer or helmsman. 5. Angus McDonald; Voyageur, midman. 6. Antoine Lafrance: Voyageur, midman. 7. Pierre Bonza or Bonga; a negro." In a footnote to Henry the Younger's list, Elliott Coues notes that "Pierre Bonza appears as interpreter N.W. Co., Lower Red r., 1804."[56] It should be noted that

Bonga

the mention of a Bonga as an interpreter would continue to be an occupation of family members for two generations. The name of Bonga has been spelled in the various ways: Bungo, Bunga, Bonza, Bongo, and Bonga.

Henry's edited work by Elliott Coues is both gripping and informative. It gives us an entirely different picture of what most today perceive is the Red River of the North. The countryside was teeming with elk, buffalo, black bear, wolves, and even an occasional grizzly. The river itself was teeming with sturgeon, catfish, and waterfowl. Henry's attention to detail and acute powers of observation in the journal allow us to visualize what the country and times were like. The journal also mentions Pierre a number of times as he fits into the operation of Red River Post that is now the site of Pembina, North Dakota.

Early in Henry's journal he frequently deals with the incredible abundance of wildlife. Henry, being flabbergasted by a particular herd of buffalo, climbed a large bur oak in this flat country of the Red River Valley to see how large the herd was and found he could not see the end of the herd. One particular spring Henry notes that thousands of dead buffalo floated by the fort in the Red River in what seemed an endless procession. Meat for the traders was plentiful. On February 25, 1801, Henry notes:

> "A herd of cows [buffalo] were crossing the ice
> near the fort; the dogs chased them, and pre-
> vented one from getting on shore. Perceiving
> this the men took a codline, which they doubled
> and then entangled her legs in such a manner
> that she fell upon her side. She lay quiet while
> they fastened the line around her horns and
> dragged her to the fort, as she was too obstinate
> to stand up. But here she jumped up and made

at the dogs, taking no notice of us. Crow and Pierre [Bonga] both got on her back, but this did not incommode her; she was as nimble in jumping and kicking at the dogs as before, although they are two stout men—Crow weighing at least 190 pounds. She was not full grown, and very lean. What must be the strength of a full-grown bull, double the weight of a cow?"[57]

Buffalo are not domestic cattle but are very dangerous wild animals and need to be given room. The fact that Pierre would get on the back of a bucking buffalo leads one to believe that Pierre indeed has a daring and bold nature about him that is typical of the voyageur personality.

About three months later Henry notes in his journal, on May 15, 1801, while at the Red River Post, "...Engaged Langlois [clerk], Desmarais [interpreter], Pierre [Bonga], and some others to settle the men's accounts."[58] This notation by Henry would lead one to believe that Pierre was rising in standing and trust with him and had abilities that the run-of-the-mill voyageur lacked. Henry was having Pierre handle some of his administrative work.

On March 12, 1802, Henry's journal notes that "Pierre's [Bonza's] wife was delivered of a daughter—the first fruit at this fort, and a very black one."[59] There is uncertainty as to whom this daughter was and who the mother was. The five surviving children of Pierre are Marguerite, Stephen, George, Jack, and Elizabeth. Marguerite was born around 1797 in Lapointe or the Fond du Lac area of Lake Superior. Stephen was also born at Fond du Lac in 1799. George states in 1872, his birth to be "...somewhere near where Duluth now is...pretty near 70 Years ago..." making his birth 1802. Jack's date of birth is uncertain but we do know he was younger than his two brothers. The birth date and place of Elizabeth is at this time unknown but Elizabeth may have been the girl born at Pembina. The wife that delivered "the first fruit at this fort..." may have been a "country wife" that so many voyageurs took and often left behind—wife and offspring. My Ojibwe friend, Juanita Blackhawk, a direct descendant of the Bongas, notes that her family's oral history says this daughter was Elizabeth. With Elizabeth's birth date and place somewhat a mystery and the oral history given by Ms. Blackhawk, I would put my money on Elizabeth being the daughter born at the Red River Post. However, examining the birth dates of those born in early North America is fairly unreliable.

It is believed that Pierre was born around the year 1771. The year 1793 would make Pierre about twenty-two years old when McKay writes of the black fiddler at the Rainy Lake Post. Jean and Jeanne Bonga, along with their children were freed in 1787 when Pierre would have been about sixteen years old. Pierre would have entered the fur trade soon thereafter.

More information concerning Pierre's wife is found in William Loren Katz's book, *Black Indian: A Hidden Heritage,* in which he states:

> "Pierre, who was apprentice to a Canadian trapper for the North West Company and was well trusted. Together with a white man, he was put in charge of the company fort when the master left on business. In time Pierre Bonga became an interpreter for the North West Company. While negotiating in a Chippewa village he met and fell in love with a Chippewa woman, and they were married...Pierre and his bride settled in Duluth half a century before a permanent European settlement was established there..."[60]

81

Barry Babcock

Evidence of Henry's growing respect and regard for Pierre is demonstrated when he left Pierre in co-charge of his important Red River Post at Pembina during a temporary absence in January 1803. Henry states in his journal on January 4, 1803: "Leaving the fort in charge of V. St. Germain and P. [Pierre Bonza], I took two men and set out on a journey."[61] Although Henry was Canadian where slavery did not exist, for him to have this degree of trust in a black man during these times most surely demonstrates a high opinion of Pierre Bonga and his abilities. Pierre was not only physically powerful but obviously intelligent too.

The next notation by Henry of Pierre is on November 6, 1803: "X.Y. [the XY Company] J. Desford [Duford of rival XY Co.] had threatened to kill my servant [Pierre Bonza] in my absence, but did not escape without a sound beating."[62] On reading this, one could assume that Pierre had no qualms about standing up for himself nor was he a man who could be intimidated. Judging from the tone of Henry's remarks, it appears that Pierre was continuing to rise in standing and surely his voyageur colleagues would be ever respectful of Pierre.

Dates of events and people in historical journals often overlap or are not in agreement. Let's look at one example of conflicting journal entries concerning the whereabouts of Pierre Bonga in November of 1803.

The Burnett County Historical Society has done a great job of reconstructing the buildings of the Northwest Trading Company post on the exact sites they occupied on the Yellow River in the St. Croix region of northwest Wisconsin. They have also done an excellent job of telling the story of the events and people whose lives were part of the history of this region. In the *Folle Avoine Chronicles*, they cite a journal entry by Michel Curot of the XY Company, a rival competitor to the NWC, which had a post constructed only several hundred feet from the NWC post. The entry, written on November 4, 1803, notes that, "Lagarde, Girard, The negro [Pierre?], and 4 of Mr. Sayers Men left for the river au serpent [Snake River in east central Minnesota], Mr. Lacroix going with them."[63] On this date in 1803, it seems unlikely that Pierre was at Folle Avoine due to a notation in the journal of Alexander Henry the Younger. On November 6, 1803, Henry writes that Pierre Bonga had a dispute with a rival trader from the XY Company while stationed at the Red River Post. Henry kept a detailed, accurate and lengthy journal of his entire career in the fur trade making it difficult to dispute his credibility. The truth we may never know. As Woodswhimsy of *Folle Avoine* states, "Historical detectives are plagued with scanty references like these from which to paint the broader picture."[64]

On June 10, 1806, Henry makes his final remarks about Pierre in his Red River Journal, writing:

> "Sent off my canoes for Kamanistiquia [Fort William]; 5 men and 22 sacks per canoe; passengers: Messrs. Alexander Wilkie, John Crebassa, Antoine Desjarlaix, Joseph St. Germain, Augustin Cadotte, Toussaint Le Sueur, and Pierre Bonza; Jean Baptiste Lambert, guide; four taureaux [80 lb. rawhide bags full of pemmican] per canoe, and one for the passengers."[65]

This is probably the end of Pierre's time at the Red River of the North.

Pierre's name can also be found in the index of Henry's edited journal, compiled by someone other than Henry as he died in 1814, where it states that Pierre Bonza, "reappears at the capture of Fort William, Aug. 13th 1816." The capture of Fort William would be in regards to Lord Selkirk of the HBC and the forceful military measures taken by him after the massacre of a Scotch settlement of Hudson Bay people at Seven Oaks (now near the present day Canadian city of Winnipeg) by NWC people, Native Americans, and Métis. This reminds us how volatile this time was due to the bitter blood feud between these two fur trading giants and how it forced all people in the *Pays d'ien Haut* to choose sides. The Bongas remained loyal Northwesters until the United States took possession below the 49th parallel and the AFC took over the trade in Minnesota and neighboring states.

Alexander Henry the Younger was a shrewd and bold trader. He knew where his profits came from and that's why he trusted Pierre Bonga. He saw something exceptional in the black voyageur.

But there is more evidence of Pierre Bonga's work in the fur trade beyond those notations of John Sayer and Alexander Henry. During the very early 1800s, records show a Bonga, most likely Pierre, as a principal trader for the NWC among the Ojibway. The Ojibwe historian, William Whipple Warren—a mixed-blood himself—states in his *History of the Ojibway People* that:

> "In 1819 the Northwest [Company] became merged into the Hudson's Bay Company, and ceased to exist. With it may be said to have ended the Augustan age of the fur trade. With deep regret do the old voyageurs and Indians speak of the dissolution of this once powerful company, for they always received honorable and charitable treatment at their hands. The principle traders who operated among the Ojibways during the era of the North West

Bonga

Company, and who may be mentioned as contemporary with John Baptiste and Michel Cadotte, are Nolin, Gaulthier, McGillis, St. Germain, Bazille Beauleau, Chabolier, Wm. Morrison, Cotte, Roussain, Bonga, J.B. Corbin, and others. These early pioneer traders all intermarried in the tribe, and have left sons and daughters to perpetuate their names."[66]

Bearing in mind that Warren's white ancestry comes from a long line of old NWC Traders, his opinion may be somewhat tainted with a mixed-blood trader bias. However, these venerable old traders were often sympathetic to the condition of the Indian and all, or nearly all, of those who married into Ojibwe families.

In the quote from Schoolcraft's *Thirty Years* it states, "The son of this Bonga [Jean] was the late [Pierre] Bonga, who died as a comme, at Lake Winnepec [Lake Winnibigoshish,] of the Fond du Lac Department." Pierre Bonga departed for the spirit world in 1831.

Throughout his life in the Northwoods, the Ojibwe affectionately called him, "*Makade wiiyaas*" meaning 'black meat.' Pierre lived an extraordinary life and created a reputation for himself in the Northwoods. The Ojibwe historian William Whipple Warren notes Pierre Bonga's name as one of the grand, respected old traders of the NWC. In examining the life of Pierre, it would be correct to say that Pierre excelled as a voyageur—amassing knowledge of the lakes and rivers and how they formed a network of watery pathways from Mackinac to the Red River of the North. His physical strength would become legendary in voyageur history. He would make a home among the Ojibwe people, having taken an Ojibwe wife, and taking residence near the mouth of the St. Louis River. He would have acquired the necessary wilderness skills, bi-lingual language skills, and necessary business skills to rise as a *commis*-clerk in the North West Company and passed them onto his progeny. He rose above those nameless, faceless ranks of voyageurs most of whom died obscure deaths, yet Pierre became a notable figure in the North Country. And lastly, he achieved the degree of monetary ability to send at least two of his children, George to Montreal and Stephen to Albany, New York, for a good education. And as Pierre and his male progeny took Ojibwe wives, their background as voyageurs in the fur trade began to meld with the culture of the Ojibwe people of whom they became a part. And Pierre carried with him the one thing his Father brought with him as a slave from Africa, his name "Bonga."

Now and then, something from the past surfaces that portrays the greatness of this family. An article titled, "Superior's First 'White' Man Intrigued Explorers—Negroid Settler Was Only Head of Lakes Resident Mentioned By Writer," by Guy M. Burnham of the *Telegram Special Correspondent*. He writes:

> "Ashland, Wis. - Bongo, the ebony hued exile from Darkest Africa, it has been said, facetiously remarked once upon a time, that he was "the first white man to make Superior his permanent home." As Bongo was reputed to have been a particularly black, Black man, his sense of humor may be appreciated. If he didn't say it, maybe someone else with a good imagination may have said it.

> Captain Marryatt, the famous novelist, went across Wisconsin and up as far as the Falls of St. Anthony in the early days. Had he continued to the Head of Lake Superior, he certainly would

have seen this picturesque African and the
world would have had another novel?

Here was the exile from a foreign land, alone in
a strange country, taking onto himself a wife
among the savages and raising a large family. If
the Chippewas of the St. Louis river had been
in the habit of choosing kings, and had made
Bongo their king, there would have been the
complete story for Captain Marryatt all ready for
printing, barring a few embellishments.

Bongo came to Lake Superior from what is now
Mackinac Island. He was the "man" of a British
officer but as the British were not slave owners,
he was obviously a free Negro. This island which
commanded the northern approaches to three
lakes, Michigan, Huron, and Superior, was very
attractive to the British, and it was quite a while
after we achieved our independence, before the
British flag was lowered at Michilimackinac.
Bongo, evidently a servant and a follower of the
British army, got to the Head of the Lakes and
there he stayed.

George T. Thomas, who knew a lot of Indian
history, used to tell about Bongo, and the latter's claim to being 'the first white settler at
Superior,' and the impression created was that
Bongo's residence at the Head of the Lakes was
at least within the memory of Thomas, who by
the way wrote a story we believe, about Bongo,
under the name of George Francis. However,
when Gen. Lewis Cass, governor of Michigan,
arrived at Superior bay in 1820, on his great

4,000 mile trip which took him to what is now Cass lake, Schoolcraft, who accompanied him, ran across Bongo at Fond du Lac.

Of all the people Schoolcraft saw at the Head of the Lakes, Bongo is practically the only one he mentions.

About three miles above the river' says Schoolcraft, 'we landed at the Indian village of Fond du Lac. While exchanging the usual salutations with them we noticed the children of an African who had intermarried with the tribe. These children were the third in descent from Bongo, a freed man.'

From this brief statement, it is impossible to say whether Bongo was then alive or dead. At least, his grandchildren were there in 1820, and in speaking of them the historian further says, 'They possessed as black skins as the father, from the fact that the marriages, were in the case of the grandfather and the father, with the pure Indian.

When Thomas speaks of 'talking' with descendants of old Bongo say 50 years ago, there were a lot of them at the head of the lake, probably a couple of hundred of them, and probably it was some of them that he heard the alleged quotation from old Bongo, that he was the first 'white' settler in that particular neck of the woods.

There are probably a lot of descendants of old Bongo in this part of the country, particularly around Fond du Lac, and perhaps on some of the reservations. Some of them will likely read this article and they may have other information about their ancestor. Fond du Lac could undoubtedly add more information about this picturesque old Negro. When he was on earth, there wasn't very much of Lake Superior to be seen yet and when Superior finally appeared on the map shortly before Civil war times, Bongo must have been in the happy hunting grounds for some time. For these reasons, the necessity for a monument to Bongo at the head of Tower Avenue need not be urged at this time."

The time has arrived to rethink the monument.

The Greatest Canoe Man in North America

Stephen Bonga

"Mr. Stephen Bungo, the oldest settler at the head of Lake Superior, and who has been in very feeble health for a long time, quietly laid down the burden of life last Tuesday evening, at the advanced age of 84 years. He was a mixture of Indian and Negro blood, and until a few years past a tall, erect and muscular man. We have not the data at hand from which to make an extended notice of the deceased, though one of great interest might be written. As we get it, his father was a negro, and was kidnapped from Montreal about one hundred years ago, and brought to this Northwest country and sold to a Frenchman connected with the Hudson Bay Fur company...and has ever since lived an honorable and upright Christian life and died in the full faith that our heavenly father meant him when he said, 'Whosoever will, let him come and take of the water of life freely,' and that he will wear the crown with the redeemed. Peace to his ashes."[67]

This obituary published in the *Superior Times* of Superior, Wisconsin on January 26, 1884, marks the passing of Stephen Bonga, the end of a most interesting man and the end of a colorful era.

Today, only a few people of the Duluth-Superior, North Shore region, northern Minnesota and Wisconsin have scant knowledge of this extraordinary man or his brothers and sisters. When asked if they know who Stephen Bonga is, most say they know of him as "the first white child born at the Head of the Lakes," a seemingly contradictory statement he made about himself.

Stephen was born in June of 1799 at Fond du Lac. He was the first of three sons born to Pierre and *Ojibwikwe*, his Ojibwe wife, and the second child as the first born was Marguerite, who was born in 1797. The other siblings, in order of age, were George, Jack, and Elizabeth for whom I have no date of birth. Stephens's brother George was also born at Fond du Lac and wrote in 1872 that he was born "pretty near 70 Years ago." Jack Bonga's birth date is uncertain but we do know he is the youngest of the three brothers. One must keep in mind that dates of birth two hundred years ago were sometimes estimates at best, even George was not certain about his birth year.

A good place to begin the story of Stephen Bonga is in 1820 with the Lewis Cass expedition to the Headwaters of the Mississippi. Minnesota and Wisconsin were then within the territory of Michigan. The region was the *Pays Sauvage* or Indian Country, where First Nations had not yet been contaminated by the pitfalls of civilization. The densely forested lands and abundant waterways seemed to these white men a deep, impenetrable wilderness. Cass had an entourage of gentlemen accompanying him, including a young Henry Rowe Schoolcraft who was included in the expedition for his background in geology and ethnology. Their mission, besides finding the Headwaters of the Mississippi River, was to see what the country offered the young nation in the way of resources. They knew there was copper on the upper peninsula of Michigan and this was an item of particular interest. They also wanted to establish relations with the Ojibwe tribes in order to create a more favorable atmosphere for the fur trade that had been previously dominated, first by the French, then the English, and then the North West Company based in Montreal. It was only seventeen years earlier, in 1803, that President Thomas Jefferson purchased from Napoleon all the land west of the Mississippi River to the continental divide of the Rocky Mountains in the Louisiana Purchase. Cass wanted to impress on British traders and Indians that this newly acquired land was now the land of the Americans—*Gichi-Mookomaanag*.

As the Cass Expedition approached the head of Lake Superior and entered the St. Louis River *(Gichi-gamiwi-ziibi)* and the village of Fond du Lac *(Nagaajiwanaang)*, Schoolcraft gave this description of what the expedition members witnessed in his 1820 narrative:

> "...we have our first glimpse of the mountains on the north side of the lake, which are distant probably forty miles. These become more distinct, and continue to increase in apparent altitude as we ascend the Fond du Lac, while on the south shore the highlands either recede so widely from the lake as to become invisible, or entirely cease. On reaching the mouth of St. Louis, or Fond du Lac river, the Cabotian mountains present a lofty barrier towards the north, and have an apparent altitude of a thousand feet above the lake. The chain runs from east to west, and as far as the eye can reach stretches off in a lofty line towards the Mississippi. It is this barrier which we have to cross with our

baggage and canoes in ascending the St. Louis river, for this precipitous stream has worn its rugged channel through these mountains, and throws itself into Lake Superior at its extreme head. The mouth of the river is not more than a hundred and fifty yards wide, but immediately on entering, it expands to a mile, and continues this width for five to six miles, and this part of it resembles a lake more then a river, having little or no current,--shallow in many places, and filled with aquatic plants. We here first saw in plenty the folle avoine, or wild rice, which is so common throughout the northwest regions, and serves the Indians as a substitute for corn."

After entering the mouth of the river, Schoolcraft notes an Indian village,

"Three miles above the mouth of the St. Louis river, there is a village of Chippeway Indians, of fourteen lodges, and containing a population of about sixty souls. Among these we notice a negro [Pierre] who has been long in the service of the fur company, and who married a squaw, by whom he has four children. It is worthy of remark, that the children are as black as the father, and have the curled hair and glossy skin of the native African. It does not appear that climate has had any more influence here, than it has along the borders of the Atlantic, in ameliorating the colour of this race."[68]

In a footnote to this, Schoolcraft notes: "Bonzo, a freedman, served a British officer at Malden in the War of 1812."[69]

Then, a short distance above this village where the Bonga family resides, Schoolcraft writes:

> "...on the opposite side of the river, are the ruins of one of the old forts and trading houses of the North West Company, which was abandoned about six years ago. The site is elevated and pleasant, but the American company have not thought proper to re-occupy it, and have fixed their establishment for the Fond du Lac department, eighteen miles above, where the first portage commences. By this change of site, they save the labour of loading and unloading their canoes at the mouth of the river."[70]

Long before 1820, Fond du Lac was the gateway to the riches of the fur trade for men who had the strength and determination to succeed. *Sieur De La Verendrye* pioneered the fur trade for the French in 1731, crossed the Grand Portage around the Pigeon River and traveled by canoe to Rainy Lake with a map drawn by an Ojibwe man by the name of *Auchagah*. Copies of this map are kept in Paris. According to Grace Lee Nute, depicted on this map with the Grand Portage and border lakes, is the St. Louis River, "...the source of the St. Louis River is shown, though it is called by its original French name, Fond du Lac River. Since one of the branches of the St. Louis River connects by a short portage with Namakan Lake..." All this points to the fact that these routes, including Fond du Lac were long in use by Native Americans who were using these routes for trade, war, transportation, hunting, and gathering, long before the arrival of the first whites.[71]

This was home to the Bongas; it was literally their backyard. They were born there, raised there, spoke the language, and were culturally linked to the land. From there they would become intimately acquainted with the lakes, rivers, and trails that would take them deep into *Le Beau Pays*. It is no wonder that throughout Stephen's life, he always returned here and in his senior years settled near Fond du Lac in this spectacularly beautiful land. Both Stephen and his father, Pierre are forever linked to this land. An article written some time ago, titled, "Head of the Lakes" when Stephen was an old man, states:

> "...In the year 1826, Gov. Doty, in a letter to
> Gen. Cass, speaks of an old negro [Pierre] re-
> siding among the Chippewas at Fond du Lac.
> He said that the negro had an Indian wife and
> a family of four children. Stephen Bungo, now
> living in the city of Superior at the advanced
> age of eighty-five years, is one of those children.
> Stephen speaks of his father, in a facetious
> way, as being the first white man (and he was
> a negro,) to permanently settle at the head of
> the lake...In time he was adopted as a member
> of the tribe, married one of their women, and
> became a progenitor of a new caste among the
> old-time proud Ojibway people. Even at this day
> there are over sixty of his descendants living in
> the neighborhood of the 'Head of the Lake.'"[72]

The article also sites Stephen relating some interesting facts about the Duluth/Superior region from the perspective of the past;

> "He says that formerly there was a low, sandy
> island in the St. Louis Bay a few miles above the
> present point, which has entirely disappeared.

It is supposed that the present sandy point
was formed from the sands of this island, carried down by the ever-onward flow of the river.
He also says that Minnesota Point, the natural breakwater so much prized by citizens of
Duluth and Superior, was once cut in twain by
a broad natural channel a mile out from the
present canal."[73]

Stephen also tells of the natural entrance to St. Louis Bay from Lake Superior through Minnesota Point was where the "barrens," opposite where Central Park now is. According to Stephen, during the spring thaw, a freshet carrying a large section of floating bog and islands came down the St. Louis River and lodged in the channel to the lake. A northeastern storm coming on further imbedded the lodged obstruction in the channel. The present entrance opposite Allouez was where the "pent-up" waters of Superior Bay broke through. Stephen's "...story is undoubtedly correct as this procedure happens almost yearly even now in a small way at the mouths of many streams on the South Shore, such as the Amnicon, Middle, and Poplar."[74]

"The Indians called the site of Duluth, fifty years ago, Onigamiinsing – Little Portage – for the reason that they had to carry their canoes over the narrow sand-point." And it goes on to cite "one of the routes often followed in early days, by the voyageur and traveler, on his way from Lake Superior to the Upper Mississippi, was by way of the St. Louis River, and a series of lakes and streams, that almost gave a continuous line from the greatest lake to the greatest river."[75]

The St. Louis River is the largest river by volume discharging into Lake Superior and is 179 miles long. The name "Fond du Lac" is French for "foot" or "bottom" of the lake but in actuality it is the 'head' as the lake discharges on the eastern or opposite end of the lake at Sault Ste. Marie.

Much focus of the fur trade history and the canoe routes used by the trade have justly focused on the famous Grand Portage border route for various reasons but the St. Louis River also accesses the border route. More importantly, it was used as the standard route by traders from Mackinac for accessing Sandy Lake, Leech Lake, and the Headwaters Country of the Mississippi River. This route, from Fond du Lac to the Mississippi River is called the Northwest Trail which leaves the St. Louis River at the mouth of the East Savanna River near the present site of the town of Floodwood about thirty-three miles upstream from Cloquet, Minnesota. On the East Savanna River is a paddle of six miles upriver to the extremely difficult six-mile Savanna Portage, which traverses a three-mile segment of knee to waist deep swamp before rising to high ground for another three miles. It terminates at the West Savanna River which flows downstream before discharging into Big Sandy Lake—*Kahmetahwungaguma*. The Savanna Portage crosses the continental divide separating the Mississippi and the St. Lawrence River watersheds.

This large and rich fur bearing region beyond the Northwest Trail has been neglected in Minnesota history. Its implications as one of the more important Indian routes play a very significant role in Dakota-Ojibwe conflicts and as access to one of the most profitable fur departments in the history of the Northwest and American Fur Companies. The Fond du Lac Department in 1805 in NWC ledgers shows "one hundred and nine men employed at a wage of sixty-three thousand nine hundred thirteen livres. Returns for 1807 indicate that the production of furs in the Fond du Lac Department was only second to Athabaska [Department]."[76]

As the late Minnesota historian Larry Luukkonen stated, the route from Fond du Lac to Big Sandy Lake is the "Northwest Trail" connecting the continents largest lake to its longest river.

Pierre Bonga had risen above the rank of voyageur to become a clerk and in doing so would have realized that if his sons were to do the same, they would be at a great advantage by getting a good education. Pierre sent George to Montreal for his schooling. One reason for choosing Montreal was because one of Pierre's two sisters, Charlotte or Rosalie, resided there. Pierre took Stephen east via the Great Lakes to Albany, New York, and enrolled him at a Presbyterian Missionary Society. Stephen did receive an adequate education in Albany but was not ordained there. Shortly before being ordained, Stephen became tired of white society and its culture and left Albany as he preferred life with the Ojibwe in Indian Country. He made his way back to Fond du Lac from Albany, New York, by canoe following the water routes from the Hudson River to the Great Lakes—an epic trip by any standards.

Stephen, who took pride in his reputation for telling the truth, was cited by Alfred Merritt, a friend and writer, who wrote of a visit he had from Stephen in his senior years concerning his time in Albany. Merritt reported:

> "Bungo used to come up and visit my broth-
> er and myself, and he always came twice each
> year, staying four or five days each time. On
> one of his trips he seemed quite excited. He
> said that they had called Bungo a liar, because
> he had said that he had seen Robert Fulton's
> steamboat at Albany on the Hudson river in
> about the year 1811. He had seen that we had
> an encyclopedia. Now he said, 'I want you to

look it up, and give me the page, and I will show these gentlemen that Bungo is not a liar."[77]

The maiden voyage of Fulton's steamboat, the "Clermont", from New York to Albany was made on August 17, 1807. The trip was a success, going from New York to Albany, a distance of 150 miles in thirty-two hours. The boiler was fueled with pine wood. The return trip was done in thirty hours. Prior to this maiden voyage, the boat was the recipient of much ridicule, being called "Fulton's Folly." The boat continued to make this trip every four days for years after the maiden voyage. This tells us that Stephen was in Albany during this period that the Clermont was in service, from 1807 to 1811. Since Stephen was born in 1799, this would make him at least eight years old in 1807.

What was Stephen doing after his arrival back at Fond du Lac from the Presbyterian school in New York? He was a voyageur—a canoe man—in the fur trade.

The Fur Trade in Minnesota

It is of value to note some background about the fur trade in Minnesota at this time. After the American Revolution and the Treaty of 1783, concerning where the border separating the two nations would be, the British and Americans temporarily agreed that the Ontario-Minnesota border would be the "customary waterway" used by traders to enter the *Pays D'en Haut* from Lake Superior. But the final agreement and survey dragged out until 1842.

Three different routes departed from Lake Superior into the interior: the Grand Portage/Voyageurs Highway, the Fort William/Kaministikwia River in Ontario, and the Fond du Lac/St. Louis River routes. The United States and Canadian border hinged upon which of these three routes would be acknowledged as the accustomed or primary route. From the time of the American Revolution, national ownership of these routes had been in dispute. After the War of 1812, the 1815 Treaty of Ghent was assigned to determine the actual "Voyageurs Highway" thereupon settling the long border dispute between the United States and Great Britain. However, the border disputes were not entirely resolved until the 1842 Webster-Ashburton Treaty agreed upon the findings and surveys done by boundary commissioners from both the United States and Great Britain from 1822 to 1824. The "customary waterway" would be the Grand Portage Route, from the Pigeon River to Lake of the Woods.

Historians speculate on how different the country would appear if the Fond du Lac or Fort William routes were to have been selected as the principal trade route rather than Grand Portage. If the Fort William route were chosen, that portion of Ontario would be Minnesota and conversely, if Fond du Lac were to be the United States border, the entire Arrowhead of northeastern Minnesota would be Canadian.

In 1802 the Fond du Lac Department was run by William Morrison who was with Alexander MacKenzie's XY Company until it merged with the North West Company in 1804. After the Treaty of Ghent in 1815, Morrison joined the American Fur Company and in 1821 signed an agreement to manage the Fond du Lac Department of the AFC. In 1816, the United States created the Exclusion Act which barred any non-Americans from working in the fur trade with the exception of voyageurs. Their importance as "the muscle" was universally recognized as paramount to the trade. No one could paddle, carry, and live in the wilds like these hardened men. One way the AFC got around the "Exclusion Act" was to hire Canadian men like Morrison as voyageurs, or some other menial job, as a guise while they actually ran the department in which they worked. Many, like William Aitkin became American citizens. Stephen worked for William Morrison until Morrison's retirement in 1826. When Morrison retired, he was replaced by William Aitkin. Stephen, himself, says he was with William Morrison when he was the first white man at the Headwaters of the Mississippi River. It is documented that Morrison was at the Headwaters in 1803-04, and 1811-12. Could it be that Stephen was with Morrison in 1811-12? He would only have been 12 or 13 years of age. Whether he was with Morrison at the headwaters or some other location downstream from the headwaters after 1812 and before 1826, is uncertain.

William Morrison was one of the toughest and most ruthless traders in the North West Territory but the Anishinaabeg liked him and felt he was fair handed. They affectionately called him *Sha-gah-nansh-eence,* meaning Little Englishman. As soon as the North West Company had merged with the Hudson Bay Company in 1821, William Morrison was placed charge of the Fond du Lac Department of the American Fur Company. He set his eyes on Grand Portage where the British could not trade due to it being south of the "customary waterway." In 1822, Ramsey Crooks, second in command of the AFC, wrote:

> "Morrison will establish some new posts along our northwestern border. The old Grand Portage is allowed to be within our line, and there the N.W. have always had a good little post, since they retired to Fort William. An outfit from the Fond du Lac department should be sent to that place under some active men; and in order to keep our opponents on their own side of the boundary, our clerks or traders are to be made customhouse officers."[78]

Barry Babcock

In 1823 a "sullen clerk" named Bela Chapman was joined by Stephen, George, and Jack Bonga as his staff. On the advice of the Grand Portage Indians, Chapman built his post at Grand Marais, a location Chapman glumly called "Fort Misery." The whole episode was a failure for both fur companies. Bela Chapman had no charisma and treated the Indians with disrespect and was extremely ill-suited for the job. The whole affair was a dismal failure. However, the Indians used their presence to play the Hudson Bay Company off against the American Fur Company. The Hudson Bay Company cut prices and sent men to winter with the Indians in order that the Indians would not trade with the Americans. The Headman of the band, a man called Espagnol, adroitly played the rivals against one another. Chapman wrote "...the Indians are not well pleased with them [HBC] for all their low prices and fair promises[.]...high time now they have opposition." At the same time, Espagnol assured the Hudson Bay men of his loyalty yet Chapman wrote, "They are partial to us and say that if we would establish a post at the Grand Marais, we would be sure of the best of their hunts." Hence, the results of being duped induced Bela Chapman to call the AFC post, "Fort Misery" as the winter was miserable and the fur business was more miserable.[79]

The Bongas were at Fort Misery for the winter of 1823-24 as "active men", as Ramsey Crooks called them, but it was a bad situation from the start. By this time in the 1800s, most of the voyageurs were second or third generation Ojibwe-French mixed-bloods. In their heart, they must have had mixed feelings when under the charge of someone as racist, insensitive, and rude to the Natives as Bela Chapman was. As voyageurs, the Bongas were at the bottom of the food chain and were certainly glad to have only spent a relatively short time at Fort Misery. By 1833 a deal was struck between the Hudson Bay Company and the American Fur Company at Grand Portage. The agreement had the HBC paying the AFC 300 livres a year—illegally—to withdraw from the border. This deal between the HBC and AFC was maintained until 1847 when the American Fur Company went out of business.[80]

The AFC did start a commercial fishing business that prospered until the economy caved and the demand for salted fish went in the tank. Jack Bonga has been listed in previous instances as a fisherman on Lake Superior. It is very likely that Jack Bonga stayed around the Grand Marais and Grand Portage areas into the thirties while the commercial fishing business flourished.[81]

From 1825—Stephen's time at Fort Misery—to 1837, Stephen was not only active as a voyageur but was elevated to the position of clerk in the American Fur Company. The great distances that Stephen paddled seems incredible to us today. Stephen's paddle frequently plied the waters of the Brule, St. Croix, Namekogen, and Yellow Rivers of Wisconsin. He also made trips in the great thirty-five foot long, *canot du maitre* (Montreal canoes) across the Great Lakes and down the St. Lawrence River into Quebec and paddled as far north in the *canot du nord* (the 25-foot-long North canoe) to Lake Winnipeg and Hudson Bay. Stephen even went as far down the Mississippi as St. Louis where better prices were paid for furs by the Chouteau Fur Company of St. Louis, a branch of the American Fur Company. Stephen, as a clerk, along the United States-Canadian border followed in the footsteps of his father, Pierre, both geographically and historically. During this period Stephen was in charge of the AFC post on Basswood Lake on the border and now part of the canoe country of the Boundary Waters Canoe Area Wilderness.

Stephen may rank among one of the greatest wilderness canoe paddlers in Minnesota and Wisconsin history, or even in North American history.

> "During the period of the American post at
> Basswood a colorful person was in charge
> – Stephen Bonga...Shortly there were many
> little half-breeds with kinky hair, which is said
> to have delighted the Indians enormously.
> Whenever they saw a Negro - the opportunity
> came seldom – they would place their hands on
> their hair and laugh merrily. It was customary
> before the campfires at night for tired voyageurs
> to recount their own prowess in canoeing and
> portaging. The tallest tale was told by a Bonga,
> it is said, who boasted of having carried eight
> packs across a portage. As the packs, or pieces,
> were made up to weigh ninety pounds each,
> the measure of his story-telling ability can be
> gauged."[82]

Stephen may have operated on the Rainy River below Rainy Lake where his Father Pierre, one of the "ordinariest negroes" as the trader John McKay had documented, played his fiddle in 1793.

Stephen's name keeps popping up all over Minnesota and Wisconsin as a trader and paddler as he seems to have had a role directly or indirectly with much of Minnesota and Wisconsin's historic events. In 1836, when Joseph N. Nicollet made his famous mapping and surveying trip to the Headwaters of the Mississippi, he notes in his journal that while at Leech Lake or *Gaa-zagaskwaajimekaag* and re-outfitting for the return trip to Fort Snelling, that:

Bonga

"Our crew is manning two canoes. The large one that we are supposed to return to St. Peter is twenty-four feet long. I am in it with Brunia [Francois Brunet], Desire Fronchet, and the mulatto Stephen, a native half-breed." In a footnote to this statement, the editor, Martha Coleman Bray states, "This was probably Stephen Bonga, a member of the well-known Negro-Chippewa family that was active in the upper Mississippi fur trade throughout the mid-19th century."[83]

The father of Itasca State Park, the crowned jewel and first state park in Minnesota, was Jacob Vradenberg Brower, who spent considerable amount of time surveying and confirming Nicollet's findings and lobbied hard in the latter part of the 1880s to save the old growth timber from the loggers axe by making it a state park. Brower wrote about the history of the Headwaters in his book titled, *The Mississippi River And Its Source: A Narrative And Critical History Of The Discovery Of The River And Its Headwaters*. In it he states, "Mr. Bungo, a representative of the colored race, in 1865, who originally claimed that he was 'the first white man who discovered Itasca lake" Some local residents of Headwaters Country think the "Mr. Bungo" Brower was referring to was George Bonga (Stephen's brother) but I think it very well could have been Stephen about whom Brower was referencing.[84]

So many names of white men are connected to the discovery of the Headwaters. All were from somewhere else and here only to profit from the fur trade or establish their names in the roster of American discovery. They did not live in the region, did not have a stake in it other than to take something. This was the land of the First Nation people who lived there, made their living there, and cared for the land. It seems rather problematic that the name Bonga does not have more historical significance in the story of the Headwaters of the Mississippi River than it does. For, as evidence seems to indicate, Jean Bonga likely found his way to the lower delta or mouth of the Mississippi which became an avenue for him out of slave country and into the Northwoods and freedom. 2,500 miles upstream and three generations later, the Bongas find themselves at the headwaters of this great river, the *Misi-ziibi,* their escape route to this safe abode in the wilderness.

The years 1836 and 37 mark the beginning of the end of the fur trade. Within a decade it would be only a remnant of what it once was. With the decline in the monetary value of furs and the influx of whites into the territories of Minnesota and Wisconsin, and with a growing nation in demand of resources, the intentions of the expanding nation became more focused on the lands held by First Nation people and the resources such as timber and minerals on these lands. Indian treaties up to this point were only for small parcels of land on which to build military forts and to bring Ojibwe and Dakota people to the peace table. Now, in 1837, the primary desire was for the rich timber in the forests of the region and use of the lakes and rivers to move the logs and power the mills to saw the timber.

Land Acquisition

The first major land acquisition treaty in Wisconsin Territory (which included much of present day Minnesota) was the Treaty of 1837 in which the Ojibwe ceded land to the United States. The land boundaries that the Ojibwe ceded in 1837 were a large tract with its western boundary at the Mississippi River and the Wisconsin River as its eastern line. The south line was the "Prairie du Chien Line" as established in the Prairie du Chien Treaty of 1825

106

(which delineated the boundaries separating the Dakota and Ojibwe) and the northern line in Wisconsin was the Lake Superior watershed. It then extended in a straight line west in Minnesota to the village of Old Crow Wing. This treaty was informally called the "White Pine Treaty" because of the demand for the virgin white pine here which was used to build the cities of Cleveland, St. Louis, and Chicago. This area included Mille Lacs Lake, the St. Croix River, and a sizable portion of east-central Minnesota and included a more significant portion of central Wisconsin. It is often called the St. Peters Treaty of 1837 due to its being held in what's now Mendota, Minnesota, near the junctions of the Mississippi River and Minnesota River (St. Peters River), at the site of Fort Snelling. The treaty negotiations were conducted by Governor Dodge of Wisconsin Territory and began on July 29, 1837.

Ojibwe bands from throughout what is now Wisconsin and Minnesota were invited even though many of these numerous bands were not directly affected by this treaty. The amount that the Indians received for the ceded lands was $800,000, mostly in goods and services. Of this amount, $100,000 would go to mixed-bloods, often referred to as the "half breed script" which included Stephen and George Bonga. An amount of $70,000 identified as debt would go to traders like William Aitkin and Lyman Warren which was not part of the original sale price. It is unclear whether the Indians understood that the money to pay off their debts was to be taken from the sale price, though they may have known as this had been standard practice by traders. The great Leech Lake Chief *Esh-ke-bug-e-koshe* (aka Flatmouth,), made the point that the traders owed them as much as they owed the traders. He also cited that many of the debt holders were now dead, killed by Dakota when they were out trapping or hunting for the traders. Furthermore, he cited that the food the traders ate and the wood they used was taken from tribal lands. He sarcastically said, "And they talk to us about paying our debts?"[85]

The official translators for the 1837 Treaty were Stephen Bonga and Patrick Quinn, who translated from English to Ojibwe, and Scott Campbell and Jean Baptiste Dubay, who translated from Ojibwe to English. The negotiations were meticulously recorded in a journal by Treaty Secretary Ver Planck Van Antwerp who included the Indian negotiators as well as Governor Dodge. The Indian statements are written in English which was done by the official government translators. There has been some criticism that the difficult job of translating was sometimes less than adequate. As an example of this, in his journal Van Antwerp noted in the margin alongside a portion of a speech by the war chief from Leech Lake, *Majigabow,* which was rendered as "nonsense" when translated "literally." He wrote that the interpreters were "unfit to act in that capacity." The *Majigabow* statement Van Antwerp is referring to is, "My father listen to me. Of all the country we grant you, we wish to hold on to a tree where we get our living, and to reserve the streams where we drink the waters that give us life." The secretary views this as a "metaphorical" reference to reserving the right to hunt, fish, and make maple sugar from maple trees. The Methodist missionary, Alfred Brunson, was present at the treaty in the role of an observer and remarked that "...there was also a Chippewa interpreter, Stephen Bonga who was also pious, and did the principle interpreting for that tribe; the government interpreter, a thick-mouthed, stammering Irishman not being able to speak intelligibly in either language."[86]

The importance of the 1837 Treaty cannot be overlooked in Minnesota and Wisconsin history, or the role Stephen had there. At the Treaty of St. Peters in 1837 and the Treaty of 1842 at Lapointe, Ojibwe from all over the Wisconsin territory made it clear in their testimony that in order to survive and maintain their culture as a people, they must maintain usufructuary rights to the land, hence:

> "Article 5. The privilege of hunting, fishing, and
> gathering the wild rice, upon the lands, the
> rivers and the lakes included in the territory
> ceded, is guaranteed to the Indians, during the
> pleasure of the President of the United States."

This article has had lasting importance to Ojibwe in the states of Wisconsin and Minnesota. In subsequent lawsuits, the federal courts have upheld these rights by issuing rulings regarding the notes and journals kept at these treaty negotiations. Courts have continually viewed the translations from the 1837 Treaty of Ojibwe headmen as precedent setting by giving Ojibwe people hunting, fishing, and gathering rights on ceded lands. The treaty also demonstrates that the Ojibwe chiefs present realized the importance of protecting the water and lands as paramount to their gathering rights.[87]

As *Esh-ke-bug-e-koshe* of Leech Lake stated:

> "My father, your children are willing to let you
> have their lands, but they wish to reserve the
> privilege of making sugar from the trees and
> getting a living from the lakes and rivers, as
> they have done heretofore and of remaining in
> the country. It is hard to give up the lands. They
> will remain, and cannot be destroyed – but you
> may cut down the trees and others will grow up.
> You know we cannot live deprived of our lakes
> and rivers. There is some game on the lands

yet and for that reason also, we wish to remain upon them, to get a living...The Great Spirit above, made the Earth and causes it to produce, which enables us to live."[88]

Another chief made the point that if whites are to receive this ceded land, they must protect the waters;

"This straw which I hold in my hands, Wild Rice is what we call this. These I do not sell. That you may not destroy the Rice in working the Timber, Also the Rapids and Falls in the Streams I will lend you to saw your timber...I do not make a present of this, I merely lend it to you."[89]

These chiefs knew then, that the fish, wild rice and game were the foundation of their existence and health. If the whites polluted the waters within the ceded lands, it had a direct negative impact on these resources thereby negating their treaty rights.

To Ojibwe people and any other Native American tribes in North America, their connection to the earth and everything on it, forms the foundation of their way of life. Stephen certainly understood this need as he was Ojibwe: he had hunted, fished, gathered maple sugar, and "knocked down" wild rice or, as the Ojibwe called it, *manoomin*. We must not forget that this region of Minnesota and Wisconsin is where Ojibwe prophesized they would settle, the place where food grows upon water, wild rice. If Indian people were restricted from harvesting rice, not only would they be culturally harmed, they would be nutritionally impaired for *manoomin* is the staff of life in this country. It is to the Ojibwe what the buffalo was to the Dakota of the plains. It provided an abundant food source. These demands were clearly under-stood by Stephen Bonga.[90]

The name Bonga can be found on almost all the sub-sequent Indian treaties in the territory but it was Stephen who capitalized on this more than either of his brothers. As his mother was a full-blood, and with his father in the backcountry much of Stephen's youth, it is not surpris-ing that he and his brothers spoke *Ojibwemowin* (Ojibwe language) fluently, living with and being raised by Ojibwe people. It has been stated a number of times that Stephen spoke very good English and we know that all the Bongas spoke French as George said of his father, Pierre, "...as he did not Speak any thing but french." As Stephen also worked as interpreter for the government in negotiations with the Dakota, it is apparent that he also spoke Dakota.

Intertribal Warfare, 1839

"War, War, War, will be carried on between the Sioux & the Chippeways...as long as there is a Brave of either Nation in existence." – Lawrence Taliaferro[91]

These are the written words, often miss-spelled, of Major Lawrence Taliaferro (pronounced Tol-li-ver), who, as the United States Indian Agent for this region, lived and worked out of St. Peter's in the 1820s and 1830s. Historians today call the conflicts between the Ojibwe and Dakota the "Hundred Years War." This long struggle dates from 1730 when the Ojibwe people marched from Fond du Lac, across the Northwest Trail against the Dakota strong-hold on Big Sandy Lake, and unofficially ends with the Dakota-Minnesota War in 1862. By the 1830s the Ojibwe people resided in roughly the northern half of the state and the Dakota in the southern half. Most of the conflicts were scattered skirmishes with a half dozen or less casualties but occasionally horrendous slaughter occurred. There were periods of relative quiet when the Ojibwe and Dakota would come together and dance, sing, compete in athletic contests, or hunt in each other's territory without molestation, but animosities would inevitably flare-up and warfare would resume.

Prior to the mid 1820s, Ojibwe people traveled to Fort St. Anthony (later renamed Fort Snelling) in Dakota country to receive annuity payments and or goods. In 1827, Taliaferro's nemesis, Henry Schoolcraft, recently appointed Indian agent for the Ojibwe, worked to change the distribution location for Ojibwe receiving annuities to Mackinac and later La Pointe. This was not a popular change for most Ojibwe, such as the Mississippi bands at Gull Lake, Mille Lacs, St. Croix, and Leech Lake. It was a lot easier for them to float down the Mississippi to St. Peter's than to make the difficult traverse via the North West Trail to Lake Superior and the lengthy travel on the world's largest lake.

Major Taliaferro was a man of contradictions. When he was first appointed Indian agent at St. Peter's in March of 1819, he was only twenty-five years of age. From "old" Virginia and of Italian ancestry, he fought in the War of 1812, having enlisted as a young man of eighteen. By the close of the war, he was a lieutenant in the regular army. From 1819 to 1839, Taliaferro was the "most important and influential civil official on the upper Mississippi." The Major was almost universally liked by all Indians and had certain personal inclinations that endeared him to Indians: his resolute conviction for the truth and his fondness for the "Indian way" which included Indian "regalia," Indian ceremonies, and the esteem Indians placed on oratory skills. In all of Minnesota's history, Major Taliaferro may have been the best white friend of the Indian.

"It is to his credit that he was cordially hated by all who could neither bribe nor frighten him to connive at lawbreaking to the harm of Indians. In spite of the complaints and machinations of traders and politicians he held his place until 1839, when he voluntarily resigned after a sixth appointment – a fact as credible to four presidents, their cabinents, and the Indian office as to the incorruptible and high-toned Virginian."[92]

The contradiction in Major Lawrence Taliaferro's persona was that he was a slave-holder and brought his slaves with him during his time at Fort Snelling. Obviously, Taliaferro's sense of humanity and decency was much different towards Anishinaabe than Black people.

The final year of Major Taliaferro's position as Indian agent in 1839, saw what would be one of the bloodiest encounters in the history of Ojibwe and Dakota warfare. It was described by Samuel Pond as "without parallel in authentic annals of intertribal warfare occurring within the boundaries of the present state of Minnesota."[93] Taliaferro, in his journal, referred to 1839 Minnesota as the "... dark and bloody ground" and with this dramatic incident in Minnesota history about to play out, we find Stephen Bonga at its vortex.

As events in the summer of 1839 unfolded toward this bloody tragedy, the most detailed description is given by the Reverend Ezekiel Gilbert Gear, who had recently arrived in the Northland as the newly appointed chaplain at Fort Snelling. Gear was an Episcopal minister who would go on to serve the Ojibwe at Crow Wing.

Taliaferro did not like Reverend Gear on first meeting him, and in his journal wrote, "I don't like his abolitionism." The Major added with grudging praise the accuracy of

Gear's manuscript in documenting the events. Gear does a good job of contextualizing the events by noting that in the Treaty of 1837, Gov. Dodge assured the Ojibwe that they would:

> "receive their payments at the Falls of the St.
> Croix river, or at some point convenient to
> them, on the lands they sold to the Government
> – though in this treaty, this matter is left to
> the discretion of the President of the United
> States. The President, it seems, ignorant of this
> assurance, has appointed Lapoint[e] on Lake
> Superior. This place may, possibly, have been
> designated, with a view to prevent future col-
> lisions with the Sioux, as it is situated some
> three or four hundred miles in an opposite di-
> rection, and in a country in which these bands
> have no interest or connextion, and they do
> not hesitate to say that the President has been
> misled by artful and designing men; and that
> their wishes have been misconceived and mis-
> represented to him."[94]

The "artful and designing men" included Henry Rowe Schoolcraft, a man much detested by Major Taliaferro.

In the summer of 1839 the Ojibwe of northern Minnesota were prepared and packed to depart for Lapointe for their annuity payments. According to Gear, when the Ojibwe began to ponder the hardships that would be encountered in the journey to Lapointe, they considered them "impract-ible and impossible, on account of the distance, the great numbers of portages, and scarcity of game; and the utter hoplessness of the attempt to bring back their property, or to subsist while there, they came to the conclusion, as they were already on the point of leaving, to come to this post, where the treaty [1837] had been made, and in the neighborhood of which they expected its fulfillment..."[95]

The authorities at Fort Snelling had no reason to expect Ojibwe people arriving as they assumed they would be well on their way to Lapointe. When word arrived at Fort Snelling that a large contingent of Ojibwe people were on their way on June 8, 1839, a "messenger" was dispatched to tell them to turn around, not come any further, that disturbances might occur between them and their old enemies, the Dakota Sioux. They were repeatedly warned to be on guard and be careful not to do anything that would offend the Dakota. The man Taliaferro picked to be the "messenger" was Stephen Bonga.

"Taliaferro received word on June 8, 1839, that the Chippewa under Hole-in-the-Day were on their way to Fort Snelling, having refused to go to Lapointe, and that 'nothing could keep them back.' The agent publicly explained to the Sioux that the visit was to be a friendly one which they must meet 'on the same grounds... and not infringe the rights of hospitality,' but he confided to his journal that in his "own private opinion" difficulty was to be apprehended. He dispatched the Negro-Chippewa fur trader, Stephen Bonga, to intercept the chief and direct him "to hold still where he is and not to come here." The Indians were already below Rum River when Bonga met them and the chief refused to stop, saying that he would stay but three days at the fort. He added that he hoped Taliaferro would keep the Sioux from interfering with him and that 'he would be quiet in turn."[96]

Knowing Major Taliaferro, it is not surprising that he chose Stephen Bonga to deliver this vitally important message. When the Major and Stephen first crossed paths is uncertain, but Taliaferro would not have failed to notice Stephen's important role at the proceedings during the negotiations of the St. Peter's Treaty of 1837. In fact, when treaty negotiations were first starting, the AFC trader Lyman Warren was making grossly inflated claims for annuity money intended for Indians as debts owed him by the Indians. Taliaferro, angered by Warren's outrageous claims, pulled out his pistol and threatened to shoot Warren unless he sit down and shut up. Hole-in-the-Day (*Bagone-giizhig*), who was present, and incensed by Warren's attempts to gouge the Indians, yelled to Taliaferro to "Shoot him, my father." Governor Dodge intervened before any violence began.[97] I only note this as to show that these people were not unknown entities but people who had a history of interactions, reputations and grudges among themselves. Taliaferro, Bonga, and the famed chief Hole-in-the-Day were not strangers to one another by any means.

Now, in early June of 1839, Stephen Bonga, alone, paddled up the Mississippi, above and around the great falls and rapids of St. Anthony where he encountered Hole-in-the-Day and his entourage somewhere below the mouth of the Rum River. Here, Bonga relayed Taliaferro's message and the great chief responded that "nothing could keep them back." So, the Ojibwe, disregarding Taliferro's message, kept coming and Stephen joined their flotilla.

Reverend Gear described the spectacular scene as the Ojibwe began arriving in full and colorful regalia at the fort in a flotilla of canoes:

"...to the number of seven or eight hundred.
They came down the Mississippi in bark canoes,

and as they shot round the bastion of the Fort, presented one of the most vivid and picturesque scenes that is possible to imagine of savage life. The party consisted of men, women and children, of all ages, from the hoary headed patriarch to the infant of a day; and acknowledged as their leader and chief, Pagonagerig [Bagonegiizhig – Hole in the Day]. This man is, perhaps, one of the finest specimens of his race, and possesses no common share of intellect, bravery and talent. His name literally signifies, hole in the sky, or bright spot in the clouds; but he is commonly called Hole in the Day. His warriors, to the number of two or three hundred, were all well-armed, and principally with guns, and appeared to be well supplied with ammunition; and their conduct, while here, was peaceable, dignified and manly. This array of strength was to be in consequence of the disturbance of last year, and with a view to over-awe their enemies."[98]

On June 20, five hundred Ojibwe arrived with Hole-in-the-Day and over the next five days the canoes kept arriving with rifle volleys from many guns to announce each group's arrival. The Ojibwe set up camp on the east side of the river, opposite the fort. By June 24, Taliaferro counted 900 Ojibwe and 856 Dakota for a total of 1,756 and moaned "I have my hands full" and predicted "trouble on trouble with Indians at war."[99]

On the next day, June 21, once all the bands arrived, a formal council was set up under a canopy near the walls of the fort which included all the chiefs and headmen of the tribes, the commanding officer of the fort, Major Joseph

Plympton, Major Taliaferro, other officers, and some citizens of the vicinity. Stephen Bonga was assigned the task of interpreter for this council. Hole-in-the-Day asked permission to spend three days, which was approved, and talks focused on payments and other matters of importance.[100] As Gear described it, the headmen of the Ojibwe:

> "expressed the deepest sorrow and regret of the disappointment of not receiving their annuities as they had expected; that they never had but one word; that they always pursued a straight course; that they were sick at heart; that they could not go to Lapoint[e] for the reason which have been mentioned; and more than insinuated that good faith had been violated."

At the conclusion of the meetings, the Ojibwe demanded that a trip be set up for them to go to Washington and meet with the Great Father in order to express their grievances. This demand was agreed upon and supported by Major Taliaferro and Major Plympton.[101]

The Ojibwe remained encamped on the east side of the Mississippi and "the utmost harmony seemed to exist between them and the Sioux." Both the Dakota and the Ojibwe, together, participated in dances, drum ceremonies, games, and friendly interaction. It appeared that a new era of permanent peace was forthcoming. Nothing occurred that would indicate any suspicion until, just before the Ojibwe were to depart, a Dakota fired a shot into an Ojibwe canoe. The Dakota man immediately fled up the St. Peter's River valley before he could be apprehended by his people who would have appropriately punished him. Another premonitory incident occurred with Strong Ground, Hole-in-the-Day's brother, who had accumulated thirty-six eagle

118

feathers by killing Dakota men on the field of battle, and was being watched with bad intentions by a number of Dakota men. He received a warning of an ambush and eluded the trap. These were the only indications of possible trouble.

On the day of Ojibwe departure, they smoked the pipe of peace with the Dakota and Taliaferro and agreed to a one-year suspension of hostilities. Just prior to departure, the Ojibwe agreed to split into two equally sized groups. One, led by Strong Ground, would go up the St. Croix in an attempt to reach Lapointe and receive their payments. The other group, under Hole-in-the-Day, would proceed up the Mississippi to their homes at Gull Lake, Crow Wing, Mille Lacs, and Leech Lake. Traveling with Strong Ground up the St Croix were some white men and mixed-bloods. One of these white men was William Aitkin, the head-man of the Fond du Lac department of the American Fur Company. Two of the mixed-bloods were Francois Brunette who guided Joseph Nicollet to the Headwaters three years earlier and Stephen Bonga.

There were two men from Hole-in-the-Day's band who had lost a relative a year earlier to the Dakota and who was buried at Camp Coldwater adjacent to Fort Snelling. With or without Hole-in-the-Day's permission, they remained behind to mourn their relative. It may be assumed that while mourning, they decided to take revenge for their brother's death and made their way to the area around a Dakota summer camp near *Bde Maka Ska*. They surprised a Dakota named Nika, who was related to Red Bird, a well-known healer among the Dakota. Nika was killed and scalped on July 2. The body was still warm when it was discovered and a war party was immediately formed and divided into two groups; one to pursue the group of Ojibwe traveling up the Mississippi and the other in pursuit of the

Ojibwe traveling up the St. Croix. The Dakota in pursuit on the St. Croix found the Ojibwe just a few miles upriver, sleeping off a bout of heavy drinking from the previous night in the river bottom with the high escarpments of the St. Croix on both sides. It was the worst ground the Ojibwe could have put themselves in the event of an attack. It was defenseless ground. The Dakota recognized the strategic superiority they had and attacked. It is said that they waited for the whites to depart before the fighting started, yet William Aitkin, Francois Brunette, Stephen Bonga, and a "Frenchman" were among the mixed-bloods and whites wounded. Alfred Brunson reports Aitkin was "slightly wounded," while Tailaferro's Journal of July 4, 1839 states, "Mr. Aitkin, & Francis Brunet, & a Frenchman were wounded. Mr. A's tent – a linen one was shot to pieces." In his Journal for July 21, "Aitkin is said to be slightly wounded a scratch on the thigh – supposed by some to have happened in his flight a scratch from a bush or stick." Brunette's wound is not known but knowing the character of the man, he was undoubtedly facing the enemy fire. As for Stephen, Alfred Brunson wrote from Fort Snelling:

> "Mr. Aitkin, a trader with the Chippeways, and Stephen Bungo, our interpreter, who were on their way to Lapoint, Lake Superior, to receive their portion of the half-breed payment [1837 Treaty], are said to have been wounded, though we have no certain intelligence of it. Both nations are very careful not to kill whitemen, half-breeds, or even Indians dressed like whitemen. But in the heat of battle, when all camped together, such accidents happen. The Sioux, who thought much of Stephen, expressed much regret on account of the occurrence – if it is so."[102]

Many of those killed were women and children; among the dead was Strong Ground's wife. One Dakota chief stated that they would have killed all the Ojibwe if they would not have waited for the whites to leave.

As bad of a situation that the Ojibwe found themselves, they rallied and made a gallant defense under the leadership of the brave and courageous Strong Ground, even driving the Dakota back. But, as one historian said, the Dakota "had not come to lose men." The attacking Dakota numbered from 100 to 150 warriors. The loss of Ojibwe life was estimated to be thirty-five to forty. Taliaferro wrote that no fewer than fifty Ojibwe were killed.

As bad as the losses were for Strong Ground, they were worse for those Ojibwe headed home on the Mississippi. The Mille Lacs band parted-ways from Hole-in-the-Day's band and the other bands, as the Mille Lacs people headed for the Rum River that would bring them to their home on Mille Lacs Lake. It was this band, the Mille Lacs Ojibwe, that suffered all the losses. They headed off in a diagonal course overland from the others and the men went on ahead to hunt as their provisions were low. The women, older men and children were behind portaging their baggage when the Dakota, led by Red Bird, caught up to them. When they did, they fired with deadly effect. Amazingly, the Ojibwe warriors nearest to the rear quickly returned to defend their women, elders, and children and made a gallant defense, making successive stands by returning the enemy's fire. One attacking Dakota said that there was continual bloodshed for a half hour as the initial killing was done mostly with knife and tomahawk. The reports of the dead Ojibwe were as high as 133; another as low as sixty or seventy. The loss to the Dakota was seventeen warriors but this included Red Bird and one of his sons.[103] Stephen would have known many of the dead on both sides.

Interpreter, Guide, and Missionary

As the fur trade was winding down, Stephen spent more of his time as an interpreter, guide, and missionary. When Stephen was one of the official interpreters at the St. Peter's Treaty of 1837, one of the observers was the Methodist missionary, Alfred Brunson. A lasting friendship developed between these two. During the 1840s, Stephen spent a great deal of time as an interpreter and guide for Rev. Brunson in Wisconsin and throughout northern Minnesota, and did some preaching of his own. Stephen was a gifted storyteller and drew an attentive audience when relating his stories.

Brunson writes of his interesting times with Stephen in the Cincinnati *Western Christian Advocate.* On July 25, 1838, Brunson writes, "We left the Sioux mission, and ascended to the St. Peters in a log canoe, not being able to get a bark one of suitable dimensions...I had with me brother Whitford, brother Randolph, and Stephen Bung[o], our interpreter." Weeks later Brunson writes, "We found here several half breeds who have attended some of the mission schools on Lake Superior or its outlet, who could sing in Chippeway, and to them and a few others, Stephen, our interpreter, gave a discourse on religious subjects, sung, and prayed." In another letter printed in the *Cincinnati Christian Advocate* under the heading, "Upper Mississippi Mission," Brunson gives us another interesting look at Stephen:

> "Stephen, our interpreter, I find has an extensive relationship; and, indeed, the Indians claim to be uncles and cousins as long as the least trace of kindred blood can be identified; hence Stephen was nephew, cousin, uncle, or brother-in-law to all these chiefs, and many of their bands. His Grandfather was a slave, brought from the West Indies to Mackinaw, and

his father was a full blooded African, married
two Chippeway women, by whom he raised a
large family, at or near Leech Lake. All these,
with other relatives, to the number of about 60,
half breeds, have adopted civilized habits, and
some of them are respectable for their literary
attainments; and they all wish to settle together
by our mission establishment; thus making a
village of some eight or ten families, comprising
sixty or seventy souls. They have hitherto been
in the employ of the traders, as sub-traders,
voyageurs, or hands; but they say they are tired
of that mode of living; and furthermore, the fur
trade is nearly extinguished, game being scare
and the price of fur being greatly reduced. Of
this association a large school could be col-
lected, and the Chippeway being their native
tongue, when educated and converted (which we
hope God will do) they would be of great use in
spreading the gospel further, among the people.
These half breeds, being natives of the country,
accustomed to its climate and the manners of
the people, and a connecting link between the
civilized and the noncivilized, will be of great
use in extending the blessings of civilization and
religion among the aboriginals."

Missionaries, like Brunson, sought out Stephen's help
as guide and interpreter due to his knowledge of the country
and the fact that he was Ojibwe. One missionary remarked,
"Bonga made our introductions to the local Indians very
easy, because he was related to about every family on the
Upper Mississippi!"[104]
Stephen married *Biwabiko-ikwe* who was the daughter

of *Chief Waabooz* (Rabbitt) of whom many of the lakes and geographic features of "Rabbit Country" on the Cuyuna Iron Range in the Crosby region of northern Minnesota are named. Stephen would play an important role in the development of missions at Little Elk and Rabbit River and assist with missions at Sandy Lake, Leech, Red Lake, and Fond du Lac in the 1840s.[105]

It is interesting to note how one historian finds attitudes towards the Bongas in the nineteenth century as compared with today, writing, "It is particularly fascinating to find them [Indians related to Bongas] typically embarrassed over their Negro blood, which was instead a matter of boasting in days when George, Stephen, and Jack were still remembered."[106]

The Ojibwe Death March of 1850

One of the blackest marks on Minnesota history is the Sandy Lake Death March of 1850. Although we have no known written account of Stephen's experience, we know he was there, as documentation shows Stephen as number seventy-nine on the Sandy Lake Annuity Role with the Fond du Lac Band.[107]

In 1849, with the decline of the fur trade and the growth of the white population, the territorial government was becoming increasingly desirous to remove Indians from areas where concentrations of white settlements and farms were developing. Therefore, on October 11, 1849, just seven months after the creation of the Minnesota Territory, the newly formed territorial legislature revoked Article five of the 1837 Treaty of St. Peters, which guaranteed Indians the right to hunt, fish, and gather on ceded lands. The territorial resolution also stated that Indians were to be removed far from white settlements which were referred to as the "removal order." On February 6, 1850, President Zachary

Taylor acted in accordance with the Minnesota Territorial Legislature by issuing an executive order rescinding the Indians right to hunt, fish, and gather on ceded lands and ordered their removal from ceded lands as stated in the treaties of 1837 and 1842 to re-settle them somewhere on the Headwaters of the Mississippi River. The removal of and resettling of Indians affected most severely the Ojibwe people from Wisconsin.

Prior to the Minnesota Territorial Legislature and President Zachary Taylor's revocation of the hunting-fishing-gathering provisions of the 1837 and 1842 treaties, Ojibwe people in Minnesota and Wisconsin traveled to Lapointe on the Madeline Islands off the south shore of Wisconsin to collect annuity payments and goods. Now, the decision of what, where, and when annuities were to be distributed was relegated to Minnesota Territorial Governor Alexander Ramsey by the Office of Indian Affairs in Washington. Governor Ramsey, as Governor, also happened to be superintendent of Indian Affairs in the territory. Since most of Headwaters Country was still unceded land, Ramsey and others considered several different locations in northern Minnesota as locations to resettle tribes per the "removal order", one being where the Leech Lake Band of Pillagers resided. This was quickly dropped as many the Leech Lakers did not want any other bands utilizing the resources that they felt only adequately supplied their own needs. After some superficial studying the location site, Big Sandy Lake was chosen as the annuity and removal site. But what was paramount on the minds of Ramsey, traders, and government officials, was not concern about a suitable site for them to subsist on the land, but rather concentrating the Indians somewhere along the Headwaters which would make it much easier for them to be fleeced by white traders and government officials. Another mitigating factor that worked against the Indians was that the United States Government was not particularly concerned about Indians. The Congress was more concerned about slavery, and what was to be free soil and what would be slave soil. Indians were way down on the governments list of priorities.

Almost all of the Wisconsin Bands of Ojibwe were opposed to leaving their homes, especially since the government had promised them that removal would not occur for a long time, not in their lifetime, but this was simply ignored by the government as it ordered the removal. Those who did not take part in the removal were told they would no longer receive annuities. Semantics and misunderstanding concerning the definition of the word "removal" was another issue. The traditional and seasonal move on the part of Indians is described by the Ojibwe word "*gosiwin*" was likely used by interpreters and translates into the traditional mode of living by Indian people in seasonal movements from hunting grounds, to rice beds, to sugar bushes, and so forth. Indian people were always "removing" from one camp to another camp. Many Indians may have understood this removal order as just temporary and that they would ultimately be moving back to their traditional homes.[108]

By November and December of 1850, thousands of Ojibwe people were arriving at Big Sandy Lake where there was a desperate shortage of food, goods, and medicines necessary to sustain the great numbers. The annuities were never appropriated by Congress and measles and dysentery were spreading through the camp like wildfire. When insufficient annuities and provisions arrived and were quickly exhausted, goods were purchased from white traders, not from government funds but from the Indian annuity payments at greatly inflated prices. Indians were dying of starvation even while insufficient rations were being consumed by 4,000 Indians. Territorial Indian Agent, John Watrous said that no fewer than 150 Indians had died. The Commandant of Fort Ripley, J.B. Todd, wrote that thirty Indians died each of the three nights he was there and "that one hundred and fifty will not cover their losses." To exacerbate matters, the hard cold, frozen winter of northern Minnesota made it extremely difficult for the Indians on their homeward journey. They had to discard their canoes as the rivers and lakes were frozen thus their journeys had to be made by foot through deep snow. Chief Buffalo of Lapointe said that 170 died during the payment and another 230 died on the journey home.[109]

While all this death and suffering was happening, the architect of this debacle, Governor Alexander Ramsey was in St. Paul celebrating Christmas. Of the shock and outrage, the most condemning words came from the great chief of the Leech Lake band of Ojibwe, *Esh-ke-bug-e-koshe,* who had his words written down and shown to Ramsey:

> "...we have been called here, and made to suffer
> by sickness, by death, by hunger and cold. I lay
> it all to him. I charge it all to our Great Father
> the Governor. It is because we listened to his
> words that we have suffered so much...We have
> been taken from our country at the most valu-
> able season of the year for hunting and fishing,
> and if we had remained at home we should
> have been far better off than we are now with
> our scanty annuity. I am not one that speaks
> of another behind his back. I say to his face all
> that I desire to say at all; and I would say to the
> governor, if he were here, all that I say to you...
> the fault rests on his shoulders...My friend, it
> makes our hearts sore to look at the losses we

have sustained while at Sandy Lake. You call us your children, but I do not think we are your children. If we were we should be white. You are not our Father and I think you call us your children only in mockery. The earth is our Father and I will never call you so. The reason we call the earth our Father is because it resembles us in color; and we call the sky our Grandfather. We did not sell the ground to our Great Father. We gave it to him in order that he might follow our example and be liberal to us."[110]

We can only imagine the ghastly scenes at Sandy Lake that Stephen witnessed and the impact it had on him. In the following year, the executive and congressional branches of government revoked President Taylor's rescission of Article V of the Treaty of 1837: the right to hunt, fish, and gather. The reinstating of Indian rights to hunt, fish, and gather, and nullifying the original removal order thus made the deaths of those Ojibwe utterly unnecessary. The Ojibwe people have yet to get an apology.

1856-57

The great American painter, Eastman Johnson, made visits to the Superior/Duluth area in 1856 and 57. Johnson had studied art in Dusseldorf, London, and the Hague. He studied Rembrandt and became so successful that his friends dubbed him the "American Rembrandt." In 1855, Johnson returned to America and the following summer, made the journey to Superior where his sister Sarah had married William H. Newton, an early white pioneer of that area.

In 1854, the entire North Shore of Lake Superior and much of the northeastern portion of Minnesota had been ceded to the whites by the Ojibwe of that region. William Newton, Johnson's brother-in-law, had made claims for land in Superior and became known as one of the "Proprietors of Superior" as he and others who owned shares in the town site were called. Superior had been platted in 1854, the same year that the Ojibwe ceded these lands. Across St. Louis Bay, in 1856, Duluth was platted. In Oneota, there was a sawmill in one of the first small communities in what's now Duluth. Small white settlements were also at Fond du Lac and fewer up the North Shore. The iron deposits of the iron ranges of northeastern Minnesota had not yet been discovered. A settler was lucky if mail was delivered once a week. The economy was based on lumber, salted fish, and a few furs.[111] The majority of people on the North Shore were Ojibwe people. In fact, there were probably five times as many Indians as there were whites in the Minnesota territory in 1849. Between 1849 and 1860, the white population increased by more than 3,700 percent! It became one of the greatest population booms in American history. 34 But northern Minnesota Territory was still wilderness and all these people coming to the state were, for the most part, settling in the southern parts on the state, along the river from Winona to St. Paul or on farms in the southern third of the state.

Probably, one of the reasons that Eastman Johnson came Minnesota Territory was the investment opportunities at the Head of the Lake. But while there, he saw a possible subject matter for his paintings—the Ojibwe in their homeland. Johnson's biographer, John I. H. Baur, wrote in *An American Genre Painter, Eastman Johnson, 1824-1906,* that he believed Johnson "may have been influenced by the [Leatherstocking] novels of [William Fenimore] Cooper." Johnson became enamored with the Ojibwe people and the rugged and beautiful country of the big lake. Although his paintings of Indian people never sold in his lifetime, they are now recognized as some of the most beautiful, complimentary and realistic depictions of Indian people at home. While in the region, Johnson had the good fortune to become friends with Stephen Bonga. Stephen served as Johnson's interpreter and guide. The two traveled, camped, and ate together as Stephen took him to the Apostle Islands, Grand Portage, Isle Royale and south to the Kettle River. Stephen and Johnson became good friends and Stephen remarked affectionately that Johnson was a "most likeable man to work for." The two undoubtedly spent a great deal of time together in a canoe visiting all the places that Stephen considered his home, and Stephen said Johnson had become an expert in handling a birch-bark canoe.[112]

The famed Ojibwe artist Carl Gawboy believes that all the time that Johnson spent with Bonga and his Ojibwe family changed his approach to painting. As for myself, I have never seen any paintings of Indian people as flattering as those done by Johnson. Johnson even provides the names of his subjects; they were real people to Johnson. Would the artist have seen the humanity in them if it were not for his trusted friend, Stephen? His paintings show Indian people in everyday activities and in their natural surroundings. There seems no doubt in Gawboy's belief that Johnson would never have gotten this close to Ojibwe people and have them sit in such a relaxed composure if it had not been that these Ojibwe people personally knew and trusted Stephen.[113]

Most of Johnson's paintings of Indian life were probably done in 1857. Johnson had built himself a small cedar log cabin on the Pokegama River, a small stream that widens into a bay as it enters the Upper Harbor of St. Louis Bay. The small cabin served as his studio, which established "himself in the woods in a primitive camp studio of his own

construction, which was everything an artist could desire."
John Bardon of Superior, who has been the source of much
Bonga and Johnson material, wrote that Johnson's cabin
was used by himself in his youth for his many hunting
trips and was identified for him by Stephen Bonga. Bardon
specified the location:

> "Twenty-eighth Street began at Old Superior on
> 6th Street near Becker Avenue. It was cut out
> through a stand of virgin timber in the early
> fifties, on a section line that intercepted the St.
> Louis River near the mouth of Big Pokegama. It
> was used by whites and Indians at all seasons
> of the year, but especially in the winter and the
> spring. The upper river would be open 10 days
> or more before the mouth. At the westerly end
> of this roadway the latter well-known painter,
> Eastman Johnson, had his studio and hunt-
> ing cabin. His right-hand man was Stephen
> Bungo..."[114]

As a young man, John Bardon recalls seeing a portrait
of Stephen Bonga in Johnson's cabin, done by Eastman
Johnson himself. The whereabouts of the Bonga portrait
are unknown. Oh, how unfortunate, as it must be a most
respectful depiction of the great old canoe-man, Stephen.
What a memorial it would be to the old voyageur if the portrait of Stephen Bonga would re-surface.

The Eastman Johnson Ojibwe paintings are now owned
and displayed at the St. Louis County Historical Society.

The Latter Years

By the time Stephen had aged into his fifties, he had
returned to settle in his beloved homeland in Old Superior,

Kenne waw be mint by Eastman Johnson, Charcoal and Crayon on Paper, 1857. Image sourced from Wikimedia Commons, Public Domain ©

the original settlement. It was near the mouth of the Nemadji River, or the left-hand river as some called it, the St. Louis River being the right-hand river.

Stephen had honed his story-telling skills and whites and Native people alike reveled in being Stephen's audience. As one citizen reminisced about Stephen:

Bonga

Kay be sen day way We Win by Eastman Johnson, Charcoal and Crayon on Paper, 1857. Image sourced from Wikimedia Commons, Public Domain☺

Ojibwe Wigwam at Grand Portage by Eastman Johnson, Oil on Canvas, 1857. Image sourced from Wikimedia Commons, Public Domain☺

"Undoubtedly the most picturesque character was Stephen Bongo – half Indian and half
Negro, with Negro features predominating...He
was a man of intelligence and full of reminiscences...He was religiously inclined and used
very good English. He was a frequent visitor
at the store and was occasionally induced to
favor his listeners with very interesting reminiscences – some of historical value, that may
never have reached the recorder of those very
remote and interesting times – if there has ever
been one. Being 'the first white man born at the
head of the lakes' as he frequently claimed in
his reminiscent moods, was probably intended
to mean that the distinction between white and
dark races depended more...on education than
on color; and while he could not deny the latter,
he presumably based his claim on the possession of the former. He was strong for education
and always interested in keeping his children in
school."[115]

John Bardon tells of how Stephen would entertain
his listeners with Ojibwe story-telling of the accounts of
Nanaboozhoo—a vitally important spiritual being in Ojibwe
creation stories—and relate the stories about Ojibwe de-
ities such as *Amik* (beaver), *Makwa* (bear) and other
"Grandfathers." Stephen also enjoyed telling of his adventures in the heyday of the fur trade, such as the voyages with the likes of William Morrison to the Headwaters
of the Mississippi or about his feats of physical prowess.
The Bongas were all legendary for their incredible physical
strength. It is easy to forget that Stephen was a *homme du
nord*—a man of the north—and also known as a *hivernant*

(winterer), which were considered by their peers to be an elite rank among voyageurs.

Concerning Stephen's strength, one account has Stephen climbing Porcupine Mountain on Lake Superior's south shore with seven hundred pounds on his back, an unbelievable feat.[116] Stephen's stories were to include his canoe voyages to the land of "little sticks" above the timber line to Hudson Bay, to St. Louis, and to Montreal. Listeners would be enthralled to hear these stories from one of the greatest canoe men who ever lived. Little did his audience realize that they were in the presence of a great man. His stories also included his skills as a woodsman and hunter.

Stephen was regarded by white and Indian alike to be one of the best bear hunters in the Head of the Lakes region. He is known to have said that he killed more bears than anyone else; but when his beloved dog died, he is thought to have said, "Bungo's dog died and Bungo did not kill anymore bear."

Another interesting incident from Stephen's later years happened when he was living at the mouth of the Brule River on the south shore of Lake Superior. The Brule River is part of one of the great water trails in the north and is also known as a great trout fishing river. Stephen had many times paddled the river which was a gateway to much of western Wisconsin and the St. Croix. While Stephen was residing there, a group of fishermen were also camped on the Brule. While the fishermen were camped there "some of the party stole all of Bungo's chickens. Bungo, who was noted for his politeness went to their camp, and said, 'Excuse me, gentlemen, Chippewa is my native language, but some of you gentlemen have stolen all my chickens.' It is needless to say Bungo was well paid for his chickens." It is easy to imagine the tall, erect, muscular old voyageur approaching the fishermen and the resulting conclusion of the fishermen that, by their own best judgment, they had better compensate this man as they correctly realized that it would be wise not to antagonize him.[117]

Stephen never gave up his calling as a lay minister, and was described by John Bardon as being "a type of traveling parson." Stephen always went to the aid of anyone in need and right up to the end was "strictly temperate and an enemy of alcohol." John Bardon noted a peculiar eating habit of old Stephen:

> "...he was unusually well regarded by both the Indians and the whites. They both seemed to appreciate him and his good qualities, but often told, laughingly, of one curious trait – that of always eating his meals alone in state, and demanding the choicest portion of whatever the family larder afforded – be it sucker head soup or muskrat with wild rice, or moose or bear cutlets. The rest of the family was then welcome to take 'pot luck.' However, there was always enough for everybody."[118]

Stephen lived a semi-subsistence life: hunting, ricing, sugar making, and making some money on the side—possibly odd jobs or some compensation from ministering to his flock. Bardon notes that there is a "noted grove" of sugar maples on a hilltop back of Oneota (West Duluth) that has always been known as "Bungo's Sugar Bush... It was a popular sugar making grove for Indians and whites." The region is rich in *manoomin* and you can be sure that Stephen was poling a canoe through some rice bed or knocking it down when ripe. He was part of the land and everything it knows.

Many interesting facts of Stephen Bonga were given

to me by my friend, Christine Carlson, who grew up in Fond du Lac and is an astute local historian. Here are a few more of Christine's interesting reminisces of Stephen: During the Minnesota Dakota Uprising of 1862, Stephen was sixty-three years of age, and joined the Superior Home Guards which was a local militia formed to protect the city. Stephen Bonga was a gifted athlete and his favorite sport was baseball. "He was a pitcher with professional accuracy and considered a favorite player in Superior. Stephen also loved to dance and attended most of the dances in the early days of Superior. He was not a medicine man but took care of many people who were in need."

Concerning Stephen's marriages and family, I cite Christine Carlson again:

"...Stephen's marriage in 1833 was to Charlotte Susan Bongo and she died in 1860. In the 1857 Minnesota Territorial and State Census for St. Louis County, Stephen is listed with Charlotte, age 45 who was born in Minnesota. The children listed are John, Samuel, James, Charlotte, and Battese. The 1870 Census for Superior lists Stephen, a fisherman, and Susan Bonga, age 60, with four children and that Susan was born in Minnesota. The children listed are Joseph, Susan, Margaret and Paul. The 1880 Census for Superior lists Stephen and Mary, age 65, with five children and that Mary, also known as Bahbewahbikwe, was born in Wisconsin. The children listed are Maggie, Sarah, James, and John. Mary, a child, and another Bonga family member were recorded as being removed from a burial site on Wisconsin Point to the Nemadji Cemetery."

137

Bahbewahbikwe may be *Biwabiko-ikwe,* the daughter of Chief Wabooz as mention earlier in reference to Carl Zapffe's "Minnesota Chippewa Treaty of 1837." Whatever the marriages and offspring, it is apparent that Stephen had many children.[119]

Stephen was human and as in most marriages, there were disputes. In a missionary's diary dated 1841, a domestic dispute between Stephen and his wife notes:

> "Friday 22 [October, 1841] I have had a na[s]
> ty case this morning. Stephen drove his wife off
> last night, about midnight, and I knew noth-
> ing about it until this morning. So I gave him
> a good sitting down about it, after which he
> asked me to speak to his wife, as he called her.
> So I did, and made him and her promise to get
> married. I also cauchened [cautioned] them
> not to sleep together until they were married,
> and further saied, 'if you do, you will commit a
> dultry [adultry]'. Now in view of this case, are
> we Missionaries clear? We have let this man
> and woman remain at our house, for some days,
> and sleep together as man & wife, and yet, they
> are in trouth, no more man & wife then I and
> Queen Victory [Victoria] are."[120]

Christine Carlson shared with me this most unusual incident with a most unusual outcome involving an eighty-one-year-old Stephen in June of 1880. The story is titled the *"Superior-Duluth Harbor Incident, 1880"*:

> "Because all 'characters' are yet known or re-
> membered, we will tell a story, a sad maritime
> story, or an almost tragedy, that occurred in the

Bonga

Superior-Duluth harbor in June, 1880. Capt. Alfred Merritt, of Duluth, owned and sailed the Nemadji River log-towing tug, 'John Martin.' He was coming back from Duluth with a string of boom-sticks to the Nemadji:

Capt. George L. Brooks of Superior owned and commanded the Superior and Duluth passenger ferry 'Minnie Lemont.' John A. Bardon, Engineer.

The Nemadji Boom Supt., a passenger on the ferry, wished to be transferred to the tug.

Usual and proper whistles were exchanged. Both boats approached each other cautiously. The 'Minnie' backed up strongly and the tug apparently likewise, but they bumped smartly, head on.

Capt. Merritt held a rope fender over the tug's bow to ease the impact.

Stephen Bungo, the aged Chippewa and negro half-breed, Superior's 'first white child,' was a passenger standing on the ferry's stern, leaning against the canopy. Because the Engineer saw they were going to collide, and the re-bound of the canopy would likely throw Bungo overboard, he made a dash to grab him.

They were both thrown overboard, Capt. Merritt likewise.

There they were – Captain of one craft and the Engineer of the other, trying their best to save

Bungo – and keep away from the reversed uncontrolled propeller of the Lemont! All were duly
picked up by the 'Martin' and then she had to
chase the 'Minnie' as no one seemed to stop the
backing engine.

Making a flying tackle from the 'Martin,' the
'Minnie' was soon under control. After exchanging a few deep sea courtesies, both crafts
proceeded unharmed, to there original destinations. It was 'all in the days work.'

Old Bungo' had proved the best swimmer of the
lot. He had shinnied up to the Martin's 'fender'
like a cat and lent a hand in hauling the other
two 'mariners' aboard."[121]

An amazing story, younger men jump in to save old
Bungo and old Bungo ends up pulling them out of the
water!

There are two known photographs of Stephen, both
appear to be taken about the same time and both are of
Stephen in advanced age. The photo most commonly seen
was taken by Will D. Baldwin. A short newspaper notation
of July of 1911 states:

"...Up to the time of his death [Stephen Bonga]
he was a favorite with all the pioneers, who will
recall the old man as their friend of the early
times, always polite, obliging and neighborly.
He furnished much of the information for the
earlier history of northern Wisconsin. The only
picture of him ever taken is reproduced on this
page. It is the work of Will D. Baldwin, a pioneer
photographer."[122]

Bonga

As Stephen got older, getting around became more than a chore, it could be dangerous. An incident in 1883 demonstrates that the proud old voyageur can find himself in a more or less humiliating position;

> "Old Stephen Bungo, the Negro Indian half-breed, had an uncomfortable experience out on the Fond du Lac road yesterday afternoon. He was walking up the railroad west of the Oneota saw mill. Coming to a cattle guard, and not daring to walk over, he threw his bundle across and went down the grade to crawl under the barbed wire fence. In this effort his clothing became entangled in the wires, and he was thrown on his back, his head and shoulders being supported by the lower wire. The poor old fellow was too feeble to help himself, and he remained in a very uncomfortable position for over an hour, when he was discovered and helped out of the trap by John H. La Vaque and the reporter who was driving by. He was completely exhausted, and would have remained there until this time had not someone happened along."[123]

In 1881 Stephen was operating a thriving fruit stand and sold photographs of himself. He was noted by all who knew him to have really "earned his own way" to the end. One acquaintance noted that old Stephen, "Instead of the usual bending over with age, he remained straight as an arrow—if anything, leaning backward."

Stephen died in January 1884 and was buried at Wisconsin Point, separating Lake Superior from St. Louis Bay. He was later moved to Nemadji Cemetery and closer to his final home.

I do not know the circumstances that contributed to Stephen's death, whether his heart gave out or pneumonia or some other debilitating factor related to old age, but whatever it was, it marked the end of a wonderful life—a man who lived the good life and walked the good path. His intelligence and kindness touched so many people, both white and Indian and his 'life and times' are an important part of Minnesota history and American history. I sense that although he has been gone for over 130 years, his spirit still resides in the land that he loved so much...Stephen's safe abode in the wilderness.

When I am in my canoe, no matter where it may be, the Namakogen & St. Croix of Wisconsin, or the great river of life, the headwaters of the Mississippi, the Boundary Waters Canoe Area or Quetico Park of Ontario or any other body of wild water in the Great Lakes region, all of which were well known by Stephen, I sense the presence of his spirit and I also feel a deep sense of regret that this kind and great man has been all but forgotten. The obituary in the Superior Times noting Stephen's passing well over a century ago stated, "We have not the data at hand from which to make an extended notice of the deceased, though one of great interest might be written."

Abraham Lincoln said, "A country with no regard for its past will have little worth remembering in its future." I hope that my humble attempt here will do more than make Stephen worth our while remembering...I hope it will make us proud of him and make him proud, too! He deserves it. He is one of the best men to have come down to us in the history of our region and is a man to emulate and hold up as what's best about us as a people and what's best about America.

The Biggest, Strongest, Smartest Man in the Northwoods

George Bonga

George Bonga wrote this letter from his home on Leech Lake in December of 1872 to Senator Henry Rice of Minnesota:

"As to My self, I was born, somewhere near where Duluth now is, that was before the N.P.R.R. had its terminus there, pretty near 70 Years ago, at that time, there was a great rivalrie, between the 2 fur Companys the old North west & the Hudson Bay. Co. My father was in the employ of the former there head quarters was at Fort William Lake Superior. I left there when I was a little school boy, as I have no recollection, of the place & went to School in Montreal, as there was no one, to take any particular interest in me. I did not get as good an education, as I might have had about the year of 1813, the great Law Suit between the above Companys took place which resulted in the Hudson Bay Co. having the Sole trade of the North west...My father came to Lake Superior with a Chippewa trader, it must be upwards of 100 years ago. At that time I beleeve there was, no traders in the interior. The North west Co. had there trading Post at a place between, were

Duluth now is & Superior City. Old McDonald,
is the first white man of there now living in thes
parts, that came to this country, he was in the
Employ of the Hudson Bay Co.   Messrs A.
Morrison I.H. Fairbanks, also Gen Sibley, H.L.
Dousman John Kenzie & my self all came in the
employ of the American fur Co.   I presume it
would be quite interesting to those who would
like such story.s to hear the above persons,
relate, what they Knew of this Country. I have
often thought, that it would be a cureousity to
some, to See a lot of these old Stagers riding on
a R.R. Together."

George mentions the year 1813 in conjunction with his
education which would make him about eleven years old.
It seems probable that several years after his schooling, he
returned to his family and home at the village of Fond du
Lac where his Ojibwe mother raised him and his siblings.
Here, in Fond du Lac, living amongst the Ojibwe, he would
be instilled with Ojibwe language, spiritual beliefs and cultural values. His father Pierre, who was at this time in the
employ of John Sayer of the North West Company, would
seldom have been at home.

Between the years 1818 to 1822, George is listed as a
voyageur in the Lac du Flambeau Department at $83.33 a
year in what would become Wisconsin.1 George Bonga was
at Fond du Lac when Cass, Schoolcraft and his entourage
of the Expedition to the Headwaters arrived at the village of
Pierre's family in 1820.[124]

Big Belly Cass

When Lewis B. Cass departed for the Headwaters of
the Mississippi in 1820, he was governor of the Territory of

Bonga

Michigan (which included most of present day Minnesota and Wisconsin) and would continue in this position for eighteen years. He would also serve as Secretary of War (1831-36), Ambassador to France (1836-42), Senator from the State of Michigan, and Secretary of State under President Buchanan. He unsuccessfully sought the Democratic nomination for President on two occasions, the third attempt for the Democratic nomination was successful but he lost the Presidential election to the Whig and Mexican-American war hero, Zachary Taylor.

Lewis Cass had a good reputation among the Indians in Lower Michigan. His respect of Indian treaty rights earned him the name Indians fondly used, "Big Belly." Cass was a proponent of government, order, military garrisons, armaments, roads, and had a vision for the growing empire. Cass would carry his plan of order—the "Cass Code"—all the way to the headwaters of the Mississippi. Lewis Cass's plan for the expedition into the region of the headwaters of the Mississippi was presented to Secretary of War, John C. Calhoun, with the intention of bringing the territory of Michigan into the "larger orbit of national policy." The president in 1820 was James Monroe. Cass's plan had six primary objectives:

> "(1)...permit a personal examination of the
> Indian tribes residing in the area, (2) pro-
> cure the extinction of Indian title to the land
> at the Straits of St. Mary's, Prairie du Chien,
> and Green Bay, (3) examine the strategically
> valuable copper mines on Lake Superior and
> perhaps purchase that land from the Indians,
> (4) ascertain the attitude of the local Indians
> toward a removal of the Six Nations to the
> Chicago area, (5) discourage the Indians from

intercourse with the British at Malden, and (6) ascertain the state of the British fur trade in that part of the Northwest Territory."[125]

Secretary Calhoun approved the plans as long as the costs did not exceed one-thousand dollars. Cass immediately commissioned Saginaw Indians to begin construction of three birch bark canoes and began a search for French-Canadian voyageurs, guides, and hunters.

Henry Rowe Schoolcraft was among eight "gentlemen" selected by Cass for their abilities as cartographers, physicians, geologists, ethnographers, and engineers. The ambitious Schoolcraft had been chosen due to previous work he had done with an expedition to Arkansas lead mines.

With everything in place, the expedition set off from Detroit in three canoes, including the diverse group of "gentleman", ten voyageurs, ten natives, and seven soldiers.

Schoolcraft in his *Narrative* states that upon reaching Mackinac, they found that the three canoes would be insufficient to accommodate the gear and additional bodies joining the expedition. It was here in Mackinac, according to historian Duane R. Lund, that an eighteen year old Hole-in-the-Day the Elder, or *Bagone-giizhig,* persuaded the traders at Mackinac to urge Cass to allow him to accompany the expedition. For the young Ojibwe leader, Hole-in-the-Day, who grew up at La Pointe in present day Wisconsin, the idea of traveling through headwaters country where the famed western vanguard of the Ojibwe resided and then down the Mississippi into Dakota country was too intriguing to miss.[126]

Arriving at the American Fur Company post near Fond du Lac, Cass enlisted eighteen-year-old George Bonga from the adjacent Indian village to serve as interpreter. This was likely the first time that George, or any Bonga, utilized their multilingual skills an interpreter. In studying the history of this region, we need to remember that *Ojibwemowin* was not the only language spoken. French was also commonly spoken by many mixed-bloods of Ojibwe and French lineage who lived in the area. George and Stephen, with educations in the east, had added English to their repertoire. To find a local resident who spoke fluent English, French, and Ojibwe would be an obvious asset for someone like Cass. Good translators were necessary. In almost all communication between whites and Indians, local interpreters were used, and frequent misunderstandings resulted from translations that were often botched by interpreters who lacked proper use of the three languages.

The fact is Lewis Cass needed an interpreter and the young George Bonga would be drawn to the arrival of this entourage of dignitaries from the United States Government. There would be some pomp and circumstance with their arrival and George and others residents at the "head of the lake" would be among the curious and the large Black Ojibwe who could communicate in three languages would most certainly have attracted the interest of "Big Belly" Cass.

The Northwest Trail

The Cass expedition would have to cross the long and difficult "Grand Portage of the St. Louis River" to get to the Mississippi. The Bongas and Indian people of the Fond du Lac area were all accustomed to the rigors of portaging and were enlisted to assist the expedition in getting them over this rugged ground. As Cass had a number of "gentlemen" on the expedition—all of whom kept journals—these journals today provide an interesting look back in time at the effort it took to carry all the necessities needed to cross this rugged country.

The portages through this area are long and extremely rugged. Schoolcraft notes that from Fort Fond du Lac on "Day XLIV, July 6, 1820:

> "The river is ascended two miles further, to the foot of the Grand Portage. Here the goods are all landed, and the carrying commences, but the canoes, without load, ascend two miles higher to the Gallery, where they are also taken out and carried across. The first part of the portage is excessively rough, and the fatigue was rendered almost insupportable by the heat of the day, the thermometer standing at 82' at noon. With the assistance of the Indians, (sixteen of whom were brought up from the mouth of the river for that purpose,) we preceded however, with all our baggage, five pauses, and encamped at twilight."

> XLV. Day.-(July 7th.) – A storm of rain commenced during the night, and continued until noon, when the sun appeared for half an hour, but the afternoon continued dark and cloudy, with showers. We commenced carrying at six o'clock, notwithstanding the rain, and with great exertions, went ten pauses and encamped on the banks of a small brook. The difficulties of the portage have been very much increased by the rain, which has filled the carrying path with mud and water. We are advancing into a dreary region. – Every thing around us wears a wild and sterile aspect, and the extreme ruggedness of the country – the succession of swampy grounds, and rocky precipices – the dark forest of hemlock and pines which overshadow the

soil – and the distant roaring of the river, would render it a gloomy and dismal scene, without the toil of transporting baggage, and the saddening influence of one of the most dreary days.

XLVI. Day. _ (July 8th) – We progressed four pauses, and reached the river at the head of the portage, in season to air our baggage – repair the canoes – and make the necessary dispositions for an early departure on the following day. The entire distance of the portage is nine miles, which is passed at nineteen pauses, divided according to the unevenness of the ground, and the facilities of traveling...The fall of the St. Louis river, between the extremes of this portage is very great, being one continued chain of rapids and falls, and at one place there is a perpendicular pitch of thirty feet. It is here that the river forces a passage through a chain of mountains consisting of short broken ridges, which give the country a very rugged appearance, and render traveling excessively toilsome..."

XLVII. Day. – (July 9th.) – On reaching the foot of the Grand Portage, we exchanged two of our canoes with the American Fur Company, for four of the smaller size adapted to navigation of the river above the portage, and now proceeded on our voyage in seven small canoes. The river is ascended to the Portage aux Coteaux, which consists of three pauses, and is a mile and a half across. The carrying path lies over an elevated tract of rough country consisting of slate in a vertical position, which is in many places

naked, and some idea may be formed of the
singular appearance of the rock, by comparing
it to the leaves of a book standing edgewise. The
effect of this arrangement of the strata, upon
the moccasins and the feet of the voyageurs,
who cross this portage has led to its name – the
portage of the knives. At the lower end of it, this
slate forms a lone standing pile, or pyramid, in
the center of the river, of eighty or ninety feet
in height, and supporting in its crevices a few
stunted pines."[127]

The extraordinary strength, stamina, and perseverance
of the voyageur make them stand out as quasi-heroic figures in this forgotten period of our history. These canoe
men were indispensable as the "engine" of the fur trade for
over 200 years.

In the following account of the Grand Portage of the St.
Louis River, David Bates Douglas, who was one of the "gentlemen" members of the Cass 1820 Expedition, depicts the
strength of one individual who may have been the young
Francois Brunette, the powerful, six-foot four-inch future
French-Ojibwe trader, whom he refers to as "Lord Byron"
while crossing the *Grand Portage*. Francois Brunette was a
lifelong friend of George and Stephen Bonga. The French
explorer, Joseph Nicollet, was extremely fond of Francois
Brunette and in 1836 wrote this about him in his *Journal*:
"a giant of great strength but, at the same time, full of the
milk of human kindness, and, withal, an excellent geographer." Nicollet also describes Brunette on a tough and
brushy portage, comparing him to the other men who suffered under the labor; "Brunia [Brunette], the giant, with
canoe tipped over head looking like an enormous seal
swimming over shrubbery, opened our path. Desire and

Bonga

Kegouedgika could barely follow him and invariably ended up questioning their own efficiency."

Douglas writes:

"...Again mounted my pack weighing about 100 pounds for the [St. Louis] portage – After ascending a very high and steep hill which the heat of the sun as well as the natural difficulty of the ascent rendered excessively fatiguing to me I proceeded with comparative ease to the dist[ance] of 3 poses...I have felt my strength much more adequate to this kind of labor at the close of the day than when I commenced, in so much that at the last pose I went back with some of the gentlemen & brought forward a bag of corn of nearly two bushels...Some of them [hired Indians] exhibit a degree of strength truly wonderful. There is one, a half Frenchman—a tall elegantly made man to whom I have given the name of Lord Byron from his striking re-semblance of contour of the head of that poet which I have seen – This man would shoulder at a load two kegs of bacon weighing not less than 125 pounds each & a bag of flour or corn of nearly a hundred pounds more & with this he would walk or rather trot off in a style which would have fatigued me had I perfectly unload-ed...but if I was astonished at the loads borne by the men I was even more so by the scarcely less burdens carried by the women...Ld. Bryon's mother carried at one load – her birch bark canoe of sufficient size to carry a whole Indian family with their baggage – at another the mats and Birch bark for a wigwam, two or three

Indian bags of skins and fishing tackle &c. a
large camp kettle with all the cooking appara-
tus & eating utensils & in short an entire Indian
lodge with all its furniture & appurtenances.
Having carried these she would making several
[trips], returning again & take up at each time a
good many loads of kegs, bags &c. I expressed
my astonishment at the great strength of the
woman & told Ld. Byron that his old mother
could carry twice as much as I could – he replied with no small air of exultation that he and
his mother would carry our largest canoe which
it had taken five or six men to carry – Two or
three other women, the wives of Indians of the
party, carried similar loads & frequently their
papooses [sic] on the top of all – Even the children would back their loads and carry a box or
small bag forward."[128]

The feats of strength acknowledged by Douglas in the
previous quote are not unparalleled. Those people today
that have heard of the Bongas, usually know of two facets
of the Bonga legend that have survived time. One is the
statements made by both Stephen and George as being
the first white men to have settled or were born at a certain locale in Indian Country. The other legend concerns
their extraordinary strength. Oral history tells of Pierre
portaging 450 pounds across the nine-mile Grand Portage
around the Pigeon River. Stephen claims, with witnesses,
that he carried 700 pounds up Porcupine Mountain on the
south shore of Lake Superior. The most incredible story,
and one which appears in a number of accounts, is that of
George portaged 700 pounds up the steep and difficult first
one-thousand feet of Fond du Lac's Grand Portage of the
St. Louis River without stopping.

Bonga

The site of this six-and-a-half-mile portage, the first leg of the Northwest Trail, is in present day Jay Cooke State Park. The ancient portage was first blazed by Native Americans untold centuries ago. Today, the portage begins at the foot of the rapids at the town site of Fond du Lac and climbs over 450 feet to the present day town of Carlton.

Pierre, though no known photograph exists, has only infrequently been described physically. Alexander Henry the Younger described him as "stout." One brief reference was that he was over six feet tall. Stephen was six feet tall or slightly more and muscularly built but was leaner than George. From the only known photographs of Stephen and George, taken late in life, it is obvious that Stephen was lighter skinned than George. Stephen appears to resemble, in racial terms, his Ojibwe Mother, while George is very dark and more so resembles his full-blooded African father, Pierre. One reference to George was that his skin was so black that it "fairly glistened." Where Stephen may have been more athletic, George was larger and stronger. The most complete description of George's physical stature asserts he was "over 200 lbs. and 6' 6" tall and commanded the respect and awe of all with whom he came into contact."[129] Another account states of George, "People remembered his enormous strength and polished manners."[130]

The Bongas had reason to be proud of their strength. At this time in the country, strength was a real asset and advantage. All the Bongas had their roots in the culture of the voyageur yet in many ways they did not fit the mold of the voyageur. Almost always, the voyageur was required by necessity to be short, under 5' 5". This general rule was due to the fact that shorter men took up less space in the canoe which left more room for trade goods and furs. Most were poorly educated. As observed by trader Daniel Harmon of the North West Company, who lived for two decades with voyageurs in the *Pays d'en Haut*, "...there is not one in a hundred of them who have the least education."[131] Obviously, the Bonga's did not fit these prerequisites. They were tall and well educated by the standards of the time. But they were strong and excellent paddlers in a canoe and they had another trait that was of high regard among the *Homes du Nord*—they were excellent singers. The ability to sing well was not for amusement, rather it was used by the voyageur to keep cadence while paddling for up to sixteen hours a day.[132]

One of the best descriptions of the 'voyageur' was given by Dr. John J. Bigsby, who accompanied the famed cartographer David Thompson of the North West Company. As secretary of the British delegation of the Boundary Commission, whose purpose was to determine the boundary of the United States and Canada under the provisions of the Convention of 1818, Bigsby wrote in his book *The Shoe and the Canoe* while on tour in 1823:

> "I was disappointed and not a little surprised at the appearance of the voyageurs. On Sundays, as they stand round the door of the village churches, they are proud dressy fellows in their party-coloured sashes and ostrich feathers; but here they were a motley set to the eye: but the truth was that all of them were picked men, with extra wages as serving in a light canoe.
>
> Some were well made, but all looked weak in the legs, and were of light weight. A Falstaff would have put his foot through the canoe to the yellow sands beneath. The collection of faces among them chanced to be extraordinary, as they squatted, paddle in hand, in two rows, each on his slender bag of necessaries. By the

Bonga

George Bonga, circa 1870. Image courtesy of the Minnesota Historical Society Collections

Stephen Bonga, circa 1880. Image sourced from Wikimedia Commons, Public Domain Ⓢ

bye, all their finery (and they love it) was left at home. One mans face, with a large nose, seemed to have been squeezed in a vice, or to have passed through a flattening machine. It was like a cheese cutter – all edge. Another had one nostril bitten off. He proved the buffoon of the party. He had the extraordinary faculty of untying the strings of his face, as it were, at pleasure, when his features fell into con-fusion – into a crazed chaos almost frightful; his eye, too lost its usual significance; but no mans countenance was fuller of fun and fancies than his, when he liked. A third man had his features wrenched to the right – exceedingly little, it is true, but the effect was remarkable. He had been slapped on the face by a grizzly bear. Another was a short, pauncy old man, with vast features, but no forehead – the last man I should have selected; but he was a hard working creature, usually called 'passé partout,' because he had been everywhere, and was famous for the weight of fish he could devour at a meal…except for the younger men, their faces were short, thin, quick in their expressions, and mapped out in furrows, like those of Sunday-less Parisians."[133]

Another voyageur, beyond seventy years of age said:

"I could carry, paddle, walk and sing with any man I ever saw. I have been 24 years a canoe man and 41 years in service; no portage was ever too long for me. Fifty songs I could sing. I have saved the lives of ten voyageurs. Have had 12 wifes and 6 running dogs. I spent all my money in pleasure. Were I young again, I should spend my life the same way over. There is no life so happy as a Voyageurs life."[134]

So the Bongas were in a real sense a different breed of voyageur. They were educated, had a degree of refinement and "polished manners." The Bongas were second and third generation voyageurs who were mostly mixed-blood French-Indian or "*Métis*" as commonly called, yet they were more: French speaking Black-Indians. There wasn't much choice of employment for the Bongas in the early 1800s as the only economic factor in the wilds was to enter the fur trade and if you weren't Scotch-English-Irish, you were to be among the ranks of the voyageur. Most voyageurs entered the fur trade as a canoe man and left as canoe man, if they lived long enough. Drowning and strangulated hernia were common causes of death amongst this breed of men.

For the Cass Expedition determined to reach the Headwaters of the Mississippi, completing the Grand Portage of the St. Louis River was just the first difficult step in a laborious process. In order to get to the Mississippi they had to cross a continental divide. Until crossing the Savanna Portage, they would be in the St. Lawrence watershed which flows to the Atlantic Ocean. Once they would cross the midway point on the Savanna Portage, they would enter the Mississippi River watershed which flows to the Gulf of Mexico.

Passing by Knife Portage, the traveler encounters four more rapids, Pine Island Rapids, the Grand Rapids of the St. Louis, Long Rapids, and the Cloquet rapids. Not too far beyond these rapids, one encounters Stoney Brook, where the St. Louis River turns west and then north at the approximate site of today's community of Floodwood. Here, the Northwest Trail departs the St. Louis River at the mouth of the East Savanna River. People who traveled the Northwest Trail described this six-mile portage as possibly the toughest portage encountered anywhere in the canoe country of Minnesota or Wisconsin. The first half of this portage was through a soggy muskeg where one often sank to his hips in muck. When one was approximately half way across the portage, the terrain changed to upland forests with a mix of pine and hardwoods. This area was and still is a frequented location for Native Americans tapping the fine sugar maples found here. The six-mile portage ended at the West Savanna River where canoes again became the mode of transportation. In the 1820 Cass Expedition, Schoolcraft did not cross the Savanna Portage, as he was sent overland from the from Knife Portage or *Portage aux Couteau* to Big Sandy Lake, but in his *Narrative* he recorded Dr. Wolcott's description of the six mile Savanna Portage:

> "The length of the Savanna portage is six miles, and is passed at thirteen pauses. The first three pauses are shockingly bad. It is not only a bed of mire, but the difficulty of passing it is greatly increased by fallen trees, limbs, and sharp knots of the pitch pine, in some places on the surface, in others imbedded one or two feet below. Where there are hollows or depressions in the ground, tall course grass, brush, and pools of stagnant water are encountered. Old voyageurs say, that this part of the portage was formerly covered with a heavy bog, or a kind of peat, upon which the walking was very good, but that during a dry season, it accidentally caught fire and burnt over the surface of the earth as to lower its level two or three feet when it became mirey, and subject to inundation from the Savanna river. The country, after passing the third pause, changes in a short distance, from a marsh to a region of sand hills covered mostly with white and yellow pine, intermixed with aspen. The hills are short and conical, with a moderate elevation. In some places they are drawn out into ridges, but these ridges cannot be observed to run in any uniform course; on the contrary they are confused in their arrangement. The country has a general rise from the East to the West Savannah, which may

be estimated at thirty feet. This is the dividing ridge between the waters of Lake Superior, and the Mississippi river. Where the portage path approaches the sources of the West Savannah there is a descent into a small valley covered with rank grass—without forest trees—and here and there clumps of willow, similar to those on the East Savannah. This valley is skirted with a thick and brushy cover of alder, aspen, hazel, &c. The adjoining hills are sandy, covered with pine. The stream here is just large enough to swim a canoe, and the navigation commences within a mile of its course. It pursues a very serpentine course to Sandy Lake, in a general direction northwest, and has several rapids."[135]

Once in the Mississippi watershed, the Northwest Trail is complete and the connection has been made from Lake Superior to the Mississippi River. The importance of the Northwest Trail cannot be over emphasized. It has been in use for hundreds of years by American Indians before the first white fur traders arrived. It is certain that the Bongas were frequent users of this route—they had to be as they made numerous trips, maybe multiple times per year, to Fond du Lac from somewhere in Headwaters Country.

From Sandy Lake to Upper Red Cedar Lake—*Gaa-miskwaawaakokaag* (place of many red cedars)—by canoe on the Mississippi, it is approximately one-hundred and fifty miles. From Upper Red Cedar Lake to the Headwaters of the Mississippi, it is another eighty-two miles. The Cass Expedition of 1820 got only as far as Upper Red Cedar Lake. Cass erroneously proclaimed Upper Red Cedar as the "Headwaters" and Schoolcraft offered to change the name to Cassina, which was shortened to Cass Lake. Legend has it that when the 1820 expedition arrived at Upper Red Cedar Lake, the region was in a drought and when Cass asked natives if there was another tributary that would lead to the true source of the river, the interpreter botched the conversion of English to Ojibwe to ask if there was any navigable tributary leading to the headwaters. During the low water of the drought, there wasn't any.

George Bonga's role as interpreter for Lewis Cass at Fond du Lac is just part one in a series of events to come that puts the children of Pierre into the real human story of the Headwaters of the Mississippi River.

The next time that George Bonga shows up in history is in the winter of 1823-24 when he and his brothers Stephen and Jack are at the bungled Fort Misery in the Fond du Lac Department of the American Fur Company. This may be the only time when the brothers served and lived together in their adult lives. From the end of Fort Misery, the brother's lives followed somewhat different paths.

An Interpreter for Missionaries

For the next decade, nothing extraordinary takes place in George Bonga's life. He appears to be establishing himself in the fur trade within the Fond du Lac Department, moving up in rank to a clerk and finding a growing demand for his skills as a translator. Mostly, we see his name mentioned at Fond du Lac and Big Sandy. It can be assumed that from 1824 to 1836, George was honing his skills as a trader and rising in the esteem of his colleagues and employers.

During this period George Bonga's ability as an interpreter was making him more in demand, and he was often sought out as an interpreter by missionaries. Indian Country was starting to see more Christian missionaries among whom were a group of four Presbyterians from the east coast. Some background on who these men of God were and how they got here is interesting. The four men who came to Wisconsin and Minnesota were Frederick Ayer, William Thurston Boutwell, Sherman Hall, and Edmund F. Ely, all were ordained Presbyterian ministers.

Frederick Ayer was the first to arrive and started his school teaching and doing mission work at Lapointe on Madeline Island at the request of Lyman Warren, the father of William Whipple Warren. William Boutwell was at Sault Ste. Marie when Henry Schoolcraft invited him along on his 1832 expedition of discovery to the Headwaters of the Mississippi at Itasca Lake. Reverend Sherman Hall, like Ayer started at Lapointe. Reverend Ely joined Boutwell in 1833 when Boutwell returned to Leech Lake to run a school and mission. Ely, without delay and at the request of William Aitkin, took up schooling and mission work at Sandy Lake in 1833 and then moved to Fond du Lac in 1834 to do the same. Aitkin wanted Ely to instruct his own children and the offspring of the mostly mixed-blood voyageurs. Rev. Edmund Ely was rather better liked than the other men of the cloth by Indians because he sang his mission teachings which the Indian children and parents found a refreshing change. Many of them moved around to different Indian settlements, such as Yellow Lake in Wisconsin and Pokegama in southern Pine County. By 1847, these four men realized that their efforts had failed and the Presbyterian missions came to an end. What these ministers contributed to our history is the letters and diaries that depict what everyday life was like for the people during the early 1800s. Within a few years the Episcopal Church had established missions in Indian Country and became the dominant church in region for the remainder of the century.[136]

Reverend Edmund Ely's diary while at Sandy Lake and

Fond du Lac makes comments about George Bonga and Francois Brunette:

> "February 2nd [1834] -- Bro. Boutwell, Mr.
> Davenport, Mr. Geo. Bonga, Mr Francois
> Brunelle [Brunette], arrived from Leech Lake
> on Friday noon last; Friday and Saturday eve-
> nings the children assembled in my room and
> some time was spent in singing. Today Mr. B
> remarked from the part of the 13th chapter of
> Luke then accompanied me to Mr. Abbott's; af-
> terwards the Indian meeting. Mr. B talked some
> to the children and others through Mr. Bonga
> who interprets excellently.[137]

> Monday, April 28 [1834] –This morning George
> Bonga sent us word that the Kij-Osaie, the most
> influential chief of this band, would be at his
> Post (Pt. Aux Pins) during the day and that if
> I wished to say anything to him, I had better
> come over, as the chief would start for Sandy
> Lake next morning. I accordingly went and G.
> Bonga interpreted to him the amount of a letter
> Mr. Boutwell left for the Chiefs. He could give no
> formal answer until he had conferred with the
> other chief who had not returned from his hunt,
> but said that no one surely would object to our
> building on that point (which Bro. Boutwell
> had contracted for with an Indian woman). He,
> (the chief) is a man about 50 or 55 years old,
> of somewhat downcast look, but behaves with
> much gravity and propriety. He is the most in-
> fluential man in his band.[138]

> Sandy Lake – Monday, June 2 [1834] Started
> a little after sunrise this morning and arrived

about 11 o'clock. A delightful day. Mons. Belcour, Bonga and the Brunettes arrived this morning; found letters from Mr. Boutwell here; he was to leave St. Peters on the 13th ult. For Yellow Lake, also a line from Bro. Ayer and some papers from New York and Boston...I expect to leave tomorrow for Fond du Lac... About 9 o'clock P.M. a boat arrived from Fond du Lac. The clerk, [George] Bonga, stated that he had seen a letter from Sandy Lake stating that the Indians of Poguvegizhik's [Bagone-giizhiig] band had, in passing that place, killed 4 of Aitkin's cattle and one horse, also 3 of the company's cattle and destroyed their crop of potatoes. The boat passed on."[139]

It appears that George Bonga and other traders and clerks moved around frequently in the greater Fond du Lac Department between the Fond du Lac, Sandy Lake, Cass Lake, Winnibigosh and Leech Lake posts. In fact it's hard to pin George down as his name comes up throughout this department.

Only 3/5ths a Human Being...

Though George Bonga lived the Northwoods, far from the seats of government and the debates of civil liberties, he was directly connected to one of the most well-known debates of civil liberty in United States history—the Dred Scott Case. Dred Scott was a slave. He was not, what was called a "field slave" in pre-Civil War era but a "house slave" and was the property of Dr. John Emerson, a Missouri army surgeon. But for the fact that Doctor Emerson had taken Scott with him to the "free ground" of Illinois and Fort Snelling (in what would become Minnesota Territory) for a two-year period in the 1830s, we would never have heard of Dred Scott. Instead, Scott would file a lawsuit ten years later that would forever catapult him into American history and would become an important event pushing the country to Civil War.

While at Fort Snelling in 1836, Dred Scott married another slave, Harriet Robinson, who was the slave of Lawrence Taliaferro. Taliaferro was the United States Indian Agent at Fort Snelling during these years including 1836 and 37. The two slaves of different owners were allowed to marry and Taliaferro transferred his ownership of Harriet to Dr. Emerson so the couple could be together. Several years later they had their first child.

After an approximate one year stay at Fort Snelling, Dr. Emerson returned to St. Louis, Missouri with the Scotts but it was not until 1846, after the death of Dr. John Emerson, and the Scotts becoming the property of Mrs. Emerson, that white friends of the Scotts advised him to sue for his freedom on account of having been on free soil for two years. This set off an eleven-year court fight over the question of slavery and freedom that became one of the most infamous Supreme Court cases in the history of the United States of America.

Dred Scott was most likely acquainted with George Bonga as noted by the Minnesota State Capital Yellow Pages website:

> "...Scott probably met and became friends with
> another famous Black Minnesotan, George
> Bonga, the son of Minnesota's first black settler
> and a fur trader and businessman who freely
> associated with the prominent politicians of
> the Territory of Minnesota. Bonga was known
> for his capture of Che-ga-wa-skung, an Ojibwa

Bonga

Indian accused of murder in 1837 that resulted in Minnesota's first criminal trial."

The possibility that George Bonga made contact and visited with Dred Scott at Fort Snelling in 1837 makes one wonder at the impression that George Bonga would have had on Dred Scott. Here is a slave who most likely had no prior experience with a man with black skin who was not only a free man but a man of consequence with an important position as a fur trader. A Black man who was the "chief agent in running down the murderer" which "was long a matter of comment in the early days," and who was a literate and educated man of the wilderness. George Bonga was big news in the territory and Scott would have been aware of this while at the fort during 1836 and 1837.

Though it's unknown whether the two men met or not, the juxtaposition of the two different lives at this time in American history is worth comparing for it gets to the essence of the Bongas. What would have gone through the mind of Scott as a slave when seeing this large Black man arriving with the fugitive and the accolades and importance that Bonga got from those in attendance to this scene? To better understand what impacts this may have had on the Dred Scott case, some background needs to be understood.

Dred Scott's attorneys first brought suit for his freedom in 1846 and were unsuccessful. However, in a re-trial in 1850 in St. Louis County, they won his freedom. This decision was appealed to the Missouri Supreme Court and, in an 1852 decision, Scott lost and was placed back in bondage. The case was beginning to receive national attention. Historian James M. McPherson writes that, "Missouri courts had previously granted freedom to slaves in cases similar to Scott's. In overturning those precedents and asserting that Missouri law prevailed despite Scott's residence in free territory, the state Supreme Court was reacting to proslavery pressures"[140] Scott's lawyers felt they could win the case if they could be heard by a federal court. Dred Scott's owner had moved to New York and Scott's attorneys thought they could be heard by appealing to the federal courts under the 'diverse citizenship clause' which gives federal courts jurisdiction over cases involving people from different states. In 1854, the circuit court for the state of Missouri accepted the case, and acknowledged Scott's status as a citizen but upheld the state court of Missouri's denial of his freedom. The next and final move for Scott's lawyers was to appeal to the United States Supreme Court.

The Supreme Court in the 1850s had nine justices: five were pro-slavery southerners, including the Chief Justice, Roger B. Taney of Maryland, two were northern Democrats, and two were anti-slavery Republicans. The proslavery elements in the country welcomed this appeal. They felt that with a proslavery, southern majority, this would clear up this mess once and for all. The case was first brought before the Supreme Court in 1856 but was held over until the 1856-57 session most likely to avoid a decision before the presidential election.

McPherson writes:

> "Three main questions before the court were:
> 1) As a black man, was Scott a citizen with a
> right to sue in federal courts? 2) Had prolonged
> residence (two years in each place) in a free
> state and territory made Scott free? 3) Was Fort
> Snelling actually free territory – that is, did
> Congress in 1820 have the right to ban slavery
> in the Louisiana Purchase north of 36* 30'? The
> court could have ducked questions one and
> three by merely reaffirming the decision of the

Missouri Supreme Court and the federal circuit
court that Missouri law governed Scott's status.
Precedents existed for doing so; the Supreme
Court itself in Strader v. Graham (1851) had
refused to accept an appeal from the Kentucky
Supreme Court which had ruled that slaves
from Kentucky taken temporarily to Ohio remained slaves under Kentucky law. And indeed,
for a time it appeared that the court would take
this way out. On February 14, 1857, a majority
of justices voted to reaffirm the Strader principle
and let it go at that. Justice Samuel Nelson of
New York began to write the decision. But a few
days later the majority reversed itself and decided a comprehensive ruling covering all aspects
of the case."[141]

As historian James McPherson asks, "Why did the court
take this step?" He explains years later that confidential
discussions and written documents give revealing insight
into the motives of the proslavery majority on the court. The
two, "non-Democrats" on the court, Justice John McLean
of Ohio and Justice Benjamin Curtis of Massachusetts,
made known their intent to dissent from the court's majority. Their dissent would uphold Scott's freedom, affirm
black citizenship, and endorse the ability of Congress to
prohibit slavery in the territories. The proslavery majority
did not want these dissents to be the Court's only verbiage
on these polarizing issues thus initiating the proslavery
majority to reverse itself and voted that Chief Justice Roger
B. Taney write a comprehensive ruling on the three points
bought before the court. But McPherson further points out
a yet more complex reasoning behind this decision. The
Congress, for years, had been trying to "pass the buck" in a

long and contentious series of compromises apparently intended to avert the final conflict. The problem boiled down to the fact that territories thus far did not prohibit slavery resulting in no such suits.

> "But here, conveniently, came a suit from another part of the Louisiana Purchase. The yearning for settlement of this question by 'judicial statesmanship' was widespread in Washington during the winter of 1856-57, especially among southerners. Alexander Stephens (soon to be Vice President of the Confederacy) wrote a letter to Justice James M. Wayne of Georgia and Justice Robert Grier of Pennsylvania (northern Democrat): 'I have been urging all the influence I could bring to bear upon the Sup. Ct. to get them no longer to postpone the case on the Mo. Restriction...I have reason to believe they will [decide] that the restriction was unconstitutional.'"

McPherson notes that Stephens was not alone in exerting pressure on the court. Alexander Stephens wrote several weeks later: "from what I hear sub rosa [the decision] will be according to my own opinions upon every point...The restriction of 1820 will be held to be constitutional. The judges are all writing out their opinions I believe seriatim. The Chief Justice will give an elaborate one."[142]

The southern Justices wanted to rule against all three questions brought before it in this suit including a ruling against Congress's right to ban slavery from the territories. They felt they needed an encompassing decision covering all aspects of the case. And they needed at least one northern justice so the opinion would "avoid the appearance of a purely sectional ruling." The weak link was Justice Robert Grier of Pennsylvania. As McPherson points out in a scheme involving then President John Buchanan, "In a response to a suggestion from Justice John Catron of Tennessee, Buchanan brought highly improper but efficacious influence to bear on Grier, who succumbed. Taney had his northern justice and could proceed with his ruling."[143]

Chief Justice Roger B. Taney of Maryland was eighty years old in 1857 and in poor health. It appears he had lived for this moment. A powerful conviction "to southern life and values, which seemed organically linked to the peculiar institution and unpreservable without it."[144] Taney had been a staunch Jacksonian Democrat "committed to liberating American enterprise from the shackles of special privilege. As Jackson's Secretary of the Treasury he had helped destroy the Second Bank of the United States. His early decisions as chief justice had undermined special corporate charters. But the main theme of his twenty-eight year tenure on the Court was the defense of slavery." It is ironic to note that Taney freed his own slaves but believed the peculiar institution was intrinsically linked to his beloved south. Taney had written in letters that his southerners had "the knife of the assassin at their throats." He also concluded that the Dred Scott decision was "essentially visceral in origin…a work of unmitigated partisanship, polemical in spirit [with an] extraordinary cumulation of error, inconsistency, and misrepresentation."[145]

Taney was writing for the majority on the Court. But beyond representing the majority on the United States Supreme Court, Taney was representing southern whites who saw any free black as a threat to their way of life. He was also writing for the whites of his home state of Maryland, a state that had the largest population of free blacks anywhere in the United States. Don E. Fehrenbacher wrote

that Taney's intentions were "to launch a sweeping coun-
terattack on the antislavery movement and...to meet every
threat to southern stability by separating the Negro race
absolutely from the federal Constitution and all the rights
it bestowed" and as McPherson phrased Fehrenbacher:

> "To do so, however, he had to juggle history,
> law, and logic in 'a gross perversion of the facts.'
> Negroes had not been part of the 'sovereign
> people' who made the Constitution, Taney ruled;
> they were not included in the 'all men' whom
> the Declaration of Independence proclaimed
> 'created equal.' After all, the author of the dec-
> laration and many of the signers owned slaves,
> and for them to have regarded members of the
> enslaved race as potential citizens would have
> been 'utterly and flagrantly inconsistent with
> the principles they asserted.' For that matter,
> wrote Taney, at the time the Constitution was
> adopted Negroes 'had for more than a century
> before been regarded as beings of an inferior
> order...so far inferior, that they had no rights
> which a white man was bound to respect."[146]

The two dissenting justices, Curtis and McLean, stated
in their minority opinion that free blacks in 1788 had legal
rights to hold and bequeath property, make contracts, seek
redress in courts, and more. In five of the original thirteen states, blacks could vote and participated in the rat-
ification process. Taney, along with the other five southern judges and the one northern judge, ruled that the two
years that Scott spent in Illinois and the same amount
of time he spent at Fort Snelling, even if the latter was
free territory, did not make him free once he returned to

Missouri. The dissenters took the position that Scott was indeed a free man by virtue of his "prolonged residence in free territory." They also cited the Constitution, "All needful rules and regulations" meant that Congress did have the power to prohibit slavery in the territories and that the first Congress in their interpretation of the Constitution upheld the Northwest Ordinance of 1787 banning slavery in the Northwest Territory. McPherson in his *Battle Cry of Freedom* cites that several framers of the Constitution were still alive during this period and that:

> "...none objected to these acts. Indeed, several
> framers served in Congress and voted for them
> or, as Presidents of the United States, signed
> them into law! If the exclusion of slavery from
> a territory violated due process, asked Curtis,
> what of the 1807 law ending importation of
> slaves from Africa? In any case, to prevent a sla-
> veowner from taking his slaves into a territory
> did not deprive him of that property."

The bottom line in all this is that instead of clearing up this mess by having a Supreme Court controlled by a pro-slave, southern majority, ruling against Dred Scott, it catapulted the country on a course leading into the bloodiest period in American history. It further polarized an already volatile and polarized Congress. The country had been teetering on Civil War from the time of the Constitutional Convention up to the Dred Scott decision and this decision did nothing to pacify the likes of fire eating southerners.

James McPherson wrote that, after the ruling of the court:

"Southerners congratulated themselves that 'southern opinion upon the subject of slavery...is now the law of the land.' The decision 'crushes the life out of that miserable...Black Republican organization.' The New York Tribune declared contemptuously that this decision by 'five slaveholders and two doughfaces' was a 'dictum...entitled to just as much moral weight as would be the judgment of a minority of those congregated in any Washington barroom'...'the remedy,' said the Chicago Tribune, was 'the ballot box...let the next president be Republican, and 1860 will mark an era kindred with that of 1776."[147]

The Dred Scott decision upheld the compromise that Northerners made with Southerners in drafting the Constitution of the United States; that Blacks would be viewed as "3/5ths human beings" and as such would be seen only as property. Full-blooded Native Americans would not gain citizenship until 1924.

In contrast, George Bonga, his heirs and siblings were not 3/5ths human beings! They were men of pride, dignity and freedom in the wilds of the Northwoods which became their safe abode in the wilderness where all things are free!

In Minnesota, the Dred Scott decision ignited a powder keg. There was polarization in Minnesota but the Republicans seemed to have the best of it. *The St. Paul Daily Times* described the Supreme Court as a "gang of slaveholders" and "The nation cannot, will not, must not be bound by it! It declares all men and women who had the impudence to be born with a black exterior, as fit only for perpetual bondage...It deprives Toil of its honest wages and Nature of its manly worth; it widens the slave-pen, strengthens the chain of oppression…Where now is our liberty?" The admission of Minnesota into the Union as a state became the focal point of long and heated debates on the Senate floor. One southern Senator spouted these fighting words:

> "Whenever the State of Minnesota shall be admitted, we shall have in this body two additional voices against what I think are the best interests of the country…I do not want representatives here from Minnesota for their voices or their power, or what they will do after they get here…I want no Minnesota Senators here. Minnesota is a Territory belonging to us, and we have the power to make all needful rules and regulations for it."[148]

The United States Supreme Court Dred Scott Decision of March 6, 1857 was twenty years after George Bonga arrived at Fort Snelling with an accused murderer lashed to a sled. The Black slave, Dred Scott, saw this free, respected and bold Black man living in the wilderness of the Northwoods become a hero with an aura of fame about him.

The Dred Scott decision was one of a number of major catalysts pushing the nation to Civil War. Behind these major catalysts are minor catalysts and it is more than plausible that the impression George Bonga made on Dred Scott may have been one of many catalysts in formulating the decision of Scott to accept the urging of friends to sue for his freedom. The Dred Scott decision wasn't a singular event but it was of paramount importance to the national question of the 'peculiar institution'.

Lincoln did not see an opportunity in his mind or in the American psyche to strike the first mortal blow against slavery until the Union victory at Antietam on September 17, 1862, which is still the single greatest loss of American life in a one day period. Lincoln had his victory and his opportunity to begin the death process for slavery. It was a momentous event in not only American history but for the world. The proclamation began:

> "Whereas, on the 22nd day of September, in the year of our Lord one thousand eight hundred and sixty-two, a proclamation issued by the President of the United States, containing among other things, the following, to wit: That on the first day January...all persons held as slaves within any State or designated part of a State, the people whereof shall then be in rebellion against the United States, shall be then, thenceforward, and forever, free..."

The official Emancipation Proclamation was to be signed and made official on Jan 1, 1863. As usual on the first of the year, a reception was held at the White House where dignitaries would line up for a hand shaking ceremony with the President. Thousands stood in line to shake Mr. Lincoln's hand at this great moment in our history. Earlier that afternoon, Lincoln took the time to personally re-copy the document, saying to Senator Sumner, "I know very well that the name connected with this document will never be forgotten." Lincoln had said previously that "If slavery is not wrong, then nothing is wrong. I cannot remember when I did not so think and feel, and yet I have never understood that the presidency conferred upon me an unrestricted right to act officially upon this judgment and feeling." Lincoln had ennobled the Civil War to a higher cause—there would be no turning back, the war was now about freeing men!

The reception ended and one task remained to be done—the President must sign the Emancipation Proclamation to make it complete. The entire Cabinet joined Lincoln in his office for this most solemn occasion. As all the Cabinet members surrounded Lincoln, some with tears in their eyes, Lincoln dipped the pen in ink and halted with the pen poised in a trembling hand and looked around and said:

> "I never, in my life, felt more certain that I was
> doing right, than I do in signing this paper. But
> I have been receiving calls and shaking hands
> since nine o'clock this morning, till my arm is
> stiff and numb. Now the signature is one that
> will be closely examined, and if they find my
> hand trembling they will say, 'he had some com-
> punctions.' But anyway, it is going to be done."

And then, slowly, but with great deliberation, Lincoln scrawled out in large, bold, exaggerated letters, ABRAHAM LINCOLN. The deed was done and history was made. To sum up what had happened, Lincoln said, "We are like whalers who have been on a long chase. We have at last got the harpoon into the monster, but we must now look how we steer, or with one flop of his tail he will send us into eternity."[149]

Abraham Lincoln and George Bonga obviously came from different roots but they did share one common trait; both grew up in the wilderness. It is also interesting to see Abraham Lincoln as the "Great Emancipator," not as a man from wealth, consequence, privilege, or high society. Rather he too, was a man born in a one room log cabin in the wilderness, born and raised in poverty, with less than a year's education in an Indiana 'blab school', labored as a rail splitter, sought out books and read them voraciously, and visualized the country through the eyes of someone who saw slavery as a curse. Certain non-obvious parallels between George Bonga and Abraham Lincoln are present.

In Carl Sandburg's, *Abraham Lincoln: The Prairie Years* he describes the world from which Lincoln emerged:

> "Often he worked alone in the timbers, all day long with only the sound of his own ax, or his own voice speaking to himself, or the crackling and swaying of branches in the wind, and the cries and whirs of animals, of brown and silver-gray squirrels, of partridges, hawks, crows, turkeys, sparrows, and occasional wildcats... Growing from boy to man, he was alone a good deal of the time. Days came often when he was by himself all the time except at breakfast and supper hours in the cabin home. In some years more of his time was spent in loneliness than in the company of other people. It happened, too, that this loneliness he knew was not like that of people in cities who can look from a window on streets where faces pass and repass. It was the wilderness loneliness he became acquainted with, solved, filtered through body, eye, and brain, held communion with in his ears, in the temple of his forehead, in the works of his beating heart...He found his life thrown in ways where there was a certain chance for certain growth. And so he grew. Silence found him; he met silence. In the making of him as he was, the element of silence was immense."[150]

Bonga

Both Lincoln and Bonga were products of wild America. The Dred Scott Supreme Court Case would not be the last time that the words or paths of these two men were to cross.

The First Resort in Northern Minnesota

From the end of the Alfred Aitkin murder trial in 1838, through the 1840s and 50s, George Bonga was seen moving about extensively. He was busy running operations at his main posts at Leech Lake and Ottertail Lake and a number of smaller posts such as a sub-post on Bungo Creek. This post and creek named after the family, is in what is now Cass County west of the town of Pine River.

One trader journal has George as clerk at the Fond du Lac post for the season of 1839-40.[151] Another account has George Bonga on Leech Lake and sending Rev. Boutwell this letter in the spring of 1838, "I have put 2 sacks of [wild] Rice & 1 Corn aside for you[.] Scortch Rice [parched] I have none."[152] And we know that George also spent time at the post and home he built on Ottertail Lake near Dakota country.

George's state-wide notoriety as a result of the Alfred Aitkin murder had created an interest and curiosity in this man of somewhat heroic proportions. Luminaries from different walks of life wanted to meet this man, and his home and posts became the lodging place for senators, railroad surveyors, state supreme court judges and other men of notable fame. In fact, it may be correctly stated that George ran the first "resort" in northern Minnesota. Men not only sought out George for his "active mind" but to have him guide them on the vast and sprawling 112,000 acre Leech Lake—*Gaa-zagaskwaajimekaag*—and personally take them by canoe *(jiimaan)* to the source of the *Misi-zibii*, the great river of life.

Shortly after the era of the fur trade had essentially

come to an end and the region was being transformed by a new breed of men, future Minnesota Supreme Court Justice, Charles Flandrau visited George Bonga at Leech Lake in 1856 and wrote the following:

"The original population of all this country was of course the Indians. The next people to arrive were the whites, who were either traders or soldiers, and in referring to the inhabitants they were always designated either as white men or Indians. At quite an early period an officer of the army of the South was stationed at Mackinac, or some other northwestern post, and brought with him two black servants, George and Jack Bonga. When he was ordered away, these two men remained behind and took service in the American Fur company as voyageurs. They married into the Chippewa tribe, and George became quite a prominent trader and a man of wealth and consequence. I was his guest for two weeks at Leech lake just forty two years ago, when I made a canoe voyage to the source of the Mississippi. He was a thorough gentleman in both feeling and deportment, and was very anxious to contribute to my pleasure during my stay with him. He loved to dwell upon the grandeur of the chief factors of the old Fur Company, and, to show me how royally they traveled, he got up an excursion on the lake, in a splendid birch bark canoe, manned by twelve men who paddled to the music of a French Canadian boat song, led by himself. George was very popular with the whites, and loved to relate to the newcomers his adventures. He was about

the blackest man I ever saw, so black that his
skin fairly glistened, but was, excepting his
brother Jack, the only black person in the country. Never having heard of any distinctions between the people but that of Indians and white
men, he would frequently paralyze his hearers
when reminiscing by saying, 'Gentlemen, I
assure you that John Banfil and myself were
the first two white men that ever came into this
country."[153]

Judge Flandrau made two errors: George and his
brother Jack were never servants and he omitted two generations, George's father and grandfather.

Flandrau's recollection renders George as someone
with a great love of the land and the former life he led. It is
easy to imagine the big man in the stern of a bark canoe on
the placid, mirrored surface of Leech Lake, joyously dwelling upon the grandeur of his home and the many episodes
of his life and leading his men by singing the old French
chansons in the melodic manner in which he was said to
have sung.

If 1840 is a good year to mark as the end of the fur
trade, it continues to show George operating as an independent trader on the Leech Lake Reservation. From the
1840s there is nothing to show that George did little else
in life other than running his store. It does appear by the
accounts of men who visited George that he did operate his
home and store as inns for overnight lodging and food. In
the account of Judge Flandrau's 1856 stay with George on
Leech Lake, George housed and fed the Judge but it also
appears that he may have guided him to the headwaters
of the Mississippi. Was George also a tour guide for some
of Minnesota's early luminaries of the scenic and historic

locations in this part of the state? Certainly, his reputation was very well known in the state.

The notion that George operated a de facto lodge is supported by an account given by Benjamin Densmore of an 1857 visit to George Bonga's home and store on Ottertail Lake. Benjamin Densmore, a railroad surveyor, along with a companion by the name of Iddings who knew Bonga, paid George and his wife a visit at their home on Ottertail Lake in 1857. Densmore wrote that:

> "Iddings had known him [Bonga] for some time...and feeling assured of a good welcome, tapped rudely at the bark door of the lodge with his walking stick. A gruff voice replete with good naturedness came from within the lodge bidding us enter.
>
> A hearty shake of the hand and he bade us to be seated upon the mat on the opposite side of the fire; he inquired if we had eaten supper and finding we had not eaten since leaving the lake, directed his...wife to prepare something. While this was being done, he entertained us with much interest in recounting events and making inquiries about elections and political matters in general, showing active thought...
>
> The supper was spread upon a clean cloth on one of the mats and consisted of boiled fish and tea...And Oh! Ye Epicures who would know what is good of the genus pisces [fish] must make a pilgrimage to Bonga's fishing lodge."[154]

Was George the first resort operator in this region or was this just another example of his hospitality and loquaciousness? Or perhaps this is just an example of Indian hospitality as anyone who lives and has friends among the native population in northern Minnesota knows, there is no hospitality like Indian hospitality.

George Bonga was married twice to two Ojibwe women. The first wife was *Nahganashikwe,* the second was *Baybahmausheak Ashwewin.* With these wives he had five children; Peter, William, Jack, Susan and George. Oral history given to me by Juanita Blackhawk says that George had more wives than the two mentioned. Juanita states that over his life George may have had as many as seven wives.

It should also be noted that while the voyageurs prided themselves on strength and stamina, they also prided themselves on downing massive amounts of alcohol. George Bonga may have been a giant among his peers in all categories including getting drunk. A fur trader at Crow Wing by the name of Augustus Aspinwall wrote in 1850:

> "I found a ½ Negro and ½ Indian [Bonga] who was trading at Leech Lake...I will say now that for several years I had Business Relations with him and Found him an Intelligent Honest Man, But the Hardest Kind of Drinker, always Drunk when he could get Whiskey...We left about 3 PM and after going about 7 miles we stopped for Dinner, my first Dinner in Camp, the Cook Took some Cold Water put it in a kettle, Put this on a Fire as to make a Thick Do, then he made this into Lengths about 6 in Long and 2 in Thick, these we Throwed in with the Pork, and in 30 Minutes more or less our Dinner was Done, Well I could not go it so went with Out my Dinner, this Meal Sobered them up some and we Started again."[155]

Treaties, Reservations, and War

In the early 1800s, the Dakota found themselves in the southern and western parts of the region that was soon to be Minnesota. By the 1850s they also found an influx of white settlers, many of Scandinavian and German stock. These people were interested in farming the rich soils of the prairie regions and were enticed to this land of promise without being informed that the land was already occupied. One thing that the Dakota realized with the arrival of these whites was depletion in the game on which they hunted and depended. The Dakota also found themselves squeezed onto reservations. The Treaty of Traverse des Sioux and the Treaty of Mendota, both signed in 1851, established settlement on reservations. The Dakota, who originally occupied the entire state, were now confined to a reservation that was a twenty-mile-wide strip of land ten miles on each side along the Minnesota River and extending 140 miles from New Ulm to Big Stone Lake near the South Dakota border. The reservations were defined as the upper and lower reservations with the Yellow Medicine River as the boundary between them.

In another agreement negotiated in 1858, the Dakota gave up the ten-mile strip of land north of the Minnesota River. This ten-mile strip was where the best hunting was found. At the time of these treaties, the Dakota population was around six thousand people. This population was made up of four tribes belonging to the *Santee* nation of the: *Mdewakanton, Wahpekute, Wahpeton,* and *Sisseton.* Three other Dakota tribes, the *Yanktons, Yanktonais,* and the *Tetons* were already in the Dakotas, having been previously forced west by the Ojibwe. It is interesting to note that the ancestors of Crazy Horse and Sitting Bull were probably residents of Mille Lacs Lake or as it was known to the Santee, Mystic Lake, before the Ojibwe pushed them onto the plains. The ancient capital of the Dakota was located on Mille Lacs Lake and was called "Izatys." The term *Isanti*, meaning people of Knife Lake, was corrupted to Santee by the whites. One of the first whites to visit this great village of Dakota was David Greysolon, Sieur du Luth in 1679. The name of this great village, *Isanti*, was mistakenly recopied from Du Luth's report as "Kathio" and the name stuck as it is now the site of Kathios State Park, in the Minnesota State Park system.

Two of the greatest deceptions and betrayals perpetrated upon the Dakota occurred during the Traverse des Sioux Treaty involving all four bands of the Santee Nation. The Santee sold all their land within the territory of Minnesota for three million dollars to be distributed in annual payments of cash and goods. In turn, a reservation twenty miles wide and one hundred miles long would be established along the Minnesota River. The creation of this narrow strip was to be for permanent use and schools, blacksmith shops, and flour mills were to be built. As the treaty papers were being signed, a second paper was signed which the Dakota believed to be a second copy, but in actuality was an agreement to pay the traders bills before dispersing the treaty payments to Indians. No service fee amounts were listed so the traders were virtually able to fill in any amount. The second deception was a clause in the treaty noting "permanent home." This language seemed to protect the Indians from being moved again at the whim of the whites. Before signing the agreed treaty, the "permanent home" language was replaced with one that gave them a home "until the Executive shall deem it expedient to direct otherwise." When the Dakota learned of this, they knew that had essentially given up all their land.[156]

Once the Dakota were moved to the reservation along the Minnesota River, they were pressured to cease their nomadic and hunting way of life, take up farming and adopt Christianity. Prior to the Civil War, over 150,000 white settlers had sunk stakes into what was Dakota land and as a result of treaties the Dakota had lost nine-tenths of their land and found themselves crowded on a narrow strip of land along the Minnesota River. Besides losing their land the Dakota found themselves at the mercy of the Indian agents and traders at the established posts on the reservation. These agents and traders outrageously abused the Dakota.

Big Eagle (*Wamditanka*) accurately described the conditions the Dakota endured on the reservation and the treatment by whites:

> "The whites were always trying to make the
> Indians give up their life and live like white men
> – go to farming, work hard and do as they did
> – and the Indians did not know how to do that,
> and did not want to anyway...If the Indians
> had tried to make the whites live like them, the
> whites would have resisted, and it was the same
> way with many Indians."

Those Dakota who lived by the hunt found themselves at odds with the traders. Very little game was left on the reservation and when the Dakota crossed into their traditional hunting grounds, conflict with whites intensified. The Dakota that took up farming had experienced several years of drought and found diminishing yields in their crops which forced them further into debt by relying on the credit system for food from agency traders. The Dakota increasingly grew resentful of the agency credit system. When annuity payments arrived from Washington, the traders had first claim on the money and no matter what the Indians actually owed, it was the word of the traders that ruled the day. Some Indians, who did keep accounts of their debt, found that the government would not accept their recorded debt which was in nearly all instances lower than the recorded amount of the traders. The Dakota believed that the 1858 Treaty had paid all debt that the Dakota owed the traders. The traders interpreted the Treaty as only giving the Indians credit after the Treaty was established. Tensions were rising and the mixed-bloods felt caught between the growing schisms. The Indian agents among the Dakota had made it a practice to hand out annuity cash payments and food only to Indians who adopted the white man's way of farming and Christianity. Those Indians, who farmed, enhanced their position by cutting their hair and dressing like whites. The end result of this is that those Dakota who refused to cultivate the land and continued to roam their ancestral lands and hunt, viewed all farmers, both white and Indian, as trespassers and a threat to the essence of their lives.

When the American Civil War broke out in April of 1861, it disrupted the flow of money and food to the reservation as agreed by Treaty. The distribution of food and money was clearly spelled out in the Treaty, but the United States Congress was under immense duress due to the Civil War and the Dakota Indians of Minnesota were not near the top of their priorities. Desperately needed money and food that rightfully belonged to the Dakota along the Minnesota River was not getting there and tensions were reaching a breaking point.

In July of 1862, several thousand hungry Santees gathered at the upper Agency on the Yellow Medicine River to collect their annuities promised by the treaty. The money due the Dakota would be used to buy needed provisions. Chief Little Crow (*Ta-oya-te-duta*) was among the Dakota intending to represent his people. Little Crow was a third descendant of Mdewkanton Chiefs, and was sixty years old and wore long sleeves to cover his crippled hands and wrists due to wounds he had received from being shot by his half-brother. A white doctor had wanted to amputate his wrists and hands, but Little Crow had sought healing through a Dakota medicine man and as a result saved his appendages and retained use of his deformed hands. Little Crow had signed the treaties that had swindled the Dakota.

Chief Little Crow asked the agent in charge, Thomas Galbraith of the Yellow Medicine Agency, why they were not being issued the food that had been promised them in the treaty when the storehouses were full of food. Galbraith replied that he could not issue the food until the annuity payments arrived and placed one hundred soldiers to guard the warehouses. Then, on August 4, about five hundred angry Santee Dakota broke into the warehouses and commandeered the flour and pork. The soldier in charge, Timothy Sheehan, in a rare gesture of compassion and sympathy, did not fire upon the Indians, but rather convinced agent Galbraith to step aside. The Indians left peacefully except Little Crow, who stayed behind until Galbraith promised that the lower agency at Redwood would also issue food. What happened next is described in Dee Brown's *Bury My Heart at Wounded Knee*:

> "Although Little Crow's village was near the
> Lower Agency, Galbraith kept him waiting sever-
> al days before arraigning a council at Redwood
> for August 15. Early that morning Little Crow
> and several hundred hungry Mdewakantons
> assembled, but it was obvious from the begin-
> ning that Galbraith and the four traders at the
> Lower Agency had no intention of issuing food

from their stores before the arrival of the annuity funds.

Angered by yet another broken promise, Little Crow arose, faced Galbraith, and spoke for his people: 'We have waited for a long time. The money is ours, but we cannot get it. We have no food, but here are these stores, filled with food. We ask that you, the agent, make some arrangement, by which we can get food from the stores, or else we may take our own way to keep ourselves from starving. When men are hungry they help themselves.'

Instead of replying, Galbraith turned to the traders and asked them what they would do. Trader Andrew Myrick declared contemptuously: 'So far as I am concerned, if they are hungry let them eat grass or their own dung.'

For a moment the circle of Indians was silent. Then came an outburst of angry shouts, and as one man the Santees arose and left the council."[157]

Then "something very important, something very bad" happened that would become the ignition source that exploded into open warfare. On August 17, 1862, four Dakota Wahpeton hunters crossed the river into the Big Woods and killed five white settlers on the farm of Howard Baker for an apparent insult near the town of Acton in Meeker County. The Indian version was related by Big Eagle:

"They came to a settler's fence, and here they found a hen's nest with some eggs in it. One of them took the eggs, when another said: 'Don't take them, for they belong to a white man and we may get into trouble.' The other was angry, for he was very hungry and wanted to eat the eggs, and he dashed them to the ground and replied: 'You are a coward. You are afraid of the white man. You are afraid to take even an egg from him, though you are half starved. Yes, you are a coward, and I will tell everybody so.' The other replied, 'I am not a coward. I am not afraid of the white man, and to show you that I am not I will go to the house and shoot him. Are you brave enough to go with me?' The one who had called him a coward said: 'yes, I will go with you, and we will see who is braver of us two.' Their two companions then said: 'We will go with you, and we will be brave too.' They all went to the house of the white man, but he got alarmed and went to another house where there were some other white men and women. The four Indians followed them and killed three men and two women. Then they hitched up a team belonging to another settler and drove to Shakopee's camp...and told what they had done."[158]

There's never been an official report on the number of settlers killed, but estimates range from 300 to 800. Historian Don Heinrich Tolzmann says that until the terrorist attacks of Sept. 11, 2001, it was the highest civilian wartime toll in U.S. history.[159]

The number of Dakota killed has never been documented but the calamity that rained down upon them in their loss of homes, near universal hatred by the white population in Minnesota, the largest mass hanging ever committed in this nation, and banishment of virtually all of the complete Dakota population from the state smacked of genocide.

Friends and Confidants – George Bonga and Bishop Whipple

One man who was not overtaken by the tide of mob hysteria was Bishop Henry Benjamin Whipple. Henry Whipple came to Minnesota at the age of thirty-seven in 1859 to become Minnesota's first Protestant Episcopal Church Bishop. Whipple was a descendant of Revolutionary stock and was said to be tall, powerfully built, and "richly endowed with bodily and mental gifts." But ill health in his youth prevented him from getting a classical education and instead found him in world of business and politics which, as historian William Watts Folwell wrote, "perhaps gave him a better training for his future work than he might have got from the odes of Horace and Pindar."

One of the first things Bishop Whipple did upon arrival in Minnesota was to visit Fort Ripley and see the conditions of the Ojibwe in the Gull Lake area. He found that of both tribes—Ojibwe and Dakota—"their wretchedness was chargeable to the indifference, not to say the rascality, of white men."

The Bishop's first wilderness journey to the Gull Lake area and his experiences in the beautiful forests and waterways kindled in the heart of the young bishop an interest in the Indian which continued to the end of his life.

> "[O]n the sixth of March, 1862 Bishop Whipple
> addressed an open letter to President Lincoln,
> in which he summarized the iniquities of the
> Indian system and insisted on the supreme
> importance of placing the Indians under a

189

government of law, administered by honest and capable men selected for their merit and fitness and not as a reward for political services."[160]

There is no account I know of that shows how George Bonga and Bishop Whipple first met but, after they did, for the remainder of their lives the white Episcopalian missionary and the Black-Ojibwe fur trader would be friends and confidants. George Bonga would become the principle source of information concerning corruption and malfeasance among corrupt Indian agents and dishonest licensed traders. Nearly all the information that Bishop Whipple received about wrong doings in Ojibwe Country originated from George Bonga. Through George's dealings with Whipple, Bonga would begin a steady series of letters to the Bishop, Indian agents, officials in the Office of Indian Affairs and legislators at both state and federal levels. George's name became well known in Washington and St. Paul and his reputation was one of honesty and honor. One top ranking official in the Office of Indian Affairs in a letter committing to rectify problems in Indian Country stated to Bishop Whipple, "...make sure George Bonga reads this letter."

In September of 1862, only a month after war raged up and down the Minnesota River Valley, Bishop Whipple wrote a courageous letter that brought an onslaught of public opinion against him from the whites in the state. The letter titled, *The Duty of Citizens Concerning the Indian Massacre,* received state wide attention. In it, the Bishop stated: "...our people cry vengeance. But if that vengeance is to be more than a savage thirst for blood, we must examine the causes which have brought this bloodshed that our condemnation may fall on the guilty."

Bonga

The Bishop goes on to decry the mistakes made in regard to the Indian. Overall, he has the system of trade and federal agents portrayed in the correct light, that being of total corruption. Whipple states:

> "The system of trade was ruinous to honest traders and pernicious to the Indian...Such a mistaken policy would be bad enough in the hands of the wisest and best men, but it is made a hundred-fold worse by making the office of an Indian agent one of reward for political services. It had been sought, not because it was one of the noblest trusts ever committed to men to try and redeem...but because, upon a pittance of salary, a fortune could be realized in a few years.

> The voice of this whole nation had declared that the Indian Department is the most corrupt in the Government. Citizens, editors, legislators, heads of the departments, and the President alike agree that it has been characterized by inefficiency and fraud. The nation, knowing this, has winked at it. We have lacked the moral courage to stand up in the fear of God and demand a reform. More than all, it was not our money. It was a sacred trust confided to us by helpless men, where common manliness should have blushed for shame at the theft...

> It hardly needed any act of wrong to incite savage natures to murderous cruelty. But such instances were not wanting. Four years ago the Sioux sold the Government part of their reservation, the plea for the sale being the need of

funds to aid them in civilization...Of the nine-
ty-six thousand dollars due to the Lower Sioux
not one cent has ever been received. All has
been absorbed in claims except eight hundred
and eighty dollars and fifty-eight cents, which is
to their credit on the books in Washington. Of
the portion belonging to the other Sioux, eighty-
eight thousand, three hundred and fifty-one
dollars and twelve cents were also taken for
claims...For two years the Indians had demanded to know what had become of their money,
and had again and again threatened revenge
unless they were satisfied. Early last spring
the traders informed the Indians that the next
payment would be only half the usual amount,
because the Indian debts had been paid at
Washington. They were in some instances refused credit on this account.

It caused deep and widespread discontent.
The agent was alarmed, and as early as May
he wrote me that this new fraud must bring a
harvest of woe, saying, 'God only knows what
will be the result.' In June, at the time fixed by
custom, they came together for the payment.
The agent could give no satisfactory reason for
the delay. There was none to give. The Indians
waited at the Agencies for two months, dissatisfied, turbulent, hungry, and then came the outbreak...The money reached Fort Ripley the day
after the outbreak. A part of the annuity had
been taken for claims and at the eleventh hour,
as the warrant on the treasury shows, was
made up from other funds to save an Indian
war. It was too late! Who is guilty of the causes

which desolated our border? At whose door is
the blood of these innocent victims? I believe
that God will hold the nation guilty."[161]

George Bonga's letters and conversations with Bishop
Whipple certainly were no epiphany for the Bishop concerning the degradation of the Indian, as he had seen the
corruption for himself. However, taking into account the
high opinion Whipple had for George Bonga, they certainly
had influence with the good bishop. Bonga, with his background and insight, would have bolstered Whipple's convictions, and at any rate, George Bonga would keep the
Bishop informed on every deed of injustice done to the
Ojibwe.

The courageous Bishop had a helpful connection in
Washington, that being his cousin, Gen. Henry Halleck,
Lincoln's chief military advisor during the Civil War. Whipple
made the trip to Washington prior to the Dakota executions
at Mankato and used his friendship with Halleck to access
President Lincoln.

As Folwell describes it:

"In the fall of 1862 Bishop Whipple was in
Washington, and with General Halleck, he
called on President Lincoln. In Whipple's remarks to the President he noted the corruption
of the agents and traders and of the events leading up to the outbreak of war. Whipple made
these remarks with such force of character
that Lincoln later remarked: 'He came here the
other day and talked with me about the rascality of this Indian business until I felt it down to
my boots.' It is not likely that this impression
had faded out when the President came to act

upon the findings of the military commission. In December Bishop Whipple published in the St. Paul newspapers a calm, clear statement of the train of events which had led to this terrible explosion. So far as is known, he was the only public man who had the courage to face the whirlwind of popular denunciation of all Indians and of the Dakota in particular. To punish the guilty would avail little if the traditional Indian policy was to be left unreformed. In some quarters the bishop came in for denunciation almost as spiteful and unsparing as that directed against the Sioux themselves, but he never retracted a syllable nor budged an inch."[162]

Bishop said of the conversation with President Lincoln:

"In the autumn the General Convention met in New York, and at the same time I visited Washington. General Halleck went with me to the President, to whom I gave an account of the outbreak [Dakota Conflict], its causes, and the suffering and evil which had followed in its wake. Mr. Lincoln had known something of Indian warfare in the Black Hawk War. He was deeply moved. He was a man of profound sympathy, but he usually relieved the strain upon his feelings by telling a story. When I had finished he said:--- 'Bishop, a man thought that monkeys could pick cotton better than negroes could because they were quicker and their fingers smaller. He turned a lot of them into his cotton field, but he found that it took two overseers to watch one monkey. It needs more than one honest man to watch one Indian Agent.'

A short time after this, President Lincoln, meeting a friend from Illinois, asked him if their old friend, Luther Dearborn, had not moved to Minnesota. Receiving an affirmative answer, he said: 'When you see Lute, ask him if he knows Bishop Whipple. He came here the other day and talked with me about the rascality of this Indian business until I felt it down to my boots. If we get through this war, and I live, this Indian system shall be reformed!'

He gave me a card to the Secretary of the Interior with the message, "Give Bishop Whipple any information he desires about Indian affairs."[163]

All of this occurred at a horrifically stressful time for Lincoln. The war couldn't be going worse for the North. The Union Army in the eastern theatre had suffered a long series of defeats at the hand of Robert E. Lee's Army of Northern Virginia. The North was growing weary and tired of the war. The Battle of Antietam occurred while Lincoln had the Emancipation Proclamation in his desk drawer, waiting for some note of optimistic news such as a victory before public release. And most pressingly, for Lincoln to give Dakota warriors a reprieve would be politically unpopular with the white voters in Minnesota which had just received statehood in 1858. Minnesota was a Republican state then and had gone for Lincoln in 1860. For Lincoln to go against the desires of the voting public in Minnesota and grant any form of leniency to Indians would be political suicide for him, but Lincoln, the man from the backwoods, did exactly that. The President stepped away from the awful situation he faced in war and politics to show an act, seen by some, of partial justice by going over every condemned warrior's name and charge against him. Of the 303 sentenced to be hung, Lincoln granted reprieve from death to all but thirty-eight – knowing that by doing so he would lose the state of Minnesota in his re-election.

In a letter George Bonga wrote to Bishop Henry Benjamin Whipple in 1863 after the mass execution of thirty-eight Dakota men following the Dakota – Minnesota War of 1862, he presents his thoughts on the changing world of the Indian. Letters like this led to a friendship, candidness, and regular correspondence between the two men. Whipple learned to listen to Bonga in regards to corrupt traders, treaty rights, bad government policy, and the general plight of the Indian:

> "...The Ind[ian] & his father before him have
> been used to the chase, although hard work,
> he is proud of it & thinks to cultivate the soil is
> only the work of hirelings... & most of the men
> are ashamed to work in that way. Many a good
> advice has been given to them, all to no pur-
> pose. Starvation will come to him first, before he
> will cut down trees & dig up roots; when he very
> well knows it would much better his condition.
> It would seem, that they can't perceive, that
> when their game is all killed off, which is dis-
> appearing very fast, they will then have to come
> down to the very lowest depth of degradation,
> if they are not exterminated, before that time
> reaches them...
>
> The little I know of the whites leads me to think,
> that they will not allow their Ind[ian]s to roam
> in their midst much longer as well as all the
> Inds. who live near the white settlements, if the

Ind[ian] could be induced to see his own good he would learn that the sooner he was removed from the whites, the better it would be for himself and his children after him. Having lived most of my life with the Ind[ian]s, I easily perceive that the Ind[ian] of today is not the same kind of Ind[ian] that was 40 years ago, although the same band. In those days we lived and mingled with them, as if we all belonged to one & the same family, our goods often out without lock & key, never fearing anything would go wrong. Far different is it now a days. There is that suspicion on either side, that when we hear of 10 or more Ind[ian]s gathered together, we feel anxious & ask each other, what that can mean, if it is not the same bad design & on the Ind[ian] side, they have always some complaint to make. Some imaginary promise that the Gov[ernmen]t has not fulfilled, has led them to that belief, that the whites are combined to try & destroy them. It appears to us all, that there is something smoldering in the breast of the Ind[ian] that it will not take much to set it a blaze. If that should ever take place, no one can foretell how far the flames will extend..."[164]

From Fur Trader to Advocate

In less than twenty years; from December of 1836 when Alfred Aitkin was murdered to the 1855 Treaty when nearly all Ojibwe land had been ceded to the whites and the majority of Ojibwe, including the *men who take by force* had been forced to settle on reservations. Then within another eight years after 1855 the woodland Dakota who had been swindled of their homes and squeezed onto a narrow strip of land along the Minnesota River would be driven from the state by the same men who stole their land by treaty in the first place. Not only had land ownership changed, but a new way of seeing the land had changed. No longer was the dominant culture one of living in concert within the plant and animal communities, but now it was how to exploit the land from farming to clear cutting of the vast virgin pinery and to plundering the earth for its wealth. At no other time in Minnesota history has such violent and dramatic change taken place, both to men and land, as between the years 1837 and 1863.

By the late summer and autumn of 1866 the era of the fur trade was gone forever. The early traders of the former North West Company and the American Fur Company were either dead or retired. Northern Minnesota was no longer ruled by the great Ojibwe chiefs as most of the major treaties had been negotiated and the First Nation people found themselves on reservations, their former country being ceded to the white man. A war had been fought with the Dakota and potential discord with the Ojibwe had been averted, but the Indian still found himself at the mercy of the corrupt system perpetuated by government agents and politically appointed licensed traders.

Most fur traders were primarily concerned with only obtaining furs. They were not interested in taking Indian land, timber, or any other resources. Even with all the faults in the fur trade, the first white traders had needed the Indian as the procurement part of the business relationship, a partnership of sorts. Now the fur trade was over and a new kind of white man came upon the scene. This new white face saw the agency system and trading policies with Anishinaabeg as a way to get rich by swindling Native people. With most Ojibwe having been placed on reservations, they came under great pressure from the government and well intentioned white missionaries to adopt the white man's way. One of the principal but mistaken goals of those trying to save the Indian from extinction was to make the Indian a farmer. Whites had no comprehension of the Indian use of land, that being one of permaculture. These missionaries included the likes of Bishop Henry B. Whipple. Although Whipple showed extraordinary compassion for Indian people, he feared that if the Indians did not adopt the ways of the white man, they would be exterminated. The Bishop saw farming as a salvation of sorts for Indian survival.

The overwhelming mind-set of white America was that the Indian was going to disappear. It was inevitable and unavoidable. America didn't really care, after all, because it was white America's destiny—manifest destiny. It was ordained that all of America rightfully belonged to the white man. Few white people stood up for the Indian other than people like Bishop Whipple, who mostly stood alone in his condemnation of the treatment of Native Americans.

It was at the onset of this transformation in Indian Country by white America that we see a shift in George Bonga's role. His letters no longer dwelled on nuances concerning the fur trade, or how the rice crop was, or the abundance of a particular fur bearer. Instead, they appeared more as letters written as an advocate. Although George Bonga exhibited some of the same mistaken goals of the missionaries and white liberals of the time advocating for the well-being of the Indian, he does differ in understanding the long cultural and subsistence needs of the Indian. After all, Bonga was a mix-blood man and had lived among the Ojibwe his entire life. He frequently referenced the importance of wild rice, maple sugar bushes, and fisheries and stated that without such resources; "...a Chippewa Ind. would be altogether at a loss how to make a living."

He harangued the "rascality" of traders and agents, and advocated for proper and sensible reservation locations where there was sufficient land with the natural resources present to support the Indian way of life. A series of letters written by George Bonga from 1866 to 1874 were almost all letters written in the interest of the Ojibwe. He noted: (1) the removal of the Crow Wing/Gull Lake bands to White Earth rather than the government idea of one big reservation at Leech Lake (2) the corruption of dishonest U.S. Indian agents and licensed traders (3) and the swindle of timber cut on reservation lands.

George Bonga's many letters and face to face visits with Bishop Whipple undoubtedly guided Whipple in formulating opinion on these issues in Indian Country. Bishop Whipple's reputation was widely regarded as an open minded man who inherently believed in gathering information and making opinion based on his first hand observations. This is not intended to take away from the many good deeds done by the good Bishop on behalf of the Dakota and Ojibwe, but clearly Bonga was an intimate and trusted source for Henry Whipple. Bishop Whipple said, "George Bonga...was a man of great intelligence and perfectly understood the Indian character. He had been my companion on many journeys through the Indian Country. I could rely implicitly upon any information he gave me, and... This man is trustworthy."30 Bonga also had a regular written communication with other policy makers such as Senator Henry Rice who played an important role, good and bad, in Indian policy in Minnesota.

I have carefully read many Bonga letters, and the more I read them and understand the politics and players of this time and place, the more I am impressed with his sagacity and clearness of thought. He carefully ponders his thoughts and calculates the effect of what he is saying.

When necessary he plays ignorant. But most importantly his understanding of the people, the resources available on the land, and intricacies of the government trading system are spot on. This is not to say he was correct all the time but those of us looking back over time have the luxury of hindsight.

It would be difficult to read the letters or understand the intent in the letters without some background of the issues and characters.

The suicide of corrupt Indian agent Lucius Walker after being exposed in 1862 resulted in the appointment of Ashley Morrill as Indian Agent for all the Ojibwe in Minnesota. Replacements automatically came about when a new President took office after an election. In the spring of 1865, Agent Morrill was replaced by Agent Edwin Clark. The licensed traders were the firm of (Wm) Aspinwall, (Chas.) Ruffee, and Nash. This department of government Indian agents and licensed traders was so corrupt that Charles Ruffee had boasted "he could make $75,000 out of this post" by fleecing the Indians. 31 So, needless to say, corruption remained business as usual—remembering too, that the money being swindled was money pledged to the Ojibwe by treaty. This corruption, plus the fact that George Bonga could not get a license himself to trade with the tribe on the Leech Lake Reservation, where he lived, rankled him greatly.

As lumberman Joel Bean Bassett stated, "His role as an informant to Bishop Whipple about the condition in Indian Country played an important part in Whipple's request to appoint a man whom he believed the right man for the job."

Bassett was a Civil War veteran. He was a native of New Hampshire who came to Minnesota after the Civil War and was a successful lumber man in Minneapolis. He also was known for starting up one of the first flour mills in the

Minneapolis and had a creek, Bassett Creek, named after him in the vicinity of the growing city. He had a wide spread reputation as an honest and trustworthy man. Whipple sought out Bassett to take the position of Indian Agent for the Ojibwe with the belief that Bassett would amend the corrupt system, mostly based on the persistent recommendations of George Bonga. In a letter dated November 14, 1866, Whipple wrote to Bassett:

> "I have today received a letter from Secy
> Browning informing me that upon my urgent
> request he has appointed you as Indian agent.
> It is the first in my life since I became a bishop
> that I have ever asked a political appointment.
> In doing it I have had to incur the ill will of some
> very dear friends and oppose one Mr. Ruffee, for
> where as a man I have had great respect...But
> for years I have labored in public & private to
> reform this abominable Indian System...I have
> had my eye on you – we were strangers, you did
> not belong to my own faith, you were not of the
> administration, but friends assured me you was
> an honest man. I believe you would...be afraid
> & ashamed to steal - I believe you would not tell
> me a lie, that is in a word I could trust you – I
> have done so to an extent that if you should dis-
> appoint me it would ruin me & make me power-
> less here."[165]

Almost three months before Whipple wrote his November 14 letter to J.B. Bassett, George Bonga began a regular correspondence with Bassett. He continued to urge Bishop Whipple to push for Bassett's appointment, believing that Joel Bean Bassett would remedy the corruption in Indian Country.[166]

Bonga

By this time, Bishop Whipple had developed a national reputation as a friend of the Indian. He had the audience of not only the Commissioner of the Office of Indian Affairs but also the President, the President's Cabinet members, and Minnesota's policy makers. He was arguably the nation's leading white activist in defending the Indian from exploitation by the whites. The Indians were beginning to feel that they had someone among the whites to represent them. The Bishop made his home in Faribault but was amazingly well traveled throughout the state. Often his first destination was the village of Old Crow Wing where he would begin journeys to the Ojibwe reservations in the Northwoods by foot, canoe, or dogsled.

By the late 1860s, the northern most town in Minnesota was Crow Wing. The historic location of this community, at the point where the Crow Wing River flows into the Mississippi, is about eight miles downstream from the present location of Brainerd. The name "Crow Wing" came from the Ojibwe word, *Gaagaagiwigwani-ziibi* (Raven-feather River), perhaps due to a large island in the mouth of the Crow Wing which was likened to the shape of a raven wing. Early French traders called the island at the junction of these two rivers, Des Corbeaus River—Corbeau being French for crow—as they had no language differentiation between crows and ravens. This is the site where in 1768, the Battle of Crow Wing took place. This was the fight in which Ojibwe men dug themselves into the bank of the river where they ambushed Dakota warriors returning with Ojibwe women captives from a raiding mission at Sandy Lake. Crow Wing had been the site of an Ojibwe village, on and off, since the Ojibwe secured the region from the Dakota. Hole-in-the-Day the Younger had a very nice home there. The first settlement was established after the 1847 Treaty. This settlement was on the east side of the

Mississippi opposite the entrance of the Crow Wing River. The Rev. J. Lloyd Breck, who established the St. Columba Mission and served there for the Episcopal Church from 1852 to 1856, described the town as having "only 32 dwellings...but 7 whiskey shops." By 1857, the entire county of Crow Wing had a population of 176, most probably residing in the village of Crow Wing. Crow Wing was the "jumping off" place into northern Minnesota and Indian Country.

A primitive foot trail had existed for perhaps centuries from St. Anthony Falls and later Fort Snelling to Crow Wing. In 1848, U.S. army Captain Napoleon J.T. Dana took a construction crew to the selected site of Fort Ripley, seven miles downstream from the village of Crow Wing. They improved the trail from Fort Ripley to Fort Snelling so it was fit for wagon travel. Since the mid 1840s the Red River Oxcart trail had two routes through the western prairie regions of the state. However, fear of the Dakota caused a third route to cut eastward from Detroit Lakes to Ottertail and then down the bank of the Crow Wing River where it crossed the river at the village of Crow Wing and continued on to St. Paul. The segment from Crow Wing to Fort Ripley was improved by Hole-in-the-Day the Younger with his own resources. He commented that by improving this seven or eight mile segment of road, he had done more to civilize the Indian than all of what the white man had done. The 1855 Treaty with the Leech Lake Pillagers provided $15,000 for improving of the Crow Wing Trail to the agency at Leech Lake. Residing at the terminus of this trail on Traders Bay of Leech Lake was the post and home of George Bonga. It was now possible to travel by road, albeit a primitive road, from Fort Snelling to Leech Lake and George's home.

Many notable figures in Minnesota history resided at one time in Crow Wing. Some notable Crow Wing residents would be William Aitkin, Allan Morrison, William

Bonga

Whipple Warren, Clement H. Beaulieu, William and John Fairbanks, and Hole-in-the-Day. Old Crow Wing became a crossroads and hub in the rapidly changing frontier of northern Minnesota and would play a role in the politics and relations of people in this part of the state. 33 Many of the Bonga letters written to Joel Bean Bassett were written from Crow Wing, as George would often stay there to better keep in touch with the political doings of his day. It was pretty handy for George as the trail virtually went from his front door on Leech Lake to the village.

In 1863, another group that Bishop Whipple had advocated for was the "Board of Visitors." The board was composed of Catholic Bishop Thomas L. Grace, American Board Missionary Thomas Williamson, and Whipple himself. They were to supervise the distribution of annuity payments, look out for the welfare of the Indian, and keep tabs on how much land the Indians had under cultivation in order to facilitate the government's grand plan of locating all the Indians on one big reservation. These open and sympathetic men listened to the Indians. What they heard was that the Indians did not want to move to the one big proposed reservation at Leech Lake. The "Board of Visitors" reported what they heard and the reasons the Indians gave for justifying their opposition to such a move. George Bonga also saw the foolishness in moving the Mississippi, Sandy Lake, Pokegama, and Mille Lacs bands to the Leech Lake Reservation. Lessons were not lost or forgotten concerning the Sandy Lake Death March of 1850 in which approximately 400 Ojibwe died resulting from this shameful fiasco motivated by greed of white government officials and Indian agents in order to enrich their pockets.

One name often mentioned in Bonga's letters is a Mr. Whitehead who was being considered as a future appointee as Indian Agent. George later argued against his appointment saying that Whitehead was a "tool" of the timber industry. Bonga often mentions the "Bishop" in his letters, this is of course Bishop Henry Benjamin Whipple. Three of George's sons who are frequently mentioned are James, Peter, and William. Senator Henry Rice is mentioned frequently; Rice was a fur trader, a Territorial representative, a state senator, and a lumber man. Also mentioned are Charles Ruffee and William Aspinwall, who are licensed traders to the Ojibwe. Charles Ruffee saw that Indian Agent Clark was on his way out and started lobbying for the job of Agent himself. People like Bonga and Whipple were only too aware of Ruffee's corrupt credentials. The Reverend Knickerbacker is David Knickerbacker, Episcopalian Priest to Gethsemane Church in Minneapolis who served as a missionary to the Ojibwe. Mr. Donnelly is state representative Ignatius Donnelly. Donnelly served as Minnesota Lieutenant Governor from 1860-62, was a representative from 1863 – 68 and a Minnesota state Senator from 1874 – 78. Donnelly was also a supporter of newly freed slaves and a supporter of women's suffrage. Mess. Peake is Ebenezer Steele Peake, an Episcopalian missionary at Gull Lake and later Crow Wing. Hole-in-the-Day the Younger is the great chief of the Mississippi Pillagers. Agent Clark is Ojibwe Indian Agent, Edwin Clark, the man who George greatly detests. Ramsey is Alexander Ramsey, Minnesota's second State Governor (1860-63) and was also was the territory's first governor. He was also a mayor of St. Paul, U.S. Senator (from 1863-1875) and made the now infamous statement, "The Sioux Indians of Minnesota must be exterminated or driven forever beyond the borders of the state." Perish Roy, Baptist Vasseaure, Joseph Desjardin, Charley Beaulieu, and Rob. Fairbanks are all mixed-blood independent traders who are also mentioned.

The series of letters from George Bonga to Joel Bean

Bonga

Bassett are below. I have copied them with the miss-spellings, capitalizations, grammar, and abbreviations as Bonga wrote them. One reason for the common use of abbreviations and shortened words and phrases was the need to conserve ink and paper in those days.

When one reads them, Bonga's personality jumps out at you. His disgust for the traders and agents is all too obvious and his style does suggest his place as an advocate. Having read them over numerous times, I feel as if I know the man and if he entered the room, I would be immediately attracted to him by his obvious charisma. Sometimes the letters seem contradictory as he, like the men of his day, saw the salvation of Native people was to take up the ways of the white man. In other ways he saw the need for Native people to preserve their culture when he made statements like an Indian can't make a living unless he has waters with fish, rice fields and sugar bushes.

J. B. Bassett Esqr   Leech Lake August 27th 1866

Respected Sir

As Mr Whitehead expects to see you I thought I would drop you a line to let you Know, that your Kindness to us, while you was in our Midst, has & I believe will always occupy Much of my thought -

I have nothing worth your attention to write about. The Ind.s seem a little More figety than they were, the first part of the summer – But this I have expected all along, for it is the character of the Inds, when he thinks (real or imaginary) that his rights are encroached upon –

I am really sorry to Say that I have lost all
hopes, in Major Clark, to act the part of a good
Agent. It seems to me, that he is so Much under
the yoke of there traders, that is impossible for
him to act, as he would wish. Respected Sir, I
have requested Mr Whitehead to call on a friend
of Mine & get his assistance if he can, for My
2 Sons to get lisence to trade, James for this
place, Peter at Red Lake or wherever the Red
Lake Inds will be paid – any advice or opinion
you could give Mr W. in the Matter, I should
certainly feel thankful to you for the trouble I
would give you – Whenever any thing occurs
worth your Notice I will write you. I am fully
convinced that your chaitable heart aches for
us all, who are under the tyranny of the Agent,
threw the Selfishness & racality of a Set of
traders – Respected Sir, Hopeing that the great
Spirit will So guide our ways, that we May Meet
again & heve another good Camp fire talk as I
call it

With Sentments of the Most Sincere respect I
remain Yours & c

G. Bonga

[Endorsed:] George Bonga

James Whitehead   Leech Lake Sep 13th [18]66

Dr Sir

I enclosed your Note, against Mr Garcelen, in
a letter & sent it down by my son Peter, for

him to Mail at Crow Wing. I hope you heve
recd it, all right – My son James, started with
another man, to build a shanty at the falls of
Prairie River   Make every thing straight with
the Docter in this Matter, so you & they will
Know what to depend upon. I don't beleeve in
after days – I rest assured that you have seen
the Bishop & and explained Matters to him –
There is agoing to be, the best hall hunts, in
Rats that we have had, for a long time – find
out what they are worth, & and also other furs
– all is well here – there will be a few articles at
Mr. Peak.s.   Please bring up for me, when you
come home.

Yours &c

G. Bonga

[P.S.] I wish you would bring for me 12 Yds nar-
row-stripe hickory (good article

J.B. Bassett Esqr   Leech Lake Sept 13th, 1866

Respected Sir

Your very Kind favour of the 27th Agust has
long been recd & also the word threw Mr
Prescott. I have some idea of up & downs in
politics & will make My self prepared for either
good or bad news – The day I cecd the news that
there was some probabiliety of Mr Raffic.s being
Agent, I wrote to the Bishop & sent the letter
by Mr Hale – I wrote his full character (a pretty

good one) it occurred to My Mind, if it was too
late then, it would come in plat by & by – I recd
a Note from B. stating he had written a letter to
the Dept 18th of Agust, concerning Ind Matters
– I have written a letter today, to the Revd Mr
Knickerbacker. I am really sorry that I did not
write the very same letter a Month ago. I feel
confident that some notice would have been
taken on it, it is My opinion he will send it on
to the Bishop – but of course the game is up by
this time. I wont trouble you about the affair
here. Suffice for me to say, all is going on as
well as could be expected – Mr Prescott is some
better today it is nothing to the Ind.s that there
is a prospect of a change of Agent, for they want
a change every day, hopeing always to get better
– I don't Know, that I ever felt so anctious, as I
feel now, & hope as soon, as you get anything
reliable you will deign to let me Know

With Sentiments of Much respect I remain
Yours &c   G. Bonga

[endorsed:] Geo Bonga

Respected Sir [Joel Bean Bassett]   Leech Lake
Sept 25, 1866

Soon after you left this, we had quite an excitement, caused by a report that the Hole in
the Day, has sent Tobacco to the Ind.s here,
for them to hold a council, for the purpose of
breaking up, the Steam Boat & destroying the
gardens &c   wheather the report was true or
not, has not been found out –

Bonga

From what I can learn from the Ind.s it appears
that the Hole in the Day & Some of his follow-
ers, wants to be removed to the rice Lake clear
water River or some where in this part of the
country, they say, this is what they understood
at the time of the treaty. It is a great pity, that
there is a strip of land, that does not come in
there reserve, which if it did, would be one of
the best countrys to locate Ind.s on, that could
be wished for, I mean that part of country, that
would take in White Earth Lake in a straight
line to the Head waters of Buffalo Creek – There
is only a little of this country that a white Man,
would think of Settleing on, whereas it would
add, to there reserve, a strip of land well adapted to there Mode of living.   There is More
Sugar trees in that country then I was aware of.
It would also add 2 or 3 extensive Rice field.s
& Many Lakes, wherein they could get, quite a
Supply of fish, which without the above Kind of
food, a Chippewa Ind. Would be altogether at a
loss how to do for a living –

I have heard some people express as there
opinion that the above country, was the best
place to establish the Agency for all the Ind.s
the idea is a foolish one, I would ask these
persons, how Many Soldiers it would require, to
drive & Keep those persons who were not willing to go.   There is no doubt but Many of them
would go & Stay as long as the Govt would feed
them.   When you traveled threw this country
last summer, you must have Noticed it was a
Very large tract.   .were it not, for some Very serious objections, a great number of Ind.s could

be removed there.   The objections are of such
a Kind that it would be idle to think of locate-
ing More then ½ of the Inds belonging to the 2
Agencys   I Mean this, & the Crow Wing Agency
–

When I first went down from Theeveing River to
the grand forks of the Red River in 1859, I said
then it was the best country, that I ever Knew
to place Inds on.   There was More fish, in that
River, than any that I ever traveled on, but
sence then the waters have been so Very low,
that Very few fish could be caught. I said too,
at the time, Knowing how hard the Missionery.s
had been working, for above 30 years past, in
trying to get the Inds. to adopt the habits of the
Whiteman. I might say, up to this time all to no
purpose, it seemed to me then & My poor opinion has not chaneged [sic], that there was the
field for there great work. My reasons for this,
beliefe are too Many, to State here – Suffice for
Me to Say, I have closely watched the workings
of Missionery.s among the Chippewas to prove
to me, that an Ind. wont try in real earnest, to
adopt the habits of the Whiteman, before he see
& feels the benefit of civilization – To affect this,
requires Soil, that can be easily brought under
cultivation, or in other words were Money will
go the furthest, by this Saveing, larger School
could be held. Knowledg diffused among Man,
instead of 10 or 12 Scholars, which is the Most
if any, of the Many, that I have seen under-
taken, in this country.   is it a wonder that
Missionerys have not succeeded, - imagine to
yourself, that of Bishop Whipple or any other

good Man, was to expend the Money, that has been expended here for educational purposes 25 or $30,000 & layed out in the above country, for the Same purpose would there not be hopes, for the riseing generation.. If such a work was once undertaken it would seem to me that the foundation, for civilizeing the Inds was laid

I know that Missionery.s here worked under great disadvantages. One great obstacle has generally been Ind. Agents, for a Selfish one considers it, so much Money out of his purse by having Missionerys in the country   Sence the talk of removeing the Ind.s has been spokin of, it has occurred to My mind how it was agoing to be effected, so as to Make it satisfactory & without any trouble. Of late years, the Ind.s have had a poor opinion of the Govt   I must Say, they have good reason for it. Most of this feeling has been brought on threw the Selfishness & negligennce [sic] of the Agents in fact the broad extent of country, that these Inds inhabite, Makes it almost impossible for one Agent to attend properly to the provisions Made in there Several treaties – Notwithstanding this, they will undertake it all, because there is More Money to be handled, without stopping to look what the consequence May be – If the Govt could be induced, to see, the propriety of having 2 Agency for all the Ind, including those of Vermillion Lake, & a Superintendent to over see the whole, a few thousand dollars aught not to be consider in the Matter – for if this State of things is allowed to go on Much longer, Must bring on trouble between the Govt & the Ind.s, which would perhaps cost Millions, as such a country as the Chippew.s inhibit   if 2 Agency.s was established one here & one at the best point on Rice or Clear water country, then there would be no room for grumbling of finding fault – This is no extravagrant [sic] idea of Mine   it was spoken of by the Ind Bureau, in 1859 - & instructions given to Major Cullen & Mr Baily to Makes this proposition to the Red Lake & Pembina Ind.s, for those 2 bands only at the time –

I beg that you will excuse me, for writing this but Knowing, the deep interest you have for the welfare of the Ind.s, I have not hessitated to Make Known to you, My poor opinion in this Matter of great importance to the Ind.s & the people of the frontier – With the Most Sincere respect I remain your Very Humble Sevt

[Endorsed:] Geo Bonga   G. Bonga

Estimate of Losses by Agents

Respected Sir [Joel Bean Bassett]   Crow Wing Oct 3d, 1866

I have today, written to Bishop Whipple & Mr Rice, this is about all I can do, for the present. If Mr Donnelly is elected, I will have to leave it to you, to heve Clark & Ruffee Kicked out of the way, to Make place for some honest Man – Mr Rice can be depend upon. *Keep this da[r]k* There is no More show for me, to get lisence   It will be too late – The anuite goods for Leech Lake started this Morning – Aspenwall & Rufee.s started yesterday, so that shows the payts are near – I thought that Ruffee could Keep up a better stiff lip, but up to this writing he is really confounded, he has asked me every time I saw him, what Mr Rice & others thought of his appointment. I think I am playing the game pretty well – but Suppose he gets his papers to Night or next Mail, how will I look in My turn – I wish you will take the trouble to call at Mr Bell.s & get packed up the 1 pr of Red Blankets that he had. The balance he has of the 2 ½ pts of the McKennaw Blankets & 5 or 6 prs of the 4 pts, the same that I got – pay out of the money I left with you – I will give an order to some one to get them, before I leave this

They say the Steam Boat could not get threw Muddy Lake – The Rice Lakers would not let the lime go – I hope you have Made it, all right with Clark. I have not yet been to the Agency – but am just going today – excuse heste

Yours &c

G. Bonga

[P.S.] Mess. Peake & Wakefield are the persons that I will get, to bring up the above Blankets I think – I understand that My Son James, is going to put up a trading Shanty, about the 10 Mile Lacke

[Endorsed:] Geo Bonga

Barry Babcock

Respected Sir [J.B. Bassett]   Crow Wing Oct 21st, 1866

I met Agent Clark & Mr Aspenwall at St Cloud, on there way to St Paul, for what, you will perhaps find out & let me know – I intend to stay & pay My board at this place for a week or two, untill I find out how the cat is going to jump –

It was a good excuse for Ruffee, that the Agent was absent, so as to get rid of me & Not offend Mr Rice.

Rumeur says that the Hole in the Day wont except his Money, from the hends of Clark – I find that I mist it a good deal, when I told Mr Rice that it would Make the Ind.s Miserable to wait 2 weeks for there payt   It is also said, that the Agent has sent for Misspe Inds to come to there payt   I will write soon again – I want to write to Mr Rice, the Bishop, Dr Knickerbacker, today over

[P.S.] let me Know if Dr K. has got home from the East.   It will Make it bad if he has not yet returned, for he is the only one I confide in, to try a purpose – try & prevail on him to attend the Leech Lake payt.

I will keep you posted while I am here   Now dear Sir, while the Major is down do speek to him about Jack.s acct & also have a full understanding about My Bill, for you know it does not do to let those things drag. The balance of My acct I will pay you after payt

216

Bonga

Respected Sir [J.B. Bassett]   Crow Wing Oct 23rd, 1866

Sence I got up here, I hear a good deal of talk about elections, & those that were Republican.s last year, will Vote on the other side, just because Mr Donnelly up holds Clark. If you care anything for the Votes of Little falls & up, you will have to be a stiring My son James has just got down, & says there is a good deal of unsatisfactory talk among the Ind.s – I think it will be best for me & My sons to lay still this winter – for if the Ind.s uses [*sic*] bad language to the Agent.s   you & I am sure will be laid to me, for I will be alone – If I was sure that the Bishep would be on the ground, I would not care – for I intend to keep My Mouth shut

[Endorsed:] Geo Bonga   Yours &c

G. Bonga

Respected Sir [J.B. Bassett]   Crow Wing Oct. 24th, 1866

The Misspi bands were enrolled yesterday. I presume there payt will begin this afternoon, where they will go next to pay, is Known only to the band of operators –

I hardly need to say that no one can get lesence   Aspenwalll & Ruffee have started there goods to all the places where the Ind.s are going to be paid. I have come to the conclusion to lay on My oars this winter, in hopes of better times by & bye – I have today written to Mr Rice & the Bishop. I wrote flat footed to the Bishop My opinion about yourself.

I also wrote the same to Mr Rice, & the many conversations we have had, about him & how you expressd yourself in My hearing at all times, & would generally wiend [sic] up by saying thet H. M. Rice had a big heart –

My suggestion.s are perhaps premature but as no one, will Know them, they can be no harm I Must admit that Clark is a playing a bold game, he is perfectly desperate, he does not seem to care who Knows of his rescility – why the board of visitors are not the ground sup-prise me, but whet good would they be with-out the Bishop – if mr Donnelly is elected I will expect, that you will pitch right into him & Govr Ramsey & have this d-d rascal threwn out of Ind country, for it is a disgrace to the Govt to heve such an Agent –

I am in a bad fix. Wakefield did not bring up My boxs from St Cloud. If they start up to Leech Lake before going to Mille Lac.s to pay I will have to go without them – I will write to you from Leech Lake.

[Endorsed:] Geo Bonga   Truly Yours &c

Bonga

Bonga

Respected Sir [J.B. Bassett]   Crow Wing Oct.
27, 1866

The payts at the Agency are over & all went well
I am told. The Hole in the Day I hear wanted to
baulk, but I suppose that Ruffee bought him in
the track, for it would not have Suited his reputation at this present Menunt for he has still
hopes of getting his papers   In the operations
of Hole in the Day and Ruffee, Perish Roy was
left out in the cold. So Perish told me himself,
this Makes another Kicker against the firm as a
Matter of course no one Knows where the band
will go next to pay, either to Leech Lake of Mille
Lac.s   it is supposed to be the latter place.
Wakefields teams brought up My box.s   I think
I will leave for home tomorrow.

I have made up My Mind not to say a word to
the Ind.s will advise them all I can to take there
pay, without any fuss, to look at the Matter
closely   it will be as well for them   they can
get no satisfaction by appealing to the honesty
or generosity of the Agent –

I wrote again today to Mr Rice – I hope you will
improve every chance, of working for us on
the frontier. I r[e]ally believe that the frontier
is in peril by the acts of these2 Men. – Robert
Fairbanks says he is a going to take goods to
Leech Lake without Lecense, if he does, and
if the Agent;s drive him off, it will Make some
fuss. I don't beleeve that Robert will try it. He is
[a] great blow   The old Red Lake cheef is here.

I gave him some insight into Ruffee.s character. Ii'll [sec] bet he wont have that confidence
in him he had – it surprises me that there is no
Board of Visitors here yet – Send the Blanket I
wrote to you about. – By express to the care of
F. W. Pecke & Co. Crow Wing – I will write you
from Leech Lake – May the Great Spirit watch &
Bless you

Most Sencerely yours

G Bonga

[P.S.] My son James, wishes you would get for
him Dark Grey Mixd cold Coat (Sack)   he is
about your size   a little larger   pretty long –
Send with the Blankets

[Endorsed:] Oct 27, Go Bonga

Respected Sir [J.B. Bassett]   Crow Wing Nov
4th 1866

I made out My application, with the Bonds, &
handed it to Agent Clark, & also the letter of
the Comr he fumbled & Mumbled about awhile,
then told me, to leave My papers & he would
send them on to Washington. I asked him if
he had any reason, to think that I was not the
proper person, to be in the Ind country he said
no, youself & sons I Know well, but B. Vasseure
& Joseph Des Jaden I only Know by sight. I told
him, that I could scratch out the names of these
2 Men, if he wished, he had nothing to say to
that. Your securities I only Know by sight. I told

him I could get 'most of all the people of Crow
Wing, to go My bonds, if that would suit him, all
he could say was leave your papers & I will send
them on to Washington – The fact is, that he is
tied body & soul, to Aspenwall % Ruffee, that
he would not dare to give lisence to his father,
while the money payts are going on   the Agent
starts today to Make the Leech & Red Lake
payts   Some of the traders, that could not get
lisence, are taking goods to the Leech Lake payt
If Agent Clark does as he did last year shut up,
there stores, I expect that there will be a big
howling by the Ind.s. Is not this a terrible state
of thing.s to be caused by the selfishness of 2
Men. They really put the frontier con[sta]ntly in
peril, to attain there end.s –

Senator Rice has always done, what he could
for me. I have not the least doubt, but what he
would endorse My application, if you should
feel inclined to ask him – senator Ramsey Might
also do it, although he is not so well acquainted,
with My character as the former – No one can
get lisence, but those who get there goods from
Aspenwall & Ruffee-

    With Sentiments of Much respect I remain
Yours &c

[Endorsed:] Geo Bonga   G. Bonga

––––––––––––––––––

Respected Sir [Bassett]   Crow Wing Nov 4th
1866

Agent Clark would not give Me or any one else
lisence. I send to you My application & Bonds
– I asked Clark, what were the reasons, if any,
that I should not gey lisence. He told me, that
Myself & Sons there was none. He said he
did not Know Baptist Vasseaure, or Joseph
DesJarden   (the latter is the Man we call at
Leech Lake Joseph Baptist)   I told him, I could
scratch these 2 mens names out, of the application, to this he made no answer, (you Know
the Agent.)   he then Mumbled something
about the Securities   I told him, I could get
the whole Crow Wing people, to go My Bonds, if
that would Satisfy him. Finally he could say no
More, but say 2 or 3 times, leave your papers 7
I will forward them to the Dept   to this I gave
him no answer, & have not seen him sence
why it is plainly to be seen, he could not give
lisence to his father – Mille Lac payt are over,
7 all went off nice, they say. Traders sold there
cheep –

Rumour says, that Clark &c will start today
for Leech lake – but the traders & Myself will
only start tomorrow. Charley Beaulieu Robt
Fairbanks, & Perish Roy Still intends to take
some goods.   Of course they will be driven
off – if you find it is necessary, you can scratch
out the Names of Baptist Vasseaure & Joseph
DesJardon – I presume the Bond.s you can fix
satisfactory. Clark told me, it was not necessary, to present the exact Invoice, only one of
some Kind provided, the articles were not down,
such as playing cards Vermillion & c – does not
this look like Clark, he also said, any amount

inside $6,000 – I also wrote you a letter if you wish to show it to Mr Rice, with the Comrs letter you can do so. I would like to get the lisence soon.

Yours Respectfully G. Bonga

[P.S.] You can do anything you think proper for me such as stamps, for the lisence &cc all the traders goods have started, at this writing the soldiers are passing the window

Yours Respectfully G. Bonga

[P.S.] I have not recd the Coat for James   just as I was going to enclose the papers, I find that I forgot to put in My application My Son William You can   Scratch out Vasseaure & ensert My Son William – I aught too to have put in Paul Bellinger. Junior instead of Joseph DesJardon

G. Bonga

Respected Sir [J.B. Bassett:]   Leech Lake Nov 9th [18]66

I drop a hasty line to say, that the Ind.s tried there best, to have More than one concern to trade – but only suceded, in getting, R. Fairbanks & Perish Roy, to open there goods a Very small lot, Say 12 or $1500 worth. Of course Clark would not heve done this Much had he not feared, that there would be trouble & he got the consent of Aspll & Frank Ray, to do this, the Inds hung to it, better then I expected

– As to My self, I did not care 1 cent as I had no goods, & I did not to run any risk – I presume this will break Beaulieu flat –

They begun to pay yesterday, will finish today. – this lake is open for the Steam Boat. I suppose they will Start for Red lake tomorrow or next day

If Mr Donnelly is elected, I will suppose that you will succeed, in getting this scoundrel out of office by the 1st of January, for at that time some honest Man aught to take hold of this work. – after the payts are over I intend to go & Stay a couple of weeks at Crow Wing. I will be More handy to correspond with My friends – I have been altogether out of the Ring so I could not say a word to the Board of Visitors, but I presume they see enough, but it is the Bishop that was wanted – I feel like an orphan   excuse haste

[Endorsed:] Geo Bonga   Yours &c

G. Bonga

––––––––––––––––––

Respected Sir [J.B. Bassett]   Leech Lake Nov 14th [18]66

We have not heard a word from below, sence I left Crow Wing of course Knew nothing of the Elections if Mr D. is elected, I rest assured that you are & will strain every nerve, to rid this country, by the 1st of January, of this infamous rascal,- the Board of Visitors I only saw once, but Know enough, to say, that they are fairly disgusted & sick of the Man – If I had a chance to point out to them 1/20 of there plans & rascality, it would have Made them crazy, to think, that there was such bare faced scoundrel.s on earth. –But doing all you can at present will Save you a good deal of writing – will I get lisence soon   By the next chance I intend to write to Mr Rice & the Bishop. I am confident that the Board of Visitors think as I do, if I thought it was any use I would write to Dr Reed – we have about 4 or 5 inches of snow

Aspenwll & Ruffee & Co will pile up the Money at the Red Lake Ind.s payt – They will be paid at the Cass Lake Portage 10 or 12 Miles from this. It wont cost the above firm 1 cent, to get there goods there, for all went in the Steam Boat – what can the Ind.s do or Say. The poor creatures are over awed by the Agent, & his cooperateors [*sic*] – Does not this call for every honest Man.['s] help, & surely God will reward him for it – excuse the haste

Yours & c

G. Bonga

Night

[P.S.] The bearer did not Start, this Morning as he intended – what I mean by saying it will Save you, a good deal of writing is, I don't see the least doubt, why the country cant get rid, of this dangerous Man, to the frontier – Steps aught to be taken for him to be removed, after the payts – his Successor, aught to have all the time, from the begening of January, to get all the Machine agoing in good shape – Why should I doubt, it is said all the Delegation are strong for his remov-al & other circumstances, goes the Same way. Respected Sir   I Know you can do a good deal towards effecting the above, *as soon as   possible*   You Know it requires a good deal of time, to Straighten out the path. It would be well to have a fair understanding with the Delegation excuse me, for My impudent suggestion

Your Humble Servant &c

G. Bonga

[Endoresed:] Geo Bonga

[P.S.] I have today written to the Bishop -& als to the Rev Mr Brick – in 2 or 3 days I will again write to Mr Rice

[Minnesota Historical Society – Letters of George Bonga [1866-72, Extracted from Journal of Negro History Vol. 12, no. 1, January 1927]

George Bonga wrote to Bishop Whipple on November 14th, 1866 stating:

"...The Red Lake Inds. are to be paid at the first portage this, to Cass Lake. About 10 or 12 Miles from this   As I am not in the Agents employ I don't Know much what is going on   the Board of Visitors left this 2 or 3 days ago for the above payt ground. They must heve a hard time of it –

Bonga

"Sence the Govt has paid annuities to the
Chippewas   Most of the Agents – has proved
themselves, to be rascals. But the present
Agent, is the Most barefaced scoundrel that
has ever came to the Ind. Country. You cannot
imagine how he acts. I presume you will hear all
from the Board of Visitors

"He very well knows that it is impossible that he
will be allowed to have his office an is playing a
desperate game to get all the money he can.

"...Rev Sir   If Mr B. could be appointed it
would seem to me, it was the will of the Great
Spirit.   for the turning point of the civilization
of them poor Indn   I have been his interpreter
for 15 months & Ive have had a Many conversations on the Subject. I Know he is honest &
sincere in his wishes for the good of the Ind.s."

In another letter written later the same day,
Bonga bemoans that condition of the Ojibwe
under the traders and agents:

"O. how long will Matters be allowed to go on in
this way. Will the Govt not put a stop to there
barefaced frauds on the Inds – I will not say
any More now. But will let the Board of Visitors,
say what they think of Matters. I regret they are
powerless to remedy the Many wrongs. I was
employed by the Agent, but gave up my salary,
for I felt I could not keep My Mouth shut (to
white Men)

"...Most rev Sir, what is wanted, is a Man that is

knewn before hand. To be honest & would take
a deep interest to better the condition of the
Ind.s in every way & one that would cheerfully
cooperate with the Missionarys, that Man I have
mentioned to you before, - Now is not the time
to try men or experiments   it is an honest Man,
that has some knowledge of Ind. Character - If
we look past, we will find that people have been
disappointed in every instance, how Agents
have turned out – Most Rev Sir, it you know
J.B. Bassett as I know him, I am certain that for
the sake of the good of the Ind.s & the frontier
country, that you would use all the influence in
your power to have him appointed Agent, as I
fear God & Know that I will have to stand before
His tribunal soon."

"...The Red Lake chief [this "Red Lake chief" is
likely the famous *May-dwa-gwa-no-nin* who beat
back government attempts to implement allotment on Red Lake] was here an anctious to see
you, as well as most of the chiefs of this place.

"From your worthy servt G. Bonga"[167]

Joel Bean Bassett, through the influence exerted by
Bishop Whipple, got the job as Indian Agent of the Ojibwe.
It appeared that nearly everyone thought better days were
ahead but things started to go wrong with Bassett almost
right away.

Contending with the new agent

There were a number of issues that were lodged against
Bassett but probably the main reason for Bishop Whipple's

anger towards him was the Treaty of March 19, 1867 which would move Gull Lake/Crow Wing, Pokegama, and Sandy Lake Bands to White Earth. Originally these same Indians were offered a treaty in February of 1864 that would concentrate all of them at Leech Lake. This they rejected due to the inadequate land size for concentrating so many people, and the likelihood of conflict with the fierce Leech Lake Pillagers who had resided there for over one hundred years. It seemed to everyone, except the Indians themselves and people like Whipple and Bonga, that such a move was the right thing. In fact, Whipple originally thought concentration at Leech Lake was right but revised that opinion quickly, probably due to Bonga's urging and his intimate knowledge of the White Earth region. It was in 1836 that Wm. Aitkin requested that Bonga establish a post at Ottertail Lake, which is in the vicinity of White Earth. Many whites and Indians were hesitant to frequent the White Earth Country due to the presence of Dakota. Bonga knew the White Earth Country and its resources from the time he managed a trading post there because of his frequent forays through its forests, *manoomin* beds, sugar maples and fisheries.

The Mille Lacs Band did not want to move and were granted exemption from the move because they had sided with the whites against Hole-in-the-Day during the turbulent times in late summer and autumn of 1862. During the war with the Dakota, it is believed that Hole-in-the-Day colluded with Little Crow to bring the war against the whites into Ojibwe Country. Before the Mille Lacs band got reprieve from this removal, an interesting story concerning their great chief, *Sha-bosh-kung* as told by Bishop Henry Whipple deserves to be retold.

Barry Babcock

"...a special agent was sent to negotiate the treaty. The man was without the slightest knowledge of the Indian character. He came to see me and begged me to help him make the treaty. After examining the paper I said: 'The Indians will not sign this treaty; they are not fools. This is the poorest strip of land in Minnesota, and is unfit for cultivation. You propose to take their arable land, their best hunting-ground, their rice fields, and their fisheries, and give them a country where they cannot live without the support of the Government.'

The agent was angry and replied:

'If you will not help me, I will negotiate it without your help'

He called all the Indians together at Crow Wing, and made this speech to them:

'My friends, your Great Father has heard how much you have been wronged, and he determined to send an honest man to treat with you. He looked in the North, the South, the East, and the West, and when he saw me he said, 'There is an honest man; I will send him to my red children.' My red brothers, the winds of fifty-five winters have blown over my head and have silvered it with gray. In all that time I have never done wrong to a single human being. As the representative of the Great Father and as your friend, I advise you to sign this treaty at once.'

As quickly as a flash of lightning, old

Bonga

Sha-bosh-kung, the head chief of the Mille Lacs band, sprang to his feet, and said:

'My father, look at me! The winds of fifty-five winters have blown over my head and have silvered it with gray. But – they haven't blown my brains away!"[168]

Bishop Whipple also made a point in his book *Lights and Shadows* to note the wit and sagacity of the great Mille Lacs chief, *Sha-bosh-kung*. In a poignant story, the Bishop relates an incident told him by the great Mille Lacs chief about a party of lost white surveyors who had wandered for days before coming upon *Sha-bosh-kung's* village. The surveyors asked for food and the chief asked his wife to prepare a meal. When it was ready, the chief left the white men standing outside. When he was done eating, he asked the white men inside, saying:

"Perhaps you wonder why I did not ask you to eat with me. When I was in Washington the Great father told me that if I wanted to be happy in this world and go to the good place when I die, I must keep my eyes open and see what the white man does, and then follow his example. I did this, and saw that the rich white man never asked the poor man to eat at his table; and if of another color, he would not receive him as a guest. Today I am the rich man; you are poor and of another color. My friends, I want to be happy in this world, and I want to go to the good place when I die, so I have followed the Great Father's advice."[169]

Shortly after Bassett's appointment, Whipple began

hearing disturbing news about treaty violations and other perceived wrongdoings under the new agent's watch. A letter from Whipple to Bassett in the autumn of 1867 questioned his motives for pressuring a premature move to White Earth. The treaty stipulated that homes, stores, blacksmith shops, and other improvements were to be made before the move. The government wanted the Indians to farm so Bassett reasoned that the band members should be located at White Earth in September so they would be established by spring planting time. When Bishop Whipple discovered that the Indians had been forced to move against assurances that they would not, he became angered at Bassett. The Gull Lake, Sandy Lake, and Pokegama bands were very low on provisions for the long northern Minnesota winter ahead. Whipple wrote Bassett on November 14, 1867:

"I write you with a sad heart, and as frankly as I would to my brother. – You know that when a stranger I trusted you as I never did a man before. – Men whom I loved ...assured me you were one I could trust.- I took precaution to ask you to tell me, in the presence of god and as under His eye who reads the heart, whether you would promise me as one who should give an account, whether you would faithfully deal, justly, honestly, by this poor Indian race. – You said you would. – I believed you. – I placed myself in a position no money on earth could tempt me to be placed, to secure a man who I believed would save this people.- ...I hear these charges openly made. First - that your interpreters and employees have often been drunkards, that no effort has been made to secure the provisions of the treaty which require married

men as employees. Second – that your clerk
and other employees have contrary to the express order of the Department, engaged in the
Indian trade and are so engaged. Third – that
the unjust removal of the Chippewas, which you
know is an express violation of the treaty, is due
to you, and it is more than hinted that you are a
party to, and have an interest in, the treaty contract...I write to ask your defense. – For I must,
as an honest man, ask your removal and give
my reasons, if these things are so."[170]

On November 15, 1867, as Joel Bassett was about a
page and a half into a letter explaining his autumn relo-
cation of Ojibwe to White Earth, he was handed Whipple's
letter. This was his response:

"I must say that I was confounded, grieved &
mortified, confounded that such an opinion had
formed of my official conduct & grieved & mortified that after all jams & anxiety & trouble I had
taken to do exact justice to the Indians and all
the parties concerned..."

Bassett's response to the charges that his employees
were "drunkards" was that:

"I have three men only in my employ that I have
ever seen drunk, these are S.A. Warren, interpreter, Paul Beaulieu, special interpreter, and
A.L. Cummings who works a part of the time
at Leech Lake in the smith shop & a part of the
time as a farmer. Warren you know well, he is
the only reliable interpreter there is about the

Agency & his services are almost indispensable. He says he cannot help drinking when he
is where he is but will move away to Rice Lake
in the Spring out of the way of whiskey, and he
believes he can then be a sober man. I have not
the heart to dismiss him...Next P.H. Beaulieu,
he came to me in rags & poverty he said he had
sinned against heaven & in my sight & was willing to become my servant, his family was suffering for food & if I would give him employment he
would never drink another drop of liquor while
so employed...he behaved well until a few days
since he fell, shall I drive him still further into
the ditch? I cannot, I will not as long as there
is hope, he too will move away in the spring
to the new reservation & I hope out of the way
of whiskey. Next is Cummings he does more
work for the Indians than any employee. I have
never seen him drink a drop while in the Indian
Country, but goes about twice a year to St. Paul
or Minneapolis & has a spree."[171]

As to Bishop Whipple's second charge of Bassett's unlicensed clerks involved in the Indian trade:

"True my clerk has during the summer and has
now a few goods but not for Indian trade but for
the purpose of supplying the employees. It was
a matter of necessity that during the summer
some one should have provisions to supply the
employees of Leech Lake & Red Lake & at my
suggestion he brought some goods. It has been
a great convenience to me as well as to the employees & I know that no Indian or white man

has suffered unless it may have been so of the traders on acct of the low price at which he sold goods. I see that trouble is likely to grow out of it and have taken the necessary steps & have the trade discontinued. George Bonga is said to have an interest in the house of Fairbanks although he says his interest is only in furnishing money. At the time of payment at Leech Lake I pasted up notices that no employee would be able to carry on any trade with an Indian. I am doing all I can to put a stop to trading by employees."[172]

Bassett response to Whipple's third charge concerning treaty violations in the early forced removal of the Mississippi Pillagers to White Earth:

"...I strenuously opposed the removal this fall on the ground that the improvements could not be made. I was met by the argument that it was not my fault I had done all I could, & the Gov'nt had directed me to remove the Indians. (Bassett's claim was denied by Chief Clerk Charles Mix of the Federal Office of Indian Affairs.) I then urged that it would be better to remove the Indians in the Spring as they would be subsisted in the summer while they were raising crops. I was met by the assurance that the gov'nt would subsist them next summer if it was necessary...Their land is plowed, their houses are nearly or quite finished and besides after they had arrived there I told them if they did not like the place and did not want to stay, they might go back and I would furnish

235

provisions to do so. I did not feel that the good
of the Indians warranted me in making more
opposition to their removal..."[173]

Bassett goes on to express concern over the destitute
condition of the Indians and how their rice crop failed and
there was a precipitous decline in the rabbit population
which they depend on. Bassett refers Whipple to Henry
Rice who was witness to Bassett's comments and thoughts
on the removal and closes his defense by stating; "As to
my having interest in the contract, I scorn to reply to any
such innuendoes, I pass it by in silence. I am nearly fifty
years old. I point you to my record not only in this state but
elsewhere."[174]

Some of the claims of wrongdoing on Bassett's part
were brought by Charles Ruffee, a man with a very check-
ered past concerning the Indian trade. Furthermore, he
was eyeing Bassett's job as he had previously been in the
running when he got wind that former Agent Clark was
on the way out. In fact, it is likely that Whipple's support
of Bassett as Agent probably stemmed from the potential
catastrophe if Ruffee were to get the job. A special investigator was sent to look into wrong doings by Joel B. Bassett,
but none were found. In fact, the investigator claimed he
was offered money to find wrong doing. The whole Office
of Indian Affairs was a "snake pit" with almost no chance
for an honest man to function above the greed and selfishness so pervasive in the department. Joel Bean Bassett
remained the Indian Agent for the Ojibwe and oversaw the
removal to White Earth Indian Reservation. Whether due
to Bassett's letter of reply to the Bishop's letter of condemnation or Whipple's unwavering inherent trust in the decency of Bassett, Bishop Whipple ultimately believed that
Bassett was a good man who had been unable to navigate

the politics and inherent corruption within a system that was incorrigible. When U.S. Grant was elected president in 1869, Bassett and most all other Agents were dismissed under an office shake-up and new policy towards American Indians.[175]

The 1873 Leech Lake Pine Scandal

In 1873, George Bonga was seventy-one years old and well into the last stanza of his life but he was still keen of mind and alert to the activity going on around him.

1873 was the year a portion of pine on the Leech Lake Indian Reservation was sold by the Office of Indian Affairs without acknowledgment or consent of the tribe. This caused a scandal that would go all the way to the headquarters of the Department of the Interior and involve Bishop Whipple, Indian Commissioner Edwin Parmalee Smith, lumber baron E.T. Wilder, William Welsh of the Board of Commissioners, Senator Henry Rice, Flatmouth the Younger, among others. Again, George Bonga was in the vortex of this controversy.

Late in 1873, Bishop Whipple, while on a visitation tour in southern Minnesota got a telegram from George Bonga stating, "The Indians at Leech Lake have killed the government cattle and stolen the government goods. I fear an outbreak." Bonga noted this was in retribution; "...The Indians at Leech Lake had heard that the Government had sold all of their pine without their knowledge or consent."

In a telegram to Department of Interior Secretary Columbus Delano, Whipple relayed George Bonga's message about the pine sale: "George Bonga had been educated in Montreal. He was a man of great intelligence and perfectly understood the Indian character. He had been my companion on many journeys through the Indian Country. I could rely implicitly upon any information he gave me."

Whipple repeated his telegram to Washington, adding, "This man is trustworthy."

In a few hours Secretary Delano telegraphed Whipple: "The President requests you to go to Leech Lake and settle the difficulty. He will ratify whatever you do."

Whipple describes his arrival at Leech Lake and meeting with Flatmouth the Younger:

> "I went to St. Paul and consulted General Terry, asking him to give Captain McKaskie, who was stationed at Fort Ripley, leave of absence to accompany me, 'for,' I said, 'if I take a Republican and settle this trouble, I shall be accused of covering up rascality; if I take a Democrat and fail to settle it, I shall be accused of stirring up an outbreak.'
>
> It was in the dead of winter, the thermometer below zero and the snow deep. It was a journey of seventy-five miles through the forest, and it took us three days to reach Leech Lake. The Indians came to their council in paint and feathers, angry and turbulent. The chief, Flatmouth, arose and said: 'I suppose you came to find out who killed the government cattle. I did. You want to know who took the government goods. I did. I told my young men to do it. Perhaps you want to know why we did it. We have been robbed. We have been robbed again and again. We will bear it no longer. Our shadows rest on our graves.' He talked a long time, angry, exasperated, and using bitter invective and stinging sarcasm. Meanwhile, I tried to think of some way to stop him, knowing that if he could be silenced I might reach the others. I

rose and said:

'Flatmouth, how long have you known me?'

'Twelve years,' he answered.

'Have I ever told you a lie?'

'No, you have not a forked tongue,' he replied.

'I shall not tell you a lie to-day,' I went on. 'I am not a servant of the Great Father; I am the servant of the Great Spirit. I shall tell you the truth. It will not be pleasant to my red brother. When you killed those cattle, you struck the Great Father in the face. When you stole those goods, you committed a crime. I am not here to tell you what the Great Father will do. He has not told me. If he does what he ought to do, he will arrest those who have committed this crime if it takes ten thousand men.'

As I expected, the chief was very angry, and, springing to his feet, began to talk violently. I folded my arms and sat down. When he paused I said quietly: 'Flatmouth, are you talking or am I talking? If you are talking, I will wait till you have finished; if I am talking you may wait till I have finished.' The Indians all shouted, 'Ho! ho!' Their chief had committed a great breach of courtesy toward me, their friend.

Overwhelmed with confusion, Flatmouth sat down, and I knew that the ground was mine. I then told them that when I heard of the pine sale I wrote to Washington and protested against it; that I went to the man who bought the pine and told him that I should oppose the sale and carry the matter into the courts. 'But,' I added, 'when I ask good men to help me, and they ask if the Indians, for whom I am pleading, are the ones who killed those cattle and stole those goods, what shall I say? You are not fools. You know that you put a gag into my mouth. Now you may talk this over amongst yourselves, and when you are ready, send for me. I shall be at the log house opposite.'

They remained in council for several hours and then sent for me. 'We have been foolish,' they said. 'You are wiser than we are. Tell us what to do and we will do it.' After promising to be peaceable, they asked me to express their sorrow to the Great Father. The sale was not confirmed.

At my next visit to Leech Lake Flatmouth asked me to go to his lodge. 'The first time I saw you,' he said, 'you wore something over your robes. I thought it was the badge of your office. I asked my wife to make one for you. Will you have it?' And he presented me a stole made of black glass beads with a cross of gold beads worked in the ends. 'I give you this,' he said, 'because you are the friend of my people.'

The argument which I made against the pine sale was this: England, Holland, France, and Spain have recognized the possessory right of the Indians to the soil, a right that can only be extinguished by treaty. The ordinance of 1787, which has the binding force of the Constitution, expressly declares that the Indians' property shall never be taken except by purchase, or in wars duly authorized by Congress. When Napoleon sold to the United States the country west of the Mississippi River, the rights of the Indians were reserved. The legislative, executive, and judicial departments of the Government have always recognized this right. The pine timber is a part of the realty. If the Secretary of the Interior has a right to sell the pine, he has also the right to sell the land. If he has the right to sell one reservation, he has the right to sell all reservations, and hence the Secretary can dispossess every Indian tribe in the United States of their homes.

The man who sold this pine was the Rev. E. P. Smith, a Congregational clergyman, who was the Indian agent. He sold it by the direction of the Department. For this he was denounced as dishonest. I knew him intimately while he was an Indian agent, and I believe that he was a devoted Christian and an official faithful to his trust. After his resignation from the office of Commissioner of Indian Affairs, he went to my uncle, the Secretary of the American Missionary Association, and said: 'They have assailed my character and have robbed me of the dearest thing in life. Give me any work, however hard, and I will do it.' The Missionary Board sent him to Africa, where he died of African fever. Mr. Smith was field-agent for the Christian Commission during the Civil War, and Commissioner of Indian Affairs, but he

died poor. He had a small family and was most
abstemious in his manner of living. The last
time we met he burst into tears as he grasped
my hand and said: 'I am so grateful, Bishop, for
your kind words. You believe me honest. God
knows I have tried to do my duty.' For my defence of Mr. Smith I was censured."[176]

The circumstances of this reservation pine sale are
indeed thorny and complicated and the people involved
show the relationships that give credence to the 'snake pit'
scenario within the Office of Indian Affairs and how no one
long involved within this framework is totally free of some
direct or indirect wrongdoing relating to the condition of
the Indian. It also clearly demonstrates that white representatives on either side can easily move back and forth
depending on partisanship or what's in it for them.

In the excerpt from Whipple's *Lights and Shadows,*
Whipple notes that E. P. Smith, then Minnesota Indian
Agent for the Ojibwe, started a contract to sell pine off the
Leech Lake Reservation without the consent of the Indians.
Sometime before the deal was finalized, E. P. Smith was
promoted to the job of Commissioner of the Office of Indian
Affairs in Washington. His replacement as Agent, Ebenezer
Douglass, completed the work begun by Smith. Edwin P.
Smith was an ordained Congregationalist Minister and was
positioned here through the work and recommendations of
President Grant's Board of Indian Commissioners.

In a letter written by the mixed-blood Clement H.
Beaulieu to Bishop Whipple from White Earth Reservation
on August 21, 1873, Beaulieu stated:

"The Pillagers of Leech Lake are dissatisfied with
Commissioner Smith for disposing of their pines

without the knowledge and consent of the chiefs & Headmen of their band. Mr. Smith told the chiefs in open counsel at this place (some of the Pillager chiefs being present) that their Great Father had sold the Leech Lake pines for the purpose of making some improvements at that place. The Pillagers are opposed of this sale, especially at the price that it was sold for $1.15 per [thousand] feet, and without their consent... since the Indians were notified of the sale...has created a terrible feeling amongst those Indians towards the whites. They say that their great Father or his representative are unjust in taking away the very last thing they have for merely a trifle to justify his white brethren. They are at a loss to know, if it is by the order of the President or the commissioner of Indian Affairs that their pines were sold. They think it was with the latter, as they say, and known to all, that he has been after the pines on all the reservation for the last 20 months. If it is the policy of the Government to take every thing that any Indian tribe claim to be his own by right, without his knowledge or consent, we shall surely have a perpetual trouble with the Indian. The Pillagers are willing to sell their pines at a reasonable price..."

In his letter to Whipple, Clement Beaulieu addressed an issue that was not commonly made before and needs to be repeated here:

"Mr. Smith being at the head of the Indian Bureau and a minister of the gospel ordained

to do the work of Christ, will be looked upon by
every denomination with anxiety - The result of
these great works – It will not do, to rule every
Indian tribe by our official with the full power
they have on hand, to visit the Indians with a
sword on one hand and a Bible in the other,
telling them, 'Submit before I pierce your heart
with this sharp weapon; resist you are doom
forever for I am a minister of the Great Spirit
sent by him, to you, for the salvation of your
soul."[177]

Clement Beaulieu later writes from White Earth
Reservation to William Welsh—first chairman of the Board
of Commissioners to advise the Office of Indian Affairs—
on September 4, 1873, concerning the need for a change
of rule from being under the yoke of Congregationalists to
Bishop Whipple and Episcopalians:

"Why not have these people under the management of the Bishop [Whipple] who has such a
control over them, which has been gain by him
by his kindness & goodness, and his honest
& upright way he has with them in his intercourse. He is looked upon by all our chippewas
as a Father and has the full confidence of all.
No one in the country has such a powerful influence over these Indians as the Bishop."[178]

In an open letter written to the Department of Interior
by William Welsh from the Board of Commissioners, from
Philadelphia on December 1, 1873, calling for an investigation into the fraudulent handling of pine on the Leech Lake
Reservation, he writes:

"...Agent Smith, about Aug. 12th, 1872, con-
tracted with F.P. Clarke for a large quanti-
ty of pine timber, belonging to the Oak Point
Chippewas, under the avowed authority of
those Indians, but without making their ap-
proval a part of the contract, and without al-
lowing sufficient time for the bidders to visit
the Reservation and ascertain the value of the
timber."

Welsh goes on to accuse Agent Smith of undertaking
to "cancel a contract that had been completed, although
he avers that he did not know of any higher offer, and had
no intercourse of any kind with Mr. Wilder, the new bidder,
until the following day..." when Welsh discovered that the
timber baron Wilder had initially and astonishingly had
made the high bid of $1.60 per thousand feet, that bid was
ignored and $1.15 was agreed upon. Clearly, Welsh viewed
the contract dealings as not passing the smell test and
called for an investigation.

Wilder, the lumber baron was in essence able to bid
downwards to $1.15 per thousand which became the agreed
contract price. Welsh's letter goes on to state, "Agent Smith
acted without authority of law in making the foregoing and
other contracts for the sale of large bodies of pine timber,
which is real-estate and cannot be disposed of without the
authority of Congress." Welsh further accuses Smith of
selling Indian timber at Red Lake and Pembina at a price
well under a higher bid. Welsh also charges Smith in a
previous fraudulent sale of Indian owned timber at Lac du
Flambeau Reservation in Wisconsin. In his letter, William
Welsh mentions Henry Rice as having copies of mentioned
contracts which verify Welsh's charges against E.P. Smith.
47 One particularly important item in Welsh's letter was

designating the timber on reservation land as "real estate" belonging to the Indians and had no more right to be sold than the house in which he lives.

A second point Welsh raised in his letter was the knowledge of Henry Rice of the pine contract. This mention of Rice was particularly bothersome to E. P. Smith who fired back in a letter to Bishop Whipple that Rice had been, as he stated:

> "Taking money for securing the passage of bills relating to Indian Affairs, while he was in Congress. There is no doubt of his receiving portions of appropriations approved by Congress, as his pay for such services...There is no doubt of his personal and profitable connections with frauds in the Chippewa Half Breed Scrip...I know that he was largely instrumental in procuring the charges against me and my administration at White Earth, and all on the plea of his love for the Indians. He has been in communications with the Beaulieus, John Geo Morrison, and Ben Fairbanks at Crow Wing, procuring grounds of accusation in any form in which these lying Half Breeds can be made to put it. He is also in communication with Bonga, particularly Bonga's son, Peter, advising the Pillagers to resist the sale of the pine, and telling them it can be set aside. Under this inspiration these Pillagers have been kept uneasy during all the summer and winter."

Smith adds that he regrets the sale, not particularly for any wrongdoing to the Leech Lake Pillagers but for "the use that has been made of it by bad persons to bring disrepute upon all efforts for helping Indians."[179]

Former Senator Henry Rice was like nearly all white men who had dealings with the Indians, they could take the high road but were equally capable at taking the low road. Rice was a Democrat and the current administration was Republican and there was an atmosphere of partisanship. George Bonga had maintained good relations with Rice throughout his career but Rice's shenanigans began to become apparent to Ojibwe people as they started to refer to him as "White Rice."

The same can be said of the "lying Half Breeds" that Smith denigrates. This happened nearly one and a half centuries ago so it is not possible to ascertain the whole truth. Clement Beaulieu and John G. Morrison are reputed to have had a role in the assassination of Hole-in-the-Day, which tarnished their reputations. But like so many of these men, they can be seen to take different sides depending on when it suits their purposes.

Columbus Delano, Secretary of the Department of the Interior, was clearly defensive about accusations of corruption by his department. On February 26, 1874, he wrote to Bishop Whipple concerning the pine sale at Leech Lake:

"I am very anxious to have you go to Leech Lake
with such associates as your own judgment
may select and endeavor to make the Indians
understand the situation which has been mis-
represented by interested and maliciously
disposed persons greatly to the injury of the
Indians and the public service. The convictions
of the Commissioners [Smith] in which I concur,
is that this difficulty has been brought about to
a very great extent by the bad conduct of Mr.
Rice, and those associated...I cannot but believe

that it is the inspiration of Mr. Rice which induces Bonga, or anybody else, to suggest his presence at the adjustment of this business."

It is noteworthy that Sec. Delano does not condemn George Bonga but rather portrays his advocacy on the part of the Indians to Henry Rice's bad influence. Commissioner Smith does not lump Bonga into the group of "lying Half Breeds" but instead states that he and his son are "advising the Pillagers to resist the sale of the pine." Both Delano and Smith are well aware of George Bonga and did not wish to turn him against them. Bonga's role as a respected elder, advocate, and friend of the Indian was strong enough for them to recognize his influence with the Indians.[180]

In February and March, Bonga wrote a series of letters to Bishop Whipple about the fraudulent pine sale. In a March 16, 1874 letter, Bonga states:

"...I have lived the most of My life (60 years) with the Inds. & I don't Know of any occurance that troubles there Minds so much as this Wilder contract. Not at this place only but threwout the whole country. The enemies of Com'r Smith have poisoned the Minds of the Inds. & have Made this pine affair a high way Robbery of what belongs to the Inds...I am aware it is a complicated affair, but it appears to me, if the Matter is well handled, all would be right. I don't see how we can get along in peace before this question is settled. Allow me to Make this suggestion if persons are appointed to settle this Pine question. White Earth, is the first place they aught to go to. The Ind Agent there would Know best, if the Mille Lac chief

would require to be present as they are a party
to the Treaty of 1867.   al the Sandy Lake &
White Oak Point Ind are of the same treaty but
they live so far apart that they don't consider
themselves connected by Treaty Stipulations &
it would be more satisfactory to both parties to
Make there own bargans. The Inds. of this place
have always given more trouble then any other
band…"[181]

While all this pine controversy was going on, the Ojibwe
Agent, Ebenezer Douglass, the man who replaced E.P.
Smith after his promotion to Commissioner, was facing
accusations of skimming annuity payments and of taking
"highly improper liberties…with many of the grown girls,
Indian and Half breed in the Government school." This
statement was made by Rev. Joseph Gilfillan, Whipple's
Episcopalian minister at White Earth, but Gilfillan did
not however concur on Douglass's corruption charges of
skimming money. In May of 1874, Douglass was replaced
by James Whitehead as Agent for the Ojibwe whom the
Indians and George Bonga did not like. George Bonga wrote
Bishop Whipple from Leech Lake on May 28, 1874, soon
after Whitehead's appointment:

"I cannot look upon the appointment of Mr.
Whitehead as Ind. Agent only as a mere tool for
those Pine speculators. I am really sorry that
Matters are in such a bad way. that we cannot
Very well expect that as long as Secy Delano &
Comr Smith holds the high office, they now do
in Govt, that the Hon. H M Rice can be got to
settle this pine question. I feel confident that he
could Settle it in such away, that the country

would be at peace again. I say so, without hesitation, for I Know it is the truth I Speak, & I am not afraid to be contradicted by one single individual in this country, except perhaps Mr. Whitehead."[182]

A month later, Bonga updated Whipple on the conditions in Indian Country:

"...No person wishes more than Myself, that this Pine Matter would be Settled Satisfactory. I have been acquainted with Most all the Agents, since the chippewas have had any, I am sorry to say that I have seen too Much of there rascality to have confidence in them...I have no chance to explain to them [Indians], who are there sincere friends, for I am aware, that Many will come, & pretend to be sheep, & will prove to be wolves to there tribes good bishop...but I Know you are doing all you can, to have good men, Settle this pine Matter for it seems to me, it is, the last chance they will ever have, to benefit there condition..."[183]

Bishop Whipple, although he viewed the pine sale as underhanded, felt that E.P. Smith was not the culprit that his antagonists felt he was. Whipple was somewhat sympathetic toward Smith and his words demonstrate this as seen in his written description of his trip to Flatmouth the Younger after receiving Bonga's telegraph alert. The Bishop felt that Wilder had taken advantage of Smith's ignorance in the value of stumpage. This greatly upset William Welsh and Welsh attributed Whipple's leniency to the fact that the lumber baron, E.T. Wilder had given money to some of

Whipple's Episcopalian schools in Faribault, Minnesota.[184] But William Welsh had also given money to some of these same schools.

The pine sale controversy fizzled out late in 1874 when tribal agricultural funds became acute. Commissioner Edwin Parmalee Smith was investigated and exonerated; he would serve as Commissioner of Indian Affairs from 1873 to 75. For decades, timber belonging to the Ojibwe would continue to be swindled by timber barons. The only difference between 1873 and later is that the timber barons would devise more ingenious methods with which to rip off the Indian of the last of the great old growth pine.

Timber swindling by lumber companies took new forms such as: 1) bidding done on reservation timber before being scaled; 2) using a method termed "round forty" in which a timber sale of reservation pine of forty acres would be logged all around the targeted forty before actual cutting within the forty; and 3) under a system where loggers could cut dead or burned timber, logging companies would start cool ground fires in healthy pine forest and use that as an excuse to cut the living pines as "burned over" timber. In one case a logging company lost a lawsuit for one million dollars in cutting green pine on the Winnibigoshish reservation but it was overturned on appeal. The corruption was unbelievable, even some of George Bonga's descendants and relatives were in on it.[185] Surely if George were alive he would not have remained quiet.

In the 1880s, the Federal Mississippi River Reservoir Dam system began a dam building project with the intent to aid in flood control and navigation. Between 1881 and 1885, dams at Pokegama Falls, Lake Winnibigoshish and Leech Lake were built. These dams displaced hundreds of Ojibwe people living in villages along these flooded waterways, damaged cranberry bogs, inundated burial grounds and permanently flooded out hundreds of acres of traditional wild rice fields.

White politicians and white business communities were not satisfied by gaining the ceded lands with the abundant and bountiful resources on those lands through treaties, they now wanted as much of what they could take from land within reservation borders through devious methods.

The Dawes Act of 1887 and the Nelson Act of 1889, often referred to as the "Allotment Acts", divided the land base within the reservations into parcels for band members. The land left over after allotment then was opened up for white settlement under the homestead laws. This resulted in a great percentage of tribal allotment lands lost by band members to white settlers through nefarious illegal taxes placed on them or through forfeiture of trust land through debt accumulated by band members to local white businesses. Today less than ten percent of the land within Leech Lake and White Earth Reservation boundaries is trust land belonging to Native people; the remainder is federal, state, county or privately owned by non-Indians.

By the close of the nineteenth century, many Leech Lakers had enough of this. *Bug-o-nay-ge-shig*, an elder and "head-man" from Bear Island on Leech Lake, was motivated to stir up trouble due to the Leech Lakers losing their treasured pines. Under trumped-up charges of running a "still" in order to quiet him due to his trouble making for timber companies, he was arrested by a handful of federal Marshalls and tribal police. Younger Anishinaabeg men wrestled him away from police and they fled to Sugar Point on Leech Lake. Being outnumbered, the Marshalls were reinforced by a train load of soldiers from the U.S. Army. The soldiers were ferried to Sugar Point by barge and tugboat and the 1898 Battle of Sugar Point took place on October 5. This last battle between the United States Army and

Bonga

Native Americans was won by the Native warriors who lost no men while the army had six men killed by Anishinaabeg fire. Though no appreciable improvement resulted in the way the Indian was treated, the conflicts, both political and through armed action, can arguably trace their origin to the 1873 Pine Scandal on the Leech Lake Reservation and involvement by George Bonga and band members. Though there was no appreciable local white interest in protecting native owned pines, these episodes concerning the loss of the great pine stands in the leech Lake and Cass Lake area resulted in a growing interest in this issue in the bourgeoning population of Minneapolis and St. Paul. The threat of losing the great virgin stands of pine was taken up by a women's group in the Twin Cities who found allies in the newly formed United States Forest Service with Gifford Pinchott as its leader and Christopher Columbus Andrews, Minnesota's first fire warden and the first Commissioner of the Minnesota Forestry Department.

Prior to 1902, with much of the timber on Indian land being stolen or swindled by timber companies the first great environmental battle in Minnesota was fought on the Leech Lake Reservation. In the USFS publication, "The Birth of a Forest," Gifford Pinchott wrote:

> "Under sloppy Indian Office handling of a latter
> amendment which permitted the logging of dead
> and down timber, much green timber was cut
> and paid for as dead and down, or was not paid
> for at all. One outfit, which included a former
> Governor of Minnesota, cut and stole more
> green timber than the dead timber they pro-
> fessed to buy...Thefts of this character, resent-
> ment over robbing the Indians, the protests of
> an honest Indian agent named Walker (who was

said to have lost his job), together with senti-
ment for preserving the primeval pine, aroused
vigorous expostulations, among others from the
Minnesota Federation of Women's Clubs and
the State Medical Society."

The Minnesota Federation of Women's Clubs were at
the forefront of a vigorous fight to create a park in the Cass
Lake area. They recognized that a special part of our states
heritage was about to be clear-cut out of existence. While
some state leaders only gave lip service to saving the primeval pines, it was:

"...Not so with the less flamboyant attack led
by the Minnesota Federation of Woman's Clubs
and notably by Mrs. W.E. Bramhall, the young,
modest, but most effective chairman of the
Federation's Forestry Committee. She was the
first of the park advocates to ask for a Forest
Reserve instead. And to her, more than any one
person goes the credit for getting it."

As a direct result of the dedicated effort by Mrs. Bramhall
and the Minnesota Federation of Women's Clubs, a bill was
authored by Representative Page Morris of Duluth. The
first draft did not include a "reserve" and was opposed by
the Women's Club, Pinchott, and a few others. On June 27,
1902, after weeks of back room negotiating and compro-
mising, the "reserve" became part of the bill and the Morris
Act became law. As Pinchott wrote:

"Its passage was a victory for public opinion
and the public interest against local opposition and the fierce hostility of the lumbering

interests, who had long ruled the roost in northern Minnesota. Without the farsighted and patriotic support of the Minnesota Federation of Women's Clubs, it would have been impossible. With it the Bureau of Forestry emerged from the period of mere advice to actual control, for the first time, of timber cutting on public land."

Although the compromise fell far short of the Women's Club's first goal of creating a park, it did allow for the logging of 200,000 acres of pine with ten percent of the stand left as seed trees, a first attempt at "best management practices" was implemented, and 25,000 acres was opened to settlement. What was most important in the Morris Act was that an area of ten sections in the neighborhood of Cass Lake was to be set aside as a "reserve" — "to be reserved from sale or settlement, together with certain islands and points in Cass and Leech Lakes, all of which were later (1908) included in the National Forest." The struggle continued over the decisions of the Ten Section Area. This fight was pioneered by Gene Bruce, a forester left in charge of these determinations by Pinchott. He formulated the Ten Section area by what was referred to as the "black line." This was a line on the map indicating the boundaries of the reserve. Included in this area are Star Island, Cass Lake, Pike Bay, Ten Section Lake, Moss Lake, Twin Lake, Little Twin Lake, and Lake Thirteen. It is this "Ten Section" that became the core of what would become Chippewa National Forest.

Although much of the original old growth timber is still standing on Cass Lake and Pike Bay, much of it in the Ten Section area was blown down in a windstorm in 1940. The Ten Section area is today managed by the USFS "to emphasize scenic values, recreation, and interpretation of natural and heritage resources. The pine will be maintained as 'big trees' for old growth."

The way I see it, the alarm cry that George Bonga sent out and the subsequent correspondence between George and officials in the Office of Indian Affairs brought forward to the public the immediate threat to one of the great remnants of old-growth pine left in the *Le Beau Pays*—the beautiful land. The efforts of these people did not save the entire old growth stands but enough of them were saved to foster the spirit of conserving these old growth forests thus the torch was passed on to another generation to take up the fight and save the unique beauty that George Bonga ostensibly started.

If George Bonga's spirit lingers over the waterways of the *Misi-ziibi*, it also resides in the 200 to 300 year old red pines of the land he loved so much.

"Hopeing that the great Spirit will So guide our ways..."

George Bonga was dead and Reverend Whipple would die in September of 1901. The two best advocates for native people were no more. When George and his siblings entered this world, all of Wisconsin and Minnesota were Indian Country. The entire region was essentially the deepest and darkest forests of what would become the United States. The only whites were fur traders with no interest in the land other than acquiring furs. These northern forests of the Great Lakes were the home of Anishinaabeg and the culture of native people was communal with Mother Earth. They, along with all members of the plant and animal communities that shared the land, were co-tenants of the living Earth. For the Anishinaabeg all life was equal. Man depended upon Mother Earth for life. All the living organisms on Mother Earth do not need us; we need them for our life.

Bonga

The culture of the white man saw man as having dominion over all life. His greed drove him as an uncontrolled consumer of what he only saw as a resource placed here for only his own greed and need of enrichment.

By 1874, during the Pine Scandal, George Bonga had reached his seventy-second year of life. Yet, even at that age, he continued to keep his paddle in the water on issues of concern to the Ojibwe and their resources. Sometime in 1870, at the age of sixty-eight, George posed in the photographic studio of Alfred Zimmerman in St. Paul for the only known photograph of the old woodsman. It would have been nice if there had been an earlier photo or painting of George but none are known to exist. He would surely have made an impressive physical image. But even the Zimmerman portrait is striking enough. The derby hat, dress jacket, vest, white shirt with bow tie, and dress pants show that George was out fitted in his best, but the most revealing aspect of the photo is that aside from all the finery George had put on, he wore moccasins on his feet. This unusual aspect of the photo is representative of the seeming ability of Bonga to move in and out of worlds. As a man who was half Black and half Indian and had not a drop of white blood in his veins, he often spoke of himself as being a white man. If a photograph could speak, it says that here is an honest, respectable and proud man.

The Bonga name lives on in some small ways in northern Minnesota. In Cass County, Bungo Township and Bungo Creek are named after George. In fact, Bungo Township was organized before there was a Cass County. In White Earth there is a lake named after George. There are many descendants of the Bongas throughout the reservations of Leech Lake, White Earth, Fond du Lac and other reservations in Northern Minnesota. I suspect there are many Bonga descendants who are unaware of the heritage they possess from these fine and great men.

George Bonga's death is given as several different dates; between 1880 and 1885, and his grave is in Onigum not far from his home on Traders Bay of Leech Lake where the "Old Crow Wing Trail" ends in his backyard. George Bonga's death in the 1880s was noted in the major newspapers in New York, Chicago, Minneapolis and elsewhere in the country and notice of his passing was also made in the United States Congress.[186]

In northern Minnesota there is only a small and ever shrinking portion of the wild places that gave Bonga his "safe abode in the wilderness where all things were free." One has only to paddle the Headwaters of the Mississippi or lounge under some old growth pine on Star Island on Cass Lake to fully appreciate that there are still places like this on earth. The notion that these places may someday cease to exist is a thought too unthinkable to ponder because these places are the American forge that enabled some of the greatest Americans to rise above the ranks and do something noble for humankind. Only true freedom can be achieved in the wilderness as it is truly the great equalizer among men. If we allow the wild places in this region or the nation to vanish, with it will go the greatest and noblest attributes of America. Even Bishop Whipple felt the power of wilderness. On one of his many forays across the forests of the north, he wrote in his diary, "None can tell how deeply solemn prayer seems as you stand under the broad canopy of heaven, studded with stars and alone before God and breathe out to him your faith, your wants, your warm gushing thoughts." And didn't the great prophets seek out wilderness as a place that brought them closer to the Great Spirit.

These special places on Earth are our sanctuaries where we can re-connect with the crucible in which we were

George Bonga, circa 1870. Image courtesy of the Minnesota
Historical Society Collections

created. Never would there have been a Bonga family for us to admire if not for this place where they could escape the trappings and inequities of racism, bondage, and enslavement. The Bonga legend far transcends black and white print on a book page as it is a story as beautiful as the land itself and begs the need for a safe abode where all of us can find freedom, knowledge, truth and walk the good path and live the good life as did the Bongas.

The Bonga story can represent what is best about America, both of the land and of men. That representation is up to us.

I close my story of the George Bonga in his own words, as he so often closed his letters;

"Hopeing that the great Spirit will So guide our ways, that we May Meet again & heve another good Camp fire talk as I call it. With Sentments of the Most Sincere respect I remain Yours & c, George Bonga"

The Real Story of the Headwaters

Yellow Head and Marguerite

"My father, the country you are going to see, is my hunting ground. I have traveled with you many days. I shall go with you farther. I will myself furnish the maps you have requested, and will guide you onward. There are many rapids in the way, but the waters are favorable. I shall consult with my band about canoes, and see who will step forward to furnish them. My own canoe shall be one of the number."

–Ozaa-windib to Henry Rowe Schoolcraft – July 10th, 1832[187]

The study of our history as human beings is important, and often complicated. Much of the historical research involves detective work and is often analogous to putting a complex jigsaw puzzle together in which some of the pieces fit, others do not, and then to further complicate the puzzle, you may find pieces from another puzzle may also fit. So it is with the question: Who discovered the Headwaters of the Mississippi River?

To emphasis a point of fact, an Indigenous North American many thousands of years ago was the first human being to gaze upon the infant Mississippi.

Caucasians are relative new-comers to the Western

Hemisphere as evident by the Native American Itasca bison kill site near the southwest end of Lake Itasca, which is 7,000 to 8,000 years old and also the Native American burial mounds found on the east side of the lake.

Henry Rowe Schoolcraft, the man credited with being the discoverer of the source of the Mississippi River in 1832, was told by his guide, *Ozaawindib*, as they neared the *Misi-ziibi*, the great river of life; "My father, the country you are going to see, is my hunting ground."

When Joseph Nicollet, in 1836, enlisted an Ojibwe man by the name of *Gay-gued-o-say* to guide him to the headwaters, he wrote of his guide:

> "His beautiful face, his handsome dark hair,
> almost curly and for which he seems to care,
> the silver ring pinching the partition of his nose,
> and his noble bearing all reveal at first glance
> a respectable personality. This impression is
> confirmed not only by his own people but also
> by the whites. Gay-gued-o-say is the only Leech
> Lake Pillager quite familiar with the region I am
> about to explore. He is the only one who has
> scoured it while hunting, hence their name for
> it; the grounds of Gay-gued-o-say. Finally he is
> one of the old ones of his nation, a wise man, A
> mediator, a keen observer – all qualities which
> lead me to place my confidence in the man."[188]

The Ojibwe name for the lake that is the source of the river is *Omashkooz* (Elk). The French called this lake *Lac La Biche*. Some whites say the Anishinaabe call it *Omashkooz* because it is somewhat shaped like an elk head when seen from the sky. But this is doubtful as this region was for eons in the transition zone of two biomes. The prairie advanced and retreated numerous times; sometime the region was prairie and sometimes forested, making it good hunting grounds for large herbivores. All these names are due to the fact that elk and deer inhabited the area for untold centuries, a place where big game resided.

Schoolcraft, at Rev. W.T. Boutwell's recommendation, came up with the name *Itasca* by capturing the last and first syllables of the Latin word Ver*itas ca*put meaning 'true head'.

The first white men laying claim to the discovery of the Headwaters are many.

On April 27, 1798, David Thompson—trader, cartographer, and explorer for the North West Company—descended the Turtle River to Upper Red Cedar Lake (Cass Lake) and announced that Turtle Lake was the headwaters of the Mississippi, which to this day is a reasonable contention as both the Turtle River and the Mississippi River flow into Cass Lake.

On February 1, 1806, Lt. Zebulon Pike arrived at Leech Lake (*Gaa-zagaskwaajimekaag*) by way of the Leech Lake River from the Mississippi River. From Leech Lake, Pike was guided to Lower and Upper Red Cedar Lakes (Lower Red Cedar is now Pike Bay and Upper Red Cedar and is now Cass Lake) and proclaimed Leech Lake to be the lower source and Upper Red Cedar Lake the upper source of the Mississippi.

On July 21, 1820, the Lewis Cass expedition reached Upper Red Cedar Lake by ascending the Mississippi from Big Sandy Lake and proclaimed Upper Red Cedar Lake the source. At the time, water levels were extremely low and the river was unnavigable above Upper Red Cedar Lake. It was here that one of his expedition members, Henry Rowe Schoolcraft, renamed Upper Red Cedar, Cassina, in honor of the expedition leader, later shortened to Cass Lake.

Barry Babcock

On August 28, 1823, the eccentric Giacomo Constantino Beltrami of Bergamo, Italy, traveling south from Red Lake, pronounced Lake Julia the Headwaters. Lake Julia is upstream from Turtle Lake, the source of the Turtle River. Beltrami was traversing what was essentially the same route that David Thompson took in 1798, but proclaimed Lake Julia as the true source.

On July 13, 1832, Henry Schoolcraft and his expedition, led by *Ozaawindib* of Star Island on Cass Lake, arrived at the east shore of the east arm of Lake Itasca. Although Schoolcraft is generally recognized as the first white man at the headwaters, he really was not. However he was a self-promoter and his literate and detailed journals persuaded the public to render him the honor as the first white man at the headwaters.

The actual first authentically documented white man at the headwaters was the fur trader, William Morrison. It was in 1803-04 on a trading visit to Rice Lake in what would become White Earth Indian Reservation over sixty years later, that Morrison ventured by *"Omashkooz."* It is documented that Morrison was at what would become officially recognized as the headwaters again in 1811-12. Morrison's assertions were authenticated by letter from his home in Canada in 1856.

As complex and lengthy as the list of explorers laying claim to the Headwaters discovery is, there is also another untold version of this story. I will lay out that history as told to me from an Anishinaabe woman who is extraordinarily well versed in Anishinaabeg history and is a direct descendant of the Bongas and has embraced her family's oral history. The oral history will present credible evidence that *Ozaawindib*, the Ojibwe man who guided Schoolcraft and his gentleman companions to the Headwaters of the Mississippi River, was in reality, Jacob Fahlstrom, the first

Bonga

Swede in Minnesota, and known to Ojibwe people he lived with, as *Ozaawindib* ("Yellow Head" as he was blond). Jacob Fahlstrom was the husband of Marguerite Bonga, the older sister to Stephen, George, Jack and Elizabeth; all children of Pierre and Ojibwikwe Bonga.

In order to understand the truth as it relates to Schoolcraft's place in history and his claims as an explorer one needs to look closer at the background of the man himself. Henry Schoolcraft's reputation for hiding and manipulating facts that would lessen his role of importance in a number of issues is historically documented. A good place to start is the relationship between Schoolcraft and John Tanner or *Shaw-shaw-wa-be-na-se* meaning the "Falcon" as he was known to native people.

Tanner had lived for thirty years with the Ojibwe and essentially was a "white Indian" who had absorbed the culture and become Anishinaabe. His life is recorded in *A Narrative of the Adventures of John Tanner (U.S. Interpreter at the Sault Ste. Marie) During Thirty Years Residence Among The Indians in the Interior of North America*, as dictated to Dr. Edwin James.

By 1828 Tanner, having spent thirty years with the Ojibwe, was in his forties and had taken residence in Sault Ste. Marie doing various jobs, such as an interpreter for Schoolcraft and a short stint as a blacksmith. Tanner's story is a Greek tragedy, a man torn between two cultures, unable to come to terms with either world in his later years. Tanner became an enemy of Henry Schoolcraft and his brother, James Schoolcraft. Henry, who initially befriended Tanner, gave him a job as an interpreter but later changed his opinion of Tanner. Both Henry and James Schoolcraft developed a strong and vehement dislike for John Tanner.

Walter O'Meara's biography of John Tanner, *The Last Portage*, depicts Schoolcraft as being envious of Tanner's greater depth and understanding of Native American culture; Tanner lived as an Indian for so long that he completely forget how to speak English. He was regarded with such a high esteem by the Indians as to be viewed with the respect normally afforded only chiefs. But in the white man's world Tanner failed at everything: a trader for the American Fur Company, a blacksmith, and an interpreter. So how is an old hunter used to living in the wilderness, prone to holding grudges, and finding himself out of place in white society to come to terms with an economy based on the puritan work ethic?

Where John Tanner forever becomes linked with the Schoolcraft's is in the murder of James Schoolcraft, Henry's younger brother. John Tanner had made threats against the life of both Schoolcrafts for various reasons and the hatred between the threesome was no secret. In Sault Ste. Marie, the year of James Schoolcraft's death, along with a number of other incidents, became known as the "Tanner Summer." On July 6, 1846, James Schoolcraft's body was found with a rifle ball in it, and the immediate cry for justice was directed at the most likely killer, John Tanner. A posse of angry whites went to Tanner's small cabin outside town to hang the old "white Injun", but he had vanished. Tanner's body was never officially found. A body was found with an old rusty musket alongside it, but confirmation of Tanner's death never occurred. Sometime later an army officer present in Sault Ste. Marie at the time of Schoolcraft's murder, made a death bed confession as to both James Schoolcraft's and Tanner's murders, but this too is speculation. Did Tanner vanish into thin air? In the last paragraph in his *Narrative*, Tanner states his desire to return to his son in Indian Country.

O'Meara says this about Schoolcraft's vehement distaste for Tanner:

Bonga

"Henry R. Schoolcraft was one of those intellectual giants who flourished in an age of amateurs. He was himself an amateur of geology, ethnology, linguistics, geography, and literary composition; and he labored and wrote prodigiously in all these fields. His 'Personal Memoirs of a Residence of Thirty Years with the Indian Tribes' – a title that stretches the facts a little, incidentally, since living at the Sault could hardly be called living with the Indian tribes – is replete with such captions as: 'Questions of the substantive verb in the Chippewa language'...'Habits of the common deer'...'Mastadon's tooth in Michigan'... 'Report on the copper mines of Lake Superior.' He also did a little exploring on the side."

O'Meara goes on to say:

"But Schoolcraft's chief interest was in the language and customs of the Ojibway; and his most important writing – if we may dismiss the suspicion that some of the best was done by his gifted wife – is on that subject. Can it be possible, one wonders, that Schoolcraft's hatred of Tanner sprang from some deep well of unconscious envy? For Tanner, after all, knew vastly more about Ojibway customs and speech than Schoolcraft, with all his erudition, could ever hope to learn...So it is only fair, perhaps, to say a few words about Schoolcraft. From his portraits, he appears to have been a heavy-jowled, thin-lipped man with a high, sloping forehead, and flinty eyes behind square, steel-rimmed

spectacles. His own writing gives him away
as pedantic, pretentious, egotistical, and not
always scrupulously accurate. Those who
knew the Schoolcrafts best reserved their warm
and affectionate adjectives for Jane, his lovely
wife."[189]

O'Meara may have had a bias for Tanner but Schoolcraft was developing the reputation of a man with a large ego by other deeds.

Looking at the governments objectives for the 1832 expedition to the Headwaters is revealing to the ulterior motives of Schoolcraft. By the determination of the War Department and the Office of Indian Affairs, three objectives were set for the expedition, none of which specifically stated that locating the Headwaters of the Mississippi was to be one of them. The first and most important objective was to end the constant warring between the Ojibwe and Dakota. Initially this had not been of great concern, even though one of Zebulon Pike's 1804 objectives was to initiate a peace, the government's concern had not yet raised to the level of great priority. A system of forts had been established, like Fort Snelling, to theoretically protect Indians from corrupt fur traders, extend the authority of the United States and protect the few white settlers present. With increased immigration of white settlers into Wisconsin and Minnesota, establishing peace between the Ojibwe and Dakota became more important. The Prairie du Chien Treaty of 1825, in which there was no cessation of land, was an agreement by both tribes, Dakota and Ojibwe, to respect a boundary line that was drawn across the state, roughly separating the two halves, north and south. The Fond du Lac Treaty of 1826 was held to bring the more northern Ojibwe into agreement with the principles set forth at Prairie du Chien. Before the ink had dried, the terms set forth at these treaties were violated and conflict continued as before. Secondly, the government was interested in assessing conditions in the fur trade in regards to the use of alcohol and the transgressions of the Hudson Bay Company on American soil. And finally, Congress had recently passed legislation for vaccinating the Indians for small pox.

In fairness to Schoolcraft, it should be noted that he had advocated for effecting a pacification of the northern tribes along with missionary work. His ardent belief in the temperance movement was well known.

Although there is no mention of the "headwaters" objective in the official government document, there is unofficial mention of it in correspondence between Schoolcraft and Cass. In a response from Schoolcraft to Governor Lewis Cass from Sault Ste. Marie, February 24, 1832 Schoolcraft writes:

> "...I gladly embrace the proposal to go to the heads of the Mississippi, to carry into effect the plan of last year. I have prepared a letter and estimates which will be submitted to you. And adopted the necessary measures here, to secure supplies for the voyage. I am in hopes that the best results will flow from it. At any rate, I shall address myself to the task with zeal and diligence, and endeavor to go over as much ground, and acquire as much information, aside from the main object, as is possible. If I do not see the "veritable source" of the Mississippi, this time, it will not be from a want of intention."[190]

In brackets at the end of this letter, the editor notes

that the letter demonstrates that Schoolcraft was more interested in the headwaters than the principle objectives of the mission and that Schoolcraft's great interest was not publicized since the Office of Indian Affairs would not want Schoolcraft using its funds for exploration. The budget for the expedition, as set by the Office of Indian Affairs and the War Department, was a $2,200 and records show that Schoolcraft was reimbursed for a sum total of $3,166.45 for the expedition.

Other evidence that leads one to believe that Henry Schoolcraft may have placed too much importance on his own reputation rather than giving providing due credit to others is found in the relationship that some of his past 'gentleman' travel companions had of him. David Bates Douglass, a member of Cass's expedition of 1820, was assigned, along with Schoolcraft, to keep a written record of that expedition. He and Schoolcraft were to jointly co-author the account of this expedition. When the expedition ended, however, Schoolcraft went ahead on his own and published the account without waiting for any contribution from Douglass which angered Douglass. Douglass's own accounts were not published until after his death.[191]

Another example involves a member of the 1832 expedition. Lt. James Allen, in charge of a ten man army escort, was to map the route and note the strength of the Indian populations. After leaving Fort Snelling for the return trip to Michigan by way of the St. Croix-Brule River portage to Lake Superior, Schoolcraft left Lt. Allen behind without a guide or proper direction. Allen, with a ten man crew of U.S. soldiers could not keep up with the French Canadian voyageurs that manned the Schoolcraft canoe. Allen's assignment to map the country also slowed him down. Without a guide, Allen often did not know where he was or what to expect. Lt. Allen was greatly irritated by the treatment he received from Schoolcraft and officially filed a grievance against Schoolcraft with the government.[192]

Schoolcraft did select four talented people to accompany him to the Headwaters in 1832. Dr. Douglass Houghton was chosen first as a surgeon but also had degrees in chemistry and natural history, training in geology and possessed an ease in all levels of society. Obviously, his training as a doctor was utilized in vaccinating the Indians for small pox, but he also possessed a valuable knowledge of geology which would serve the greater interests of the expedition. He would later make Michigan his home and become renowned there. His expertise in copper and its mining earned him the title "Father of copper mining in the United States." He warned against prospectors running to Michigan to strike it rich: "Look closely before the step is taken, which will most certainly end in disappointment and ruin," he wrote. His life would end in 1845 at the young age of thirty-six by drowning in Lake Superior. It is said that he went out onto the lake against the advice of voyageurs, due to worsening weather conditions. He has a city, county, and lake named after him in Michigan.

Lt. James Allen, who commanded the military escort of U.S. soldiers, all of whom were promised extra pay for fatigue duty, was another good choice. Allen was a West Point graduate and possessed excellent map making skills. Aside from making maps of the country traversed he was to keep a journal of the "manners and customs of the various Indian tribes," which translated into observing "their strength in numbers, their attitude toward the United States, and the influence of foreign traders."[193]

The third "gentleman" was the Reverend William Thurston Boutwell. Boutwell was selected by Schoolcraft due to Schoolcraft's belief that the Indian had to be culturally stripped of his "heathen" beliefs in order to civilize him. Boutwell would show shock and horror at the habits of the Indians. However, upon completion of the expedition, Boutwell would take an Indian wife and remain in Indian Country, spending a good portion of it on Leech Lake among the Pillagers. His letters and other writings would prove invaluable in enabling historians to later learn of the events that took place in Headwaters Country.

The fourth and most underestimated member was George Johnston of Sault Ste. Marie. Johnston was a mixed-blood interpreter for the expedition; he was also Schoolcraft's brother-in-law. His mother was the daughter of White Fisher or *Waub-o-jeeg,* the great Ojibwe chief of Wisconsin. George and his mother were responsible for quelling the potential armed conflict between Sault Ste. Marie Ojibwe and the Lewis Cass Expedition in 1820 of which Schoolcraft was a member. Cleve Stillwell, local historian in the Bemidji/Laporte area, wrote about the abuses George Johnston received from Schoolcraft and others after the 1832 expedition:

> "...Both Cass and Schoolcraft, who was George's brother-in-law having married Jane Johnston, promised to exert influence to have him paid for his assistance. But agents changed and no payment was forth coming. In 1856 five chiefs made their mark for a claim of $1,600 which was to be paid by the government for food, shelter and medicine supplied to them by George Johnston. George wrote letter after letter for aid in collecting his just dues, and at last sent a memorandum to Congress enumerating his claims, but no one was powerful enough or interested enough to help him.
>
> In 1847, Schoolcraft was head-quartered in

Bonga

Washington as Superintendent of Indian Affairs.
Congress had appropriated about $30,000
for the first of five volumes to be prepared,
of his Historical and Statistical Information
Respecting the History, Condition and Prospects
of the Indian Tribes of the U.S.

One letter from Schoolcraft to George, while
the book was being prepared, says, 'You are
favorably situated for collecting traditions and
traits of the red race and their character and
history; and possessing as you do a full knowledge of their language with more than the or-
dinary share of English literature and letters,
you would be almost inexcusable not to employ
your leisure moments in putting on record all
you can find among them worthy of it. It is a
debt you owe to them and to the country and
such labor, if well directed and well executed
will form your best claim to remembrance. Life
is at best short and he only lives well who does
something to benefit others. So far as you may
transmit to me, anything you can collect in
name or lodge-tales, picture writing or any other
branch, I can assure you that you shall have
final and full literary credit.'

George Johnston sent much material to
Schoolcraft, who thanked him in many letters
for either a legend, song, a translation or other
information, but the promise of "final and full
literary credit" was never fulfilled.

In a book of reminiscences by George are found
carefully copied passages from the Bible and

some writings of his own. One reads, 'No friend have I, no hopes of any. What a world to live in. O God, judge and assert my rights.' Another, 'Direct my paths in virtue to pursue.' At age 65, George left his home one winter day. When he failed to return, practically all his neighbors turned out on snowshoes and dogs to search for him. He was found north of his home, across the canal near the rapids frozen to death.

Longfellow's "Legend of Hiawatha" was inspired by Schoolcraft's writings. As we read it we might give a thought also to George Johnston's contributions to it."[194]

It is rather a shame that Schoolcraft rarely mentions George Johnston or the deeds of George prior to the 1832 expedition. The entire Johnston family played a great role in the history of the North West. Only in Schoolcraft's *Thirty Years* does he write about the Johnston family. It is in character that when Schoolcraft named a small lake (now Little Portage Lake) on the connection from Pike Bay to Leech Lake—"*Shiba*"—each initial representing to the last name of each of his "gentleman" travelers, we find no 'J' for Johnston. Possibly the "I" is meant for "interpreter"?

In chapter one of the section, "Exploratory Trip Through the St. Croix and Burntwood (or Brule) Rivers" in his 1832 journal, Schoolcraft gives a thumbnail sketch of *Waub-o-jeeg*, the great Ojibwe chief of Chequamegon and northern Wisconsin, but completely fails to mention that George Johnston is his grandson.[195]

Schoolcraft's omissions of such valuable information in the historical record are too frequent to assume it is inadvertent. It leads one to suspect that these omissions are intentional so as to maintain his own role as the central figure. It also asks what contributions from others may have been left out of his 'official' record of both the 1820 and 1832 expeditions?

Another possible covert deception by Schoolcraft involves the journals of Nicollet. These journals are some of the most accurate and best portrayals of native people and their lives written by any white visitor to Indian Country. These papers by this kindly and respectful man were lost for many years and their surfacing and editing by Martha Coleman Bray are truly a treasure for those of us interested in our history.

As Ms. Bray notes in her "Editors Preface" to her magnificent work:

> "Nicollet's official papers...were deposited with the Corps of Topographical Engineers, where they lay untouched until 1921, when the old war department records were moved to new quarters and scholars were called in to identify the contents of a dusty box with iron handles which had a 'very European look.' The manuscripts here published for the first time are among those eventually transferred to the Library of Congress. These papers include correspondence; the St. Croix journal; a few scattered pages from what was apparently a personal notebook, the rest of which is lost... Two of the groups of documents published in this volume – the journal of a trip to the sources of the Mississippi and the Indian materials on separate sheets in no particular order – were at some time dissociated from Nicollet's other papers and came eventually to rest in the Library of Congress among the papers of Henry

Barry Babcock

Rowe Schoolcraft, who explored the sources of
the Mississippi in 1832. There they were discovered only a few years ago [Mrs. Bray's work
copyrighted 1970 by MNHS] by John Frances
McDermott, research professor of history at
Southern Illinois University, in the course of his
own untiring investigation into the history of the
Mississippi valley."[196]

These valuable papers may very well have been lost to
history if not for Mr. McDermott and causes one wonder if
this was Schoolcraft's intention?

I state the above not to go off on an unrelated tangent
or divert away from the story of the Bonga family role but to
lay before the reader some unknown facts about the mind
and ego of Henry Schoolcraft as it relates to missing pieces
of the jigsaw puzzle concerning credible people associated with the Headwaters who have been deleted from the
record.

Finally, we must address the problem of the largest
missing puzzle piece of all: the story of Jacob Fahlstrom
and his role in the discovery of the Mississippi Headwaters.

Much has been written about Jacob Fahlstrom, the first
Swedish settler in Minnesota. Surprisingly, there is unwrit-
ten family history which has been passed down through
generations of his descendants.

The written record on Fahlstrom includes information
from various sources, including a monument at Kellogg
Boulevard and Roberts Street in St. Paul with the inscrip-
tion: IN MEMORY OF THE FIRST SWEDISH SETTLER IN
MINNESOTA – JACOB FAHLSTROM – FUR TRADER – MAIL
CARRIER – MISSIONARY – 1793 – 1857 – WHO FARMED
IN THIS REGION BEFORE 1838.

The many versions of how a youthful lad from Sweden

found himself in North America vary Some say that he was orphaned, others say he was separated from his Father and another version says his parents died, and while visiting London with an uncle, he became separated from his uncle. Whatever the case, young Jacob became a cabin boy on a Lord Selkirk HBC ship.

As to how he went from cabin boy to being taken in by a group of Native Americans, one story is that the ship was wrecked and he made to it land and was found by Indians. Another story is that while at one of the HBC posts, he became lost and stumbled into an Indian village and was cared for and stayed on. In Emeroy Johnson's essay "Was Oza Windib A Swede?" he cites a number of Swedish historians: Allan Kastrup, Theodore A. Norelius, Robert Gronberger, and A.E. Strand among others who wrote of the interesting and intriguing life of Fahlstom. One account states that Fahlstrom "...wandered in the woods until found by a band of Indians and lived with them, learned their language and customs, endured dreadful hardships and had many narrow escapes from death by starvation or otherwise."[197] Johnson also cites a Swedish novel by Samuel Sollerman based on Fahlstrom's life that was titled *Gula Skalpen* and is interpreted as "Yellow Scalp."

In an essay for the "Minnesota Swedish Pioneer Centennial Committee", Charles J. Peterson wrote the following:

> "Jacob Fahlstrom was born in Stockholm, Sweden, July 25, 1793, son of a potter. When 12 years old, young Jacob went to sea as a cabin boy. The ship was wrecked on the coast of England, but Jacob was rescued and soon entered the employ of Lord Selkirk, the director of the Hudson's Bay Company. He went with

Lord Selkirk to Canada. There he remained for several years, becoming a cour-de-bois and expert canoe man. During the struggle between the North West Company and the Hudson Bay Company, Fahlstrom made his way to the mouth of the St. Louis River where he came to a Chippewa village of fourteen lodges. After a time he was accepted as a member of the tribe. There he married the beautiful Margret, daughter of Bungo, a West Indian, and his Chippewa wife..."

One story has Jacob traveling across the Canadian border and assumedly following the North Shore of Lake Superior to Fond du Lac or traveling upstream on the St. Louis River until he arrives at Fond du Lac where he was welcomed by those at the Ojibwe village and there he meets the beautiful Marguerite, daughter of Pierre Bonga, and falls in love. If Jacob is listed as an employee of the American Fur Company in 1817 and as Jacob is believed to have been born 1793, he would have been in his mid-twenties when he met Marguerite.

"Bungo" the "West African" is Pierre Bonga living at Fond du Lac. In 1797, Pierre and *Ojibwikwe* had their first child; a daughter. Some records show her birth place as Lapointe on Madeline Island, others have it at Fond du Lac. Wherever she was born, she was given the name Marguerite, though one document has it as *Ominwasino-ikwe*. As a small girl she was called *Maanaadizi* which is a nickname meaning "ugly" a name given to overly attractive girls to suppress any conceit and maintain a strong virtue of humility.[198] Little if any background of Marguerite is available until she marries. For several decades her life would have been immersed in the Ojibwe culture and her home, the Bonga settlement at Fond du Lac.

Bonga

Historian Larry Luukkonen writes about some of the early residents along the Northwest Trail:

"One of the more well-known figures was also the first Swede in Minnesota. Jacob Falstrom, whose son was born at Sandy Lake, was recorded on the roster of the American Fur Company employees in 1817 and for subsequent years as "Jacob Falstraw." In recorded history Jacob's Swedish name is often spelled differently; Fahlstrom, Folstrom, Folstrum and Falstraw.[199]

Jacob and Marguerite had many children and I have been told that their descendants, besides in northern Minnesota, are also in east central Minnesota and west central and northern Wisconsin. The names and ages of these children have been recorded in two sources. One is the 1850 census which includes contradictory information:

"The age of their oldest son John is given as 27 and daughter Nancy's also as 27. This would suggest that they were twins, born in 1823, but the place of birth is not the same for both. John was born at Sandy Lake, Nancy at Lake Superior. The other children were all born at Lake Superior, Cecelia in 1835, James in 1837, George in 1844."[200]

Another source referencing children born to Jacob and Marguerite is that of Edward D. Neil who states that in the 1880s:

"The oldest son, John was born at Leech Lake and married Margaret Reul, who died March 28,

1865. Nancy was born at Sandy Lake and is still living. Sarah, was born at Gull Lake, now the wife of B. Fournier. Jane, wife of J. McKnight, died February 22, 1861; James and George died when small. George the second is now living and married Catherine H. Simondet. James the second, now living. Cecelia, the wife of Chas. Villendren."[201]

Now to the important question: Was Jacob Fahlstrom actually *Ozaawindib*? In Schoolcraft's *Expedition to Lake Itasca* the first mention of *Ozaawindib* is made here, when Schoolcraft writes:

"At the mouth of the Brule River, a small party of the Chippewas was encountered, from the sources of the Mississippi. It turned out to be the family of Ozaawindib, one of the principle Chippewas, from Cass Lake. He was persuaded to return, and proved himself to be a trusty and experienced guide through the most remote and difficult parts of the route."[202]

Schoolcraft portrays the meeting as pure chance. He notes that this native man, *Ozaawindib*, happens to have a home on Star Island. Things could not have turned out better for the explorer as that is where he is going and he requests that *Ozaawindib* be his guide. In Johnson's essay he notes that "...Jacob and his wife have been able to establish a home on the south shore of Lake Superior, near the mouth of the River Bois de Brule, and another home on the island in Cass lake, probably also more or less permanent homes at Leech Lake and Sandy Lake." There is every possibility that Jacob and Marguerite did have a home at or near the mouth of the Brule River, as Jacob was employed by the AFC and the Brule was a major travel corridor into northwestern Wisconsin and the St. Croix River. This raises the possibility that Schoolcraft may have known of Jacob and his connections and knowledge of Headwaters Country. When confronted with these occurrences and encounters, it raises the question, could this all be just random chance?

The greatest revelation concerning Jacob and *Ozaawindib* was given to me by my friend, Juanita Blackhawk, an enrolled White Earth Reservation Band member. Juanita is a highly respected Elder, a member of the Loon (*Maang*) Clan, an accomplished quill artist and painter, a noted bead work artist for native regalia and a historian in her own right. Juanita has a detailed family tree that shows her Great, Great, Great, Great Grandparents are Jacob Fahlstrom and Marguerite Bonga Fahlstrom. Before meeting Juanita, I was a bit timid to propose that Jacob actually was *Ozaawindib* as so many whites have stolen so much of Anishinaabeg history. When I first asked Juanita if this were so, she laughed and said her relatives have known that Jacob Fahlstrom was *Ozaawindib* for generations. Juanita's oral history, as with most oral history, has remained very important to them and their ancestors. After studying the information I have written about Jacob and Marguerite and seeing Juanita Blackhawk's comprehensive family tree, I believe that Jacob was *Ozaawindib*, the guide for Schoolcraft. Juanita Blackhawk's astute and intimate knowledge her family and Ojibwe history in the Northwoods is impressive. Having heard Juanita's oral history, there is no doubt in my mind as to who *Ozaawindib* was. Juanita Blackhawk's narrative reveals in more complete and astonishing detail the truth about the role of her ancestors and the vital role they played in the story of the Mississippi Headwaters.

Juanita begins her story when the youngster, Jacob Fahlstrom, who may or may not have been an orphan, and was accompanying his uncle to England via ship. Jacob's uncle was a Swedish logger and was transporting a ship-load of timber he had sold in England. The vessel was ill-for-tuned and was wrecked off the English coast. Jacob was rescued, and through unknown circumstances became a cabin boy on a Hudson Bay Ship of Lord Selkirk.

On the journey aboard this Lord Selkirk ship to Hudson Bay, young Jacob was nine or ten years old. Once at the fort, the HBC crew went hunting in search of needed food and young Jacob became separated and lost. He wandered for days, subsisting on berries or whatever presented itself as food for the scared, hungry, and lost young boy. After many days of aimless wandering in the vast wilderness, Jacob was found by some Indians and turned over to an Ojibwe woman by the name of *Ka-ji-ji*, who took Jacob in and gave him the love, care, and oversight any mother would give to her own. *Ka-ji-ji* became Jacob's loving Mother and Jacob and *Ka-ji-ji* bonded. Over the years, Jacob became a "white-Indian", adopting their culture and language. He eventually forgot his native Swedish language and spoke only Ojibwemowin. He became as close to *Ka-ji-ji* as though she were his biological Mother as they were devoted to one another. As Jacob matured and settled in what would become Minnesota, he brought his adopted Mother, *Ka-ji-ji,* into the region to be close to him.

Through his life with the Ojibwe, Jacob developed hunt-ing and trapping skills, woodsmanship, and an intimate knowledge of the land, plants, and wildlife around him. He also became adept at canoe handling and travel. The vast area in which they lived and traveled became part of

Bonga

Jacob's world. Like his adopted Indian family, Jacob could travel great distances without a map. All these skills made him a perfect fit within the world of his time.

When I asked Juanita about how Jacob and *Ka-ji-ji* first came into the United States from Canada, she correctly noted that Indians recognized no borders and due to their seasonal movements, frequently crossed back and forth across the Canadian-Minnesota border. International borders were not part of their lexicon.

Eventually, Jacob enlisted in the American Fur Company and became a trader.

As white history indicates, Jacob had made his way as far south as Fort Snelling before the expedition of Schoolcraft. Oral history agrees that Jacob was hired as a mail carrier on the Mississippi below Fort Snelling where he was taken captive by Dakota and later released. Could the Dakota have mistaken Jacob as an Ojibwe?

When perusing through the material I have on Jacobs's life, it struck me as possibly too unlikely that Jacob could be in northern Minnesota one year and the next year in what would become St. Paul or Fort Snelling. But Juanita's oral history has Jacob even walking all the way to Fort Snelling from one or more of the AFC posts in the northern parts of the state. Those of us in the twenty-first century have a hard time comprehending the great distance that people, especially native people traveled in those days but nonetheless, it's true. Most Indians or fur traders thought nothing of traveling by canoe from Leech Lake to Sault Ste. Marie or walking and snowshoeing over 200 miles. This is where "Indian time" comes from. When destinations are hundreds of mile away, stating you will be there on a certain date and time, doesn't work when the weather and other factors come into play. You'll be there when you get there. People could not operate as we do today on precise schedules, there were too many factors out there to delay and inhibit travel.

As an employee of the American Fur Company in a specific department, in this case, the Fond du Lac department, Jacob came to know intimately all the other traders. As Juanita told me, Jacob knew George, Stephen, Pierre and other Bonga family members well, as he would have known all the traders in the Fond du Lac outfit.

White history has Jacob making his way to Fond du Lac on the St. Louis River and there meeting Marguerite and falling in love with her. Juanita told me that Jacob met Marguerite, not randomly at Fond du Lac, but through Pierre Bonga, Marguerite's father. Pierre was in his later years and had a superlative reputation among all native people as a good trader and Jacob, as a trader for the AFC, knew Pierre. Jacob Fahlstrom, as noted in an old photo and a portrait appears to be a well built and handsome man. This was verified by Juanita. She says he was six feet tall, broad shouldered, and a powerful physical specimen.

As Juanita notes in her knowledge of her family, Jacob and Marguerite were married the "Indian way" and were recognized husband and wife. It was later in their lives that Jacob and Marguerite were married in a church the white man's way.

Juanita notes they had numerous cabins throughout the region, possibly including northwestern Wisconsin, giving additional credibility to the thought that a cabin was at or near the mouth of the Brule River on the south shore of Wisconsin. It is also common knowledge in oral history that they had a home on Star Island of Cass Lake among many others.

When I asked Juanita Blackhawk about the circumstances enabling Jacob to become the guide for Schoolcraft on his 1832 expedition, she laughed and said in a very matter-of-fact manner, "why George Bonga set it up... it was all George!" We know that George was at Fond du Lac in 1820 when Schoolcraft was a travel companion of Louis Cass and Cass enlisted the multi-talented eighteen-year-old George Bonga as interpreter while in Fond du Lac. Surely, one could not help but notice this imposing, articulate and savvy Black Indian. Surely, Schoolcraft would have been very much aware of George as he most certainly

Jacob Fahlstrom, known as "Yellow Head" or *Ozaawindib*. Image sourced from Wikimedia Commons, Public Domain Ⓢ

Jacob Fahlstrom and Marguerite Bonga. Image sourced from Wikmedia Commons, Public Domain ©

rose in the esteem of the Cass Expedition members. It is more than plausible that Schoolcraft took the opportunity to ask for help, in the way of a guide in 1832, from the highly respected George Bonga.

At one point, Jacob Fahlstrom "... became a mail carrier between Fort Crawford, near Prairie du Chien, and Fort Snelling. The mail was transported in birch canoes. On one of his trips he was made prisoner by the hostile Sioux Indians. After his release, Jacob decided on a less strenuous life and became a farmer for a while on what is now downtown St. Paul."[203]

When Jacob took up farming on land that would become St. Paul, Jacob and the other settlers thought it was "public domain" and they would be able to remain there permanently but:

"About the time Major Plympton was appointed commandant [of Fort Snelling], the settlers suspected that they were to be turned out of the reserve as soon as the Indian treaties went into effect. When Lieutenant Smith began his survey of the population in October, 1837, their suspicions were confirmed and they decided that the time for action had arrived. Accordingly a meeting was held and a memorial adopted which was sent to President Van Buren...Among the petitioners were... Jacob Falstrom...The petition failed to produce the desired results and after the order of July 1838 many of the settlers left the reservation, most of them going to Wisconsin."[204]

"...The petition failed to produce the desired results and in 1838 the settlers were driven off and their cabins burned by troops from the fort. The majority went to Wisconsin but Jacob stakes a claim and made his home in the town of Afton on Section 5, Town. 28, Range 20. Along the north boundary of this section runs present U.S. 12."[205]

Sometime after 1832 Jacob had taken to the bottle and was seen as a drunk but somehow had an awakening and abstained from alcohol and found the white man's religion.

Jacob became a lay preacher in the Methodist religion and moved around a great deal within the Fort Snelling, Red Rock, Cold Water and surrounding region.

> "In 1841...but the conversion of one white man and his family was worth, in the estimation of Elder Brunson, the whole cost of the Kaposia mission. This man was one Jacob Falstrom, a Swede who emigrated from the Selkirk settlement years before the building of Fort Snelling and had engaged in the service of the American Fur Company..."[206]

> Having embraced Methodism, Jacob enrolled in the newly established M. E. Church mission at the village of Kaposia on the site of present day South St. Paul. The class records show the names of Mr. and Mrs. Fahlstrom and their daughters Nancy, Jane and Sally. After the removal of the mission to Red Rock, Jacob remained a valued assistant and interpreter for the mission until his death in 1857."[207]

Emery Johnson cites the Swedish-American historian, Eric Norelius, who gives an account of an old farmer/missionary by the name of Bolton in the Red Rock area, downstream from present St. Paul, who remarked of Marguerite; "...he said that she was part Chippewa and part Negro, that they spoke the Chippewa language in their home, and otherwise used the English language, and that when other Swedes came and settled in the region Fahlstrom regained the use of the Swedish language, which he had long forgotten." One item of interest in Johnson's essay is that, after the statement by Norelius that Fahlstrom's wife was "part Negro", Johnson writes; "It is highly unlikely that a Negro woman was in northern Wisconsin [LaPointe] and married to an Indian in the latter part of the 18th century." Obviously, Emery Johnson was not aware of the Bonga family.

Emery Johnson also writes that W.H.C. Folsom who has a long history in Minnesota and Wisconsin speaks of *the* "fine mind" of Falstrom's wife, and he states that Mr. and Mrs. Falstrom were "consistent Christians and members of the Methodist Church for many years."

"Mrs. Fahlstrom lives to the year[Feb. 6th] 1880. Mr. and Mrs. Fahlstrom are both buried at Afton." Jacob died in July 1859.[208]

In looking at the span of Jacob and Marguerite Fahlstrom's life without the oral history of Juanita Blackhawk, the probability of Jacob being *Ozaawindib* seems possible as there are so many relevant connections. With the oral history, the likelihood becomes more than probable as it is now logical.

The influential fur trader George Bonga, Jacob's brother-in-law and partner in business believed that Jacob would be a superb choice as a guide for the man that was now chief Indian agent (Schoolcraft) for the Ojibwe in northern Minnesota. These are my speculations concerning the arrangement. The most important fact is the oral history of a Bonga descendant, Juanita Blackhawk, saying George Bonga was the man responsible for suggesting Jacob Fahlstrom, known as "Yellow Head" or *Ozaawindib*, to guide Henry Rowe Schoolcraft to the source of the river of life. This time and place had far deeper meaning in the lives of the Bongas and Anishinaabeg than for Schoolcraft; it was their home.

Barry Babcock

What would be the reason Schoolcraft did not disclose that his guide was a white man? Would it negate Schoolcraft as being the first white man to discover the Headwaters? This appears credible with Schoolcraft's reputation. What is most important is putting the rightful people back into national and regional history where they belong.

The connections between the Bongas and all the explorers of the Headwaters are intertwined and interwoven. The story of the Bongas and the Headwaters is now complete. It has taken some luck in meeting Juanita and finding pieces from different sets of puzzles, but the puzzle is now finished. The story of how the great river of life lead Jean out of slavery; Pierre to find his safe abode in the wilderness and where his children lived as free men and free women; where the first Swede in Minnesota fell in love and married a Black-Ojibwe woman and how this entire family is forever linked to the great river of life, the *Misi-ziibi*. When I am too old to paddle in the backcountry, this land will still have great meaning to me, as within it is a story about what is good about who we are supposed to be as Americans. This heritage and history of the Headwaters can be ours.

When I am again in my canoe in some backcountry spot in Headwaters Country I can stop and maybe sense the spirit of big George there too in the land that he loved so deeply. Perhaps I will feel his dignified and benevolent face smiling upon me. This is for you and your family George. Long live the story of the Bongas.

Acknowledgments

So many people have helped and encouraged me to write the Bonga story that it would be difficult to list them all. Those who come immediately to mind and stand out are Robert Truer, who supported and urged me to write this story. Leo Soukup, who is the heart and soul of the Beltrami County Historical Society in Bemidji, Minnesota. Leo gave me an incredible amount of his time, support, and help, especially with corrections concerning dates and other accurate historical records. Without Leo's help, it is doubtful the book would have happened. Carol Jaakola, a direct descendant of Stephen Bonga, and an enrolled band member of the Fond du Lac Tribe of Ojibwe and author and historian Christine Carlson of the Fond du Lac community at the "foot" of Lake Superior are both, fully responsible for providing me a plethora of information, especially pertaining to Stephen, that without them, much of the story would be incomplete. I would be totally remiss if I did not acknowledge Henry (Hank) Bonga who encouraged me and did all he could to forward my work. Hank wanted so much to see the book become a reality as he saw it as his legacy but tragically Hank fought cancer through all this and died before the book materialized. Special thanks goes to Juanita Blackhawk of the White Earth Band of Ojibwe, a direct descendant of Marguerite Bonga and Jacob Fahlstrom. She spent an entire day giving me her family's oral history which was of paramount importance to me. If not for the Minnesota Historical Society and the archives they make available for the public and people like me to access letters and documents that I desperately needed to fill in so many gaps and holes in the story. I need to thank Philip Schwartzberg of Meridian Mapping for the excellent, last-minute maps he created for this book. The support and encouragement I received from so many of my Anishinaabe friends from the reservations of Leech Lake, White Earth, and Red Lake was of great spiritual and moral importance to me. If I were to cite one person that was most important in this endeavor, it is my wife, Linda Mae, who tolerated so much of my time and efforts being directed away from our immediate needs so this story could be told. I owe Colin Mustful, a wonderful historian and author himself, my heartful appreciation in finalizing this book. With Colin's help and guidance, I am immensely proud of the version of this book the public will see. I cannot express sufficiently what he means to this book!

Bibliography

Books

Allen, Anne Beiser. *And the Wilderness Shall Blossom: Henry Benjamin Whipple Churchman Educator Advocate for the Indians*. Afton MN: Afton Historical Society Press, 2008.

Bigsby, John Jeremiah. *The Shoe and Canoe; Or Pictures of Travel in the Canadas: With Facts and Opinions on Emigration, State Policy, and Other Points of Public Interest*. Vol. 1. London: Chapman and Hall, 1850.

Brower, Jacob Vrandenberg. *The Mississippi River And Its Source: A Narrative and Critical History of the Discovery of the River and its Headwaters, Accompanied by the Results of Detailed Hydrographic and Topographic Surveys*. Minneapolis, MN: Harrison & Smith State Printers, 1893.

Brown, Dee. *Bury My Heart at Wounded Knee: An Indian History of the American West*. London: Holt, Rinehart & Winston, 1970.

Cleland, Charles E. "Preliminary Report of the Ethnohistorical Basis of the Hunting, Fishing, and Gathering Rights of the Mille Lacs Chippewa," in *Fish in the Lakes, Wild Rice, and Game in Abundance*. Compiled by James M. McClurken. East Lansing, MI: Michigan State University Press, 2000.

Coleman, Sister Bernard, Sister Verona LaBud, and John Humphrey. *Old Crow Wing:History of a Village*. Brainerd MN: Evergreen Press of Brainerd LLC, 2000.

Collections of the State Historical Society of Wisconsin. Ed. Reuben Gold Thwaites. Volume 20. Madison, WI: Wisconsin Historical Society, 1911.

Douglas, David Bates. Appendix E, "Letters of David Bates

Douglas," in *Schoolcraft's Narrative Journal of Travels: Through the northwestern regions of the United States, extending from Detroit through the great chain of American lakes to the sources of the Mississippi River, in the year 1820.* Ed. Mentor L. Williams. East Lansing, MI: Michigan State University Press, 1992.

Ely, Edmund F. *The Ojibwe Journals of Edmund F. Ely, 1833–1849.* Ed. Theresa M. Schenck. Lincoln, NE: University of Nebraska Press, 2012.

Folwell, William Watts. *A History of Minnesota.* Vol. 1 and 2. St. Paul, MN: Minnesota Historical Society, 1921.

Gilman, Rhoda R. *The Story of Minnesota's Past.* St. Paul, MN: Minnesota Historical Society Press, 1989.

Harmon, Daniel Williams. *Harmon's Journal 1800–1819.* Ed. William Kaye Lamb. Surrey, BC, Canada: TouchWood Editions, 2006.

Henry, Alexander, and David Thompson. *New Light on the Early History of the Greater Northwest: The Manuscript Journals of Alexander Henry, Fur Trader of the Northwest Company, and of David Thompson, Official Geographer and Explorer of the Same Company, 1799–1814.* Ed. Elliott Coues. Volumes 1 and 2. New York: NY: Francis P. Harper, 1897.

Horrigan, Brian. "Introduction" in Kenneth Carley, *Minnesota in the Civil War: An Illustrated History.* St. Paul, MN: Minnesota Historical Society Press, 2006.

Lund, Duane R. Ph.D. *Our Historic Upper Mississippi.* Cambridge, MN: Adventure Publications, 1991.

—————. *The Lives and Times of Three Powerful Ojibwe Chiefs.* Cambridge, MN: Adventure Publications, 2003.

Luukkonen, Larry. *Between the Waters: Tracing the Northwest Trail from Lake Superior to the Mississippi.* United States: Dovetailed Press LLC, 2007.

Mackey, Frank. *Done with Slavery: The Black Fact in Montreal, 1760-1840.* Montreal, Quebec: McGill-Queen's University Press, 2010.

Bonga

McKeig, Cecelia, and Renee Geving. *The 1898 Battle of Sugar Point: The Last Encounter Between the U.S. Army and the Indians of North America.* Walker, MN: Cass County Historical Society, 2011.

McKenney, Thomas Loraine. *Sketches of a Tour to the Lakes: Of the Character and Customs of the Chippeway Indians, and of Incidents Connected with the Treaty of Fond Du Lac. By Thomas L. McKenney ... Also, a Vocabulary of the Algic, Or Chippeway Language, Formed in Part, and as Far as it Goes.* Baltimore, MD: F. Lucas, jun'r., 1827.

McPherson, James M. *The Illustrated Battle Cry of Freedom: The Civil War Era.* New York, NY: Oxford University Press, 1988.

Neill, Edward D. "History of the Ojibways, and Their Connection with Fur Traders, Based Upon Official and Other Records," in *Collections of the Minnesota Historical Society.* Vol. 5. St. Paul, MN: Minnesota Historical Society, 1885.

—————. *History of Washington County and the St. Croix Valley.* Minneapolis, MN: North Star Publishing Company, 1881.

Nelson, George. *My First Years in the Fur Trade: The Journals of 1802-1804.* Eds. Laura Lynn Peers and Theresa M. Schenck. St. Paul, MN: Minnesota Historical Society Press, 2002.

Nicollet, Joseph Nicolas. *The Journals of Joseph N. Nicollet: a Scientist on the Mississippi Headwaters: With Notes on Indian Life, 1836-37.* Ed. Martha Coleman Bray. St. Paul, MN: Minnesota Historical Society, 1970.

Nute, Grace Lee. *Rainy River Country: A Brief History of the Region Bordering Minnesota and Ontario.* St. Paul, MN: Minnesota Historical Society, 1950.

O'Meara, Walter. *The Last Portage.* Boston, MA: Houghton Mifflin, 1962.

Peterson, C.J. "The First Swedish Settler in Minnesota," in *Swedish Pioneer Centennial Celebration: Rockford*

Illinois June 1948. Rockford, Il: Swedish Pioneer Centennial Association Rockford Committee, 1948.

Sandburg, Carl. *Abraham Lincoln: The Prairie Years.* New York, NY: Blue Ribbon Books, 1926.

——————. *Abraham Lincoln: The War Years.* Vol. 2. San Diego, CA: Harcourt, Brace, 1939.

Schenck, Theresa M. *William W. Warren: The Life, Letters, and Times of an Ojibwe Leader.* Lincoln, NB: University of Nebraska Press, 2007.

——————. *The Voyageur.* New York and London: D. Appleton & Co, 1931.

——————. *The Voyageur's Highway: Minnesota's Border Lake Land.* St. Paul: MN, Minnesota Historical Society Press, 2002.

Schoolcraft, Henry Rowe. *Personal Memoirs of a Residence of Thirty Years with the Indian Tribes on the American Frontiers: With Brief Notices of Passing Events, Facts, and Opinions, A.D. 1812 to A.D. 1842.* Philadelphia, PA: Lippincott, Grambo and Company, 1851.

——————. *Schoolcraft's Expedition to Lake Itasca: The discovery of the source of the Mississippi.* APPENDIX C. "Journal and Letters of Lieutenant James Allen." East Lansing, MI: Michigan State University Press, 1993.

——————. *Schoolcraft's Expedition to Lake Itasca: The discovery of the source of the Mississippi.* Ed. Philip P. Mason. East Lansing, MI: Michigan State University Press, 1993.

——————. *Schoolcraft's Narrative Journal of Travels: Through the northwestern regions of the United States, extending from Detroit through the great chain of American lakes to the sources of the Mississippi River, in the year 1820.* Ed. Mentor L. Williams. East Lansing, MI: Michigan State University Press, 1992.

Stevens, Hiram Fairchild. *History of the Bench and Bar of Minnesota.* Minneapolis, MN: Legal Publishing and Engraving Company, 1904.

Upham, Warren, James Heaton Baker, Lucius Frederick

Hubbard, and William Pitt Murray. *Minnesota in Three Centuries, 1655-1908*. Mankato, MN: Publishing Society of Minnesota, 1908.

Vennum, Thomas Jr. *Wild Rice and the Ojibway People*. St. Paul, MN: Minnesota Historical Society Press, 1988.

Warren, William W. *History of the Ojibway Nation*. Vol. 5. St. Paul, MN: Minnesota Historical Society, 1885.

——————. *History of the Ojibway People*. Ed. Theresa M. Schenck. St. Paul, MN: Minnesota Historical Society Press, 2009.

Whipple, Henry Benjamin. *Lights and Shadows of a Long Episcopate : Being Reminiscences and Recollections of the Right Reverend Henry Benjamin Whipple D.d. Ll. D. Bishop of Minnesota*. New York, NY: Macmillan, 1912.

Zapffe, Carl Andrew. *Minnesota's Chippewa Treaty of 1837*. Brainerd MN: Historic Heartland Association, 1994.

Manuscript Sources

Bertrand, Achille H. *Recollections of Old Superior, 1923*. Wisconsin Historical Society Archives, Superior Area Research Center, Superior Public Library.

Chippewa Halfbreeds to Daniel P. Bushnell, July 24, 1839. *The Territorial Papers of the United States*. Ed. John Porter Bloom. Vol. 28. Washington, D.C.: The National Archives, 1975.

Governor Dodge to Commissioner Crawford, February 8, 1839. *The Territorial Papers of the United States*. Ed. John Porter Bloom. Vol. 27. Washington, D.C.: The National Archives, 1969.

Lucius Lyon to Commissioner Crawford, July 16, 1839. *The Territorial Papers of the United States*. Ed. John Porter Bloom. Vol. 28. Washington, D.C.: The National Archives, 1975.

Whipple, Henry B. *Henry B. Whipple Papers, 1833–1934*.

Manuscripts Collection, Minnesota Historical Society, St. Paul, MN.

William Aitkin to Ramsay Crooks, January 4, 1837. *American Fur Company Papers, 1831–1849*, microfilm, M151, Reel 24. Minnesota Historical Society, St. Paul, Minnesota.

Periodicals

Blegen, Theodore C. "Armistice and War on the Minnesota Frontier." *Minnesota History,* 24, no. 1 (1943): 11–25.

Bonga, George. "Letters of George Bonga." *The Journal of Negro History,* 12, no. 1 (1927): 41–54.

Densmore, Benjamin. "Benjamin Densmore's Journal of an Expedition on the Frontier." *Minnesota History Bulletin,* 3, no. 4 (1919): 167–209.

Durbin, William. "Who Was George Bonga." *Minnesota Conservation Volunteer.* (November-December, 2010). http://files.dnr.state.mn.us/mcvmagazine/young naturalists/young-naturalists-article/george_bonga/ george_bonga.pdf.

Heilbron, Bertha L. "A Pioneer Artist on Lake Superior." *Minnesota History,* 21, no. 2 (1940): 149–157.

Johnson, Emeroy. "Was Oza Windib a Swede?" *Swedish American Historical Quarterly.* 35, no. 3 (July 1984): 207–220.

Meehan, Thomas A. "Jean Baptiste Point Du Sable, the First Chicagoan," *Journal of the Illinois State Historical Society.* 56, no. 3 (1963): 439–453. http://www.jstor. org/stable/40190620.

Porter, Kenneth W. "Relations Between Negroes and Indians Within the Present Limits of the United States." *The Journal of African American History.* 17, no. 3 (July 1932): 287–293

The Journal of Negro History. Ed. Carter G. Woodson. Vol. 12. Lancaster, PA: The Association for the Study of Negro Life and History, Inc., 1927.

Bonga

Walton, William. "Eastman Johnson, Painter." *Scribner's Magazine,* 40, issue 3 (Sept. 1906): 263–274.

Woodwhimsy. "The Bonga Saga." *Inter-County Leader.* 79, no. 13 (2011).

Websites

"About Congo." *Embassy of the Republic of Congo in Washington, D.C..* Accessed February 20, 2023. http://www.ambacongo-us.org/en-us/aboutcongo/peopleculture/people.aspx.

Armor, David A. "Robertson, Daniel." *Dictionary of Canadian Biography.* Vol. 5. University of Toronto/ Université Laval, 2003–. accessed February 21, 2023. http://www.biographi.ca/en/bio/robertson_daniel_5E.html.

"Chapter Five: Roots of the Community," in "Grand Portage: The Grand Portage Story." *National Park Service, U.S. Department of the Interior."* Last Updated July 15, 2009. Accessed February 24, 2023. https://www.nps.gov/parkhistory/online_books/story/chap5.htm.

"George Sayer/ Sayers (1812-1882) Catherine Caplette (1817-?)." *Red River Ancestry.ca.* Last Updated April 8, 2017. Accessed February 21, 2023. https://www.redriverancestry.ca/SAYER-GEORGE-1812.php.

Hemphill, Stephanie. "Eastman Johnson's Legacy in Art." *MPR News.* Published July 4, 2006. Accessed February 27, 2023. https://www.mprnews.org/story/2006/06/30/eastmanjohnson.

"Jean Baptiste Point du Sable." *Wikipedia.* Last Updated February 20, 2023. Accessed February 21, 2023. https://en.wikipedia.org/wiki/Jean_Baptiste_Point_du_Sable.

Steil, Mark, and Tim Post. "Hundreds of Settlers Killed in Attacks." *Minnesota Public Radio.* Published September 26, 2002. Accessed March 5, 2023. http://news.minnesota.publicradio.org/features/200209/23_steilm_1862-m/part4.shtml.

"The Bongas of Cass County." *Iplivecams.* Accessed March 3, 2023. https://www.iplivecams.com/travel/the-bongas-of-cass-county/.

Wisconsin Historical Society. "Additional Information" in "Portrait of Stephen Bonga." Image ID: 55160. Viewed online at https://wisconsinhistory.org/Records/Image/IM55160.

About the Author

Aside from canoeing all the navigable rivers and lakes in the Headwaters region of northern Minnesota, Barry has paddled thousands of miles in remote wilderness areas such as the Boundary Waters Canoe Area, Quetico Provincial Park, and Woodland Caribou Provincial Park of Ontario. His love of canoe travel developed into a keen interest of the fur trade from the 1660s to the 1840s. Barry's love of wild places led himself, his wife Linda, and their dogs to live a sustainable life style off-the-grid in a remote setting in the north woods for twenty years. For his entire adult life, Barry has been a tireless advocate for wild places and wild things. For the last three years, Barry, Linda and their dogs now reside in a small home on Gitchi Ma'iingan Lake on his beloved Headwaters of the Mississippi River.

Endnotes

A Dark Cloud Approaching from the East (pages 15-55)

1   William W. Warren, *History of the Ojibway Nation*, Vol. 5, (St. Paul, MN: Minnesota Historical Society, 1885), 256.

2   Duane R. Lund, Ph.D., *Our Historic Upper Mississippi*, (Cambridge, MN: Adventure Publications, 1991), 36.

3   Henry Rowe Schoolcraft, *Schoolcraft's Expedition to Lake Itasca: The discovery of the source of the Mississippi*, APPENDIX C, "Journal and Letters of Lieutenant James Allen," (East Lansing, MI: Michigan State University Press, 1993), 209–210.

4   Larry Luukkonen, *Between the Waters: Tracing the Northwest Trail from Lake Superior to the Mississippi*, (United States: Dovetailed Press LLC, 2007), 211.

5   Henry Rowe Schoolcraft, *Personal Memoirs of a Residence of Thirty Years with the Indian Tribes on the American Frontiers: With Brief Notices of Passing Events, Facts, and Opinions, A.D. 1812 to A.D. 1842*, (Philadelphia, PA: Lippincott, Grambo and Company, 1851), 540.

6   Ibid.

7   Ibid.

8   Joseph Nicolas Nicollet, *The Journals of Joseph N. Nicollet: a Scientist on the Mississippi Headwaters: With Notes on Indian Life, 1836-37*, ed. Martha Coleman Bray (St. Paul, MN: Minnesota Historical Society, 1970), 83.

9   Ibid., 86.

10   Warren Upham, James Heaton Baker, Lucius Frederick Hubbard, and William Pitt Murray, *Minnesota in Three Centuries, 1655-1908*, (Mankato, MN: Publishing Society of Minnesota, 1908), 125–126.

11   William Aitkin to Ramsay Crooks, January 4, 1837, *American Fur Company Papers, 1831–1849*, microfilm, M151, Reel 24, Minnesota Historical Society, St. Paul, Minnesota.

12   Luukkonen, *Between the Waters*, 224.

13   Ibid., 223.

14 Upham, *Minnesota in Three Centuries,* 127.

15 Nicollet, *The Journals of Joseph N. Nicollet,* 215.

16 George Nelson, *My First Years in the Fur Trade: The Journals of 1802-1804,* eds. Laura Lynn Peers and Theresa M. Schenck (St. Paul, MN: Minnesota Historical Society Press, 2002), 17.

17 Upham, *Minnesota in Three Centuries,* 127.

18 Ibid.

19 Schoolcraft, *Schoolcraft's Expedition to Lake Itasca,* 47.

20 Upham, *Minnesota in Three Centuries,* 127.

21 Schoolcraft, *Personal Memoirs,* 554.

22 Upham, *Minnesota in Three Centuries,* 127–129.

23 William Whipple Warren, *History of the Ojibway People,* ed. Theresa M. Schenck, (St. Paul, MN: Minnesota Historical Society Press, 2009), 265.

24 Full blooded Indians would not receive citizenship until 1924 yet mixed-bloods were recognized as citizens and could vote.

25 Upham, *Minnesota in Three Centuries,* 129–130.

26 Ibid., 130.

27 Ibid.

28 Governor Dodge to Commissioner Crawford, February 8, 1839, *The Territorial Papers of the United States,* ed. John Porter Bloom, Vol. 27, (Washington, D.C.: The National Archives, 1969), 1186.

29 Lucius Lyon to Commissioner Crawford, July 16, 1839, *The Territorial Papers of the United States,* ed. John Porter Bloom, Vol. 28, (Washington, D.C.: The National Archives, 1975), 12–13.

30 Chippewa Halfbreeds to Daniel P. Bushnell, July 24, 1839, *The Territorial Papers of the United States,* ed. John Porter Bloom, Vol. 28, (Washington, D.C.: The National Archives, 1975), 16–18.

31 Brian Horrigan, "Introduction" in Kenneth Carley, *Minnesota in the Civil War: An Illustrated History,* (St. Paul, MN: Minnesota Historical Society Press, 2006), xviii.

Bongo from the Congo
(pages 56-70)

32 Carl Andrew Zapffe, *Minnesota's Chippewa Treaty of 1837*, (Brainerd MN: Historic Heartland Association, 1994), 253–255.

33 "About Congo," *Embassy of the Republic of Congo in Washington, D.C.,* Accessed February 20, 2023, http://www.ambacongo-us.org/en-us/aboutcongo/peopleculture/people.aspx.

34 *The Journal of Negro History,* ed. Carter G. Woodson, Vol. 12, (Lancaster, PA: The Association for the Study of Negro Life and History, Inc., 1927) 53–54.

35 "Jean Baptiste Point du Sable," *Wikipedia,* Last Updated February 20, 2023, Accessed February 21, 2023, https://en.wikipedia.org/wiki/Jean_Baptiste_Point_du_Sable.

36 Thomas A. Meehan, "Jean Baptiste Point Du Sable, the First Chicagoan," *Journal of the Illinois State Historical Society,* 56, no. 3 (1963): 445. http://www.jstor.org/stable/40190620.

37 Ibid., 446.

38 David A. Armor, "Robertson, Daniel," *Dictionary of Canadian Biography*, vol. 5, University of Toronto/Université Laval, 2003–, accessed February 21, 2023, http://www.biographi.ca/en/bio/robertson_daniel_5E.html.

39 Frank Mackey, *Done with Slavery: The Black Fact in Montreal, 1760-1840*, (Montreal, Quebec: McGill-Queen's University Press, 2010), 402.

40 *The Journal of Negro History,* 54.

41 Armor, "Robertson, Daniel," http://www.biographi.ca/en/bio/robertson_daniel_5E.html.

42 Ibid.

43 Mackey, *Done with Slavery,* 402.

44 Schoolcraft, *Personal Memoirs,* 450–451.

Where All Things Are Free
(pages 71-89)

45 Thomas Loraine McKenney, *Sketches of a Tour to the Lakes: Of the Character and Customs of the Chippeway Indians, and of Incidents Connected with the Treaty of Fond Du Lac. By Thomas L. McKenney ... Also, a Vocabulary of the Algic, Or Chippeway Language, Formed in Part, and as Far as it Goes*, (Baltimore, MD: F. Lucas, jun'r., 1827), 351.

46 Grace Lee Nute, *The Voyageur*, (New York and London: D. Appleton & Co, 1931), 38.

47 Ibid., 7.

48 Ibid., 10.

49 Grace Lee Nute, *Rainy River Country: A Brief History of the Region Bordering Minnesota and Ontario*, (St. Paul, MN: Minnesota Historical Society, 1950), 16.

50 "George Sayer/ Sayers (1812-1882) Catherine Caplette (1817-?)," *Red River Ancestry.ca*, Last Updated April 8, 2017, Accessed February 21, 2023, https://www.redriverancestry.ca/SAYER-GEORGE-1812.php.

51 Ibid.

52 Ibid.

53 *Fur Trade Manuscript Sources*, Author's Private Collection, 34.

54 Alexander Henry and David Thompson, *New Light on the Early History of the Greater Northwest: The Manuscript Journals of Alexander Henry, Fur Trader of the Northwest Company, and of David Thompson, Official Geographer and Explorer of the Same Company, 1799–1814*, ed. Elliott Coues, Volume 1, (New York: NY: Francis P. Harper, 1897), 49–50.

55 *Fur Trade Manuscript Sources*, Author's Private Collection, 34.

56 Henry, *New Light*, 49–50.

57 Ibid., 170–171.

58 Ibid., 180.

59 Ibid., 194.

60 Ibid., 207.

61 Ibid.

62 Ibid., 231.

63 *Collections of the State Historical Society of Wisconsin*, ed. Reuben

Gold Thwaites, Volume 20, (Madison, WI: Wisconsin Historical Society, 1911), 440.

64 Woodwhimsy, "The Bonga Saga," *Inter-County Leader,* 79, no. 13 (2011): Section B, page 9.

65 Alexander Henry and David Thompson, *New Light on the Early History of the Greater Northwest: The Manuscript Journals of Alexander Henry, Fur Trader of the Northwest Company, and of David Thompson, Official Geographer and Explorer of the Same Company, 1799–1814,* ed. Elliott Coues, Volume 2, (New York: NY: Francis P. Harper, 1897), 276.

66 Warren, *History of the Ojibwe Nation,* 381.

The Greatest Canoe Man in North America
(pages 90-143)

67 "Obituary for Stephen Bonga," *Superior Times,* January 26, 1884.

68 Henry Rowe Schoolcraft, *Schoolcraft's Narrative Journal of Travels: Through the northwestern regions of the United States, extending from Detroit through the great chain of American lakes to the sources of the Mississippi River, in the year 1820*, ed. Mentor L. Williams, (East Lansing, MI: Michigan State University Press, 1992), 137–139.

69 Ibid., 139.

70 Ibid.

71 Grace Lee Nute, *The Voyageur's Highway: Minnesota's Border Lake Land,* (St. Paul: MN, Minnesota Historical Society Press, 2002), 21–22.

72 John Bardon, "Stephen Bungo, First White Child," *Superior Times,* December 22, 1925.

73 Ibid.

74 Ibid.

75 Ibid.

76 See Larry Luukkonen's, *"Between the Waters"* for one of the most comprehensive and detailed accounts of the North West Trail and the History of the Fur Trade in the Fond du Lac Department. Grace Lee Nute, "A Description of Northern Minnesota by a Fur-Trader in 1807," *Minnesota History Bulletin* 5, no. 1 (1923): 28–39.

77 Alfred Merritt, "Society Formed by Old Settlers in 1886; First Meeting Was Superior," *Superior News Tribune,* March 8, 1925.

78 "Chapter Five: Roots of the Community," in "Grand Portage: The Grand Portage Story," *National Park Service, U.S. Department of the Interior,"* Last Updated July 15, 2009, Accessed February 24, 2023, https://www.nps.gov/parkhistory/online_books/story/chap5.htm.

79 Ibid.

80 Ibid.

81 Ibid.

82 Nute, *The Voyageur's Highway,* 45–46.

83 Nicollet, *The Journals of Joseph N. Nicollet,* 118.

84 Jacob Vrandenberg Brower, *The Mississippi River And Its*

Bonga

Source: A Narrative and Critical History of the Discovery of the River and its Headwaters, Accompanied by the Results of Detailed Hydrographic and Topographic Surveys, (Minneapolis, MN: Harrison & Smith State Printers, 1893), 186.

85 Theresa M. Schenck, *William W. Warren: The Life, Letters, and Times of an Ojibwe Leader*, (Lincoln, NB: University of Nebraska Press, 2007), 13–14.

86 Charles E. Cleland, "Preliminary Report of the Ethnohistorical Basis of the Hunting, Fishing, and Gathering Rights of the Mille Lacs Chippewa," in *Fish in the Lakes, Wild Rice, and Game in Abundance,* compiled by James M. McClurken, (East Lansing, MI: Michigan State University Press, 2000), 29.

87 Ibid., 31.

88 Ibid.

89 Thomas Vennum, Jr., *Wild Rice and the Ojibway People,* (St. Paul, MN: Minnesota Historical Society Press, 1988), 289.

90 Cleland, *Preliminary Report,* 28–29.

91 Theodore C. Blegen, "Armistice and War on the Minnesota Frontier," *Minnesota History,* 24, no. 1 (1943): 11.

92 William Watts Folwell, *A History of Minnesota,* Vol. 1, (St. Paul, MN: Minnesota Historical Society, 1921), 141–142.

93 Blegen, "Armistice and War," 12.

94 Ibid., 17.

95 Ibid.

96 Ibid., 17–18.

97 Upham, *Minnesota in Three Centuries,* 280.

98 Blegen, "Armistice and War," 15–16.

99 Ibid., 18.

100 Edward D. Neill, "History of the Ojibways, and Their Connection with Fur Traders, Based Upon Official and Other Records," in *Collections of the Minnesota Historical Society,* Vol. 5, (St. Paul, MN: Minnesota Historical Society, 1885), 488.

101 Blegen, "Armistice and War," 19.

102 Rev. Alfred Brunson, *Western Christian Advocate,* November 9, 1839.

103 Folwell, *A History of Minnesota,* 21–25.

104 Rev. Alfred Brunson, *Western Christian Advocate,* November 9, 1839.

105   Zapffe, *Minnesota's Chippewa Treaty,* 253–255.

106   Ibid.

107   *Wisconsin Historical Society,* "Additional Information" in "Portrait of Stephen Bonga," Image ID: 55160, viewed online at https://wisconsinhistory.org/Records/Image/IM55160

108   Schenk, *William W. Warren, 88.*

109   Ibid., 92–93.

110   Ibid., 95–97. Flatmouth's speech was written down and at Chief Flatmouth's request, it was sent to Gov. Ramsey so the Governor would know who was truly responsible for this horrible disaster.

111   Bertha L. Heilbron, "A Pioneer Artist on Lake Superior," *Minnesota History,* 21, no. 2 (1940): 151.

112   Ibid.

113   According to Stephanie Hemphill, "Johnson's guide was probably George Bonga, a son of Pierre Bonga, a freed slave. Pierre had married an Ojibwe woman and settled with her people in northern Wisconsin. Carl Gawboy is convinced spending time with this mixed-race family drew Eastman Johnson into a new reality, which changed his approach to painting people. Just as he was able to capture the humanity of Ojibwe people in this part of the country."Gawboy says Johnson was so friendly with the Bonga family that others in the community were willing to pose for him. Because of that, he was able to create portraits full of detail and feeling. "I mean obviously these Indians are relaxed, and that's a real important part of his paintings," Gawboy says. "They aren't formal, stiff portraits -- as happened with many photographers at a later time." Stephanie Hemphill, "Eastman Johnson's Legacy in Art," *MPR News,* Published July 4, 2006, Accessed February 27, 2023, https://www.mprnews.org/story/2006/06/30/eastmanjohnson.

114   William Walton, "Eastman Johnson, Painter," *Scribner's Magazine,* 40, issue 3 (Sept. 1906), 268.

115   Achille H. Bertrand, *Recollections of Old Superior, 1923,* Wisconsin Historical Society Archives, Superior Area Research Center, Superior Public Library.

116   Zappfe, *Minnesota's Chippewa Treaty,* 255.

117   Alfred Merritt, "Society Formed By Old Settlers in 1886," *Duluth Sunday News Tribune,* March 8, 1925.

118   John A. Bardon, "Stephen Bungo Story is Told,"

Bonga

Superior Times, November 22, 1925.

119   Christine Carlson, "Stephen Bonga and Family," *Fond du Lac Newsletter,* March 2011.

120   Luukkonen, *Between the Waters,* 255.

121   Christine Carlson, "Stephen Bonga and Family," *Fond du Lac Newsletter,* March 2011.

122   *Lake Superior Recorder,* July 7, 1911.

123   *Duluth Tribune Superior Times,* August 4, 1883.

Barry Babcock

The Biggest, Strongest, Smartest Man in the Northwoods
(pages 144-261)

124   *Fur Trade Manuscript Sources,* Author's Private Collection, 34. – Also see: Kenneth W. Porter, "Relations Between Negroes and Indians Within the Present Limits of the United States," *The Journal of African American History,* 17, no. 3 (July 1932), 287–293.

125   Schoolcraft, *Schoolcraft's Narrative Journal,* 12.

126   Duane R. Lund, Ph.D., *The Lives and Times of Three Powerful Ojibwe Chiefs,* (Cambridge, MN: Adventure Publications, 2003). Pages 37 to 42 tell of how Hole-in-the-Day was a principle player in preventing violence at Michilimackinac and then accompanied the Cass Expedition to Fond du Lac.

127   Schoolcraft, *Schoolcraft's Narrative Journal,* 141–143.

128   David Bates Douglas, Appendix E, "Letters of David Bates Douglas," in *Schoolcraft's Narrative Journal of Travels: Through the northwestern regions of the United States, extending from Detroit through the great chain of American lakes to the sources of the Mississippi River, in the year 1820,* ed. Mentor L. Williams, (East Lansing, MI: Michigan State University Press, 1992), 375.

129   "The Bongas of Cass County," *iplivecams,* Accessed March 3, 2023, https://www.iplivecams.com/travel/the-bongas-of-cass-county/

130   Rhoda R. Gilman, *The Story of Minnesota's Past,* (St. Paul, MN: Minnesota Historical Society Press, 1989), 79.

131   Daniel Williams Harmon, *Harmon's Journal 1800–1819,* ed. William Kaye Lamb (Surrey, BC, Canada: TouchWood Editions, 2006), 178.

132   Ibid.

133   John Jeremiah Bigsby, *The Shoe and Canoe; Or Pictures of Travel in the Canadas: With Facts and Opinions on Emigration, State Policy, and Other Points of Public Interest,* Vol. 1, (London: Chapman and Hall, 1850), 132–133.

134   Nute, *The Voyageur,* 7.

135   Schoolcraft, *Schoolcraft's Narrative Journal,* 150–151.

136   Folwell, *A History of Minnesota,* Vol. 1, 173–181.

137   Edmund F. Ely, *The Ojibwe Journals of Edmund F. Ely,*

1833–1849, ed. Theresa M. Schenck, (Lincoln, NE: University of Nebraska Press, 2012), 73.

138   Ibid., 89.

139   Ibid., 102.

140   James M. McPherson, *The Illustrated Battle Cry of Freedom: The Civil War Era,* (New York, NY: Oxford University Press, 1988), 133.

141   Ibid., 134.

142   Ibid., 135.

143   Ibid., 136.

144   Ibid.

145   Ibid.

146   Ibid., 137.

147   Ibid., 138.

148   Horrigan, "Introduction" in Kenneth Carley, *Minnesota in the Civil War,* **xxiii–xxiv.**

149   Carl Sandburg, *Abraham Lincoln: The War Years*, Vol. 2, (San Diego, CA: Harcourt, Brace, 1939), 8–28.

150   Carl Sandburg, *Abraham Lincoln: The Prairie Years*, (New York, NY: Blue Ribbon Books, 1926), 27.

151   Vennum, Jr., *Wild Rice,* 116.

152   Ibid.

153   Hiram Fairchild Stevens, *History of the Bench and Bar of Minnesota,* (Minneapolis, MN: Legal Publishing and Engraving Company, 1904), 216.

154   Benjamin Densmore, "Benjamin Densmore's Journal of an Expedition on the Frontier." *Minnesota History Bulletin,* 3, no. 4 (1919): 199-201.

155   Peg Meier, "Black Frontiersman," *Minneapolis Star Tribune,* February 6, 1995.

156   Anne Beiser Allen, *And the Wilderness Shall Blossom: Henry Benjamin Whipple Churchman Educator Advocate for the Indians*, (Afton MN: Afton Historical Society Press, 2008), 79.

157   Dee Brown, *Bury My Heart at Wounded Knee: An Indian History of the American West,* (London: Holt, Rinehart & Winston, 1970), 40.

158   Ibid., 42.

159   Mark Steil and Tim Post, "Hundreds of Settlers Killed in Attacks," *Minnesota Public Radio,* Published September 26, 2002, Accessed March 5, 2023, http://news.minnesota.publicradio.org/features/200209/23_steilm_1862-m/part4.shtml.

160   Henry Benjamin Whipple, *Lights and Shadows of a Long Episcopate : Being Reminiscences and Recollections of the Right Reverend Henry Benjamin Whipple D.d. Ll. D. Bishop of Minnesota*, (New York, NY: Macmillan, 1912), 138–141.

161   Ibid., 126–127.

162   William Watts Folwell, *A History of Minnesota,* Vol. 2, (St. Paul, MN: Minnesota Historical Society, 1924), 208.

163   Whipple, *Lights and Shadows,* 138.

164   George Bonga to Rev. Henry B. Whipple, October 22, 1863, *Henry B. Whipple Papers, 1833–1934*, Location P823, Box 3, Manuscripts Collection, Minnesota Historical Society, St. Paul, MN.

165   Henry Benjamin Whipple to D.M. Cooley, September 28, 1866, *Henry B. Whipple Papers, 1833–1934*, Location P823, Box 4, Manuscripts Collection, Minnesota Historical Society, St. Paul, MN.

166   Sister Bernard Coleman, Sister Verona LaBud, and John Humphrey, *Old Crow Wing:History of a Village*, (Brainerd MN: Evergreen Press of Brainerd LLC, 2000).

167   George Bonga, "Letters of George Bonga," *The Journal of Negro History* 12, no. 1 (1927): 41–54.

168   Whipple, *Lights and Shadows,* 248–249.

169   Ibid., 249–250.

170   Henry Benjamin Whipple to Joel Bean Bassett, November 14, 1867, *Henry B. Whipple Papers, 1833–1934*, Location P823, Box 5, Manuscripts Collection, Minnesota Historical Society, St. Paul, MN.

171   Joel Bean Bassett to Henry Benjamin Whipple, November 15, 1867, *Henry B. Whipple Papers, 1833–1934*, Location P823, Box 5, Manuscripts Collection, Minnesota Historical Society, St. Paul, MN.

172   Ibid.

173   Ibid.

174   Ibid.

175   Ibid.

176   Whipple, *Lights and Shadows,* 45–50.

177   Clement H. Beaulieu to Henry Benjamin Whipple, August 21, 1873, *Henry B. Whipple Papers, 1833–1934*, Location P823, Box 10, Manuscripts Collection, Minnesota Historical Society, St. Paul, MN.

178   Clement H. Beaulieu to William Welsh, September 4, 1873, *Henry B. Whipple Papers, 1833–1934*, Location P823, Box 10, Manuscripts Collection, Minnesota Historical Society, St. Paul, MN.

179   Ibid.

180   Columbus Delano to Henry Benjamin Whipple, February 26, 1874, *Henry B. Whipple Papers, 1833–1934*, Location P823, Box 10, Manuscripts Collection, Minnesota Historical Society, St. Paul, MN.

181   George Bonga to Henry Benjamin Whipple, March 16, 1874, *Henry B. Whipple Papers, 1833–1934*, Location P823, Box 10, Manuscripts Collection, Minnesota Historical Society, St. Paul, MN.

182   George Bonga to Henry Benjamin Whipple, May 28, 1874, *Henry B. Whipple Papers, 1833–1934*, Location P823, Box 10, Manuscripts Collection, Minnesota Historical Society, St. Paul, MN.

183   George Bonga to Henry Benjamin Whipple, June 1874, *Henry B. Whipple Papers, 1833–1934*, Location P823, Box 10, Manuscripts Collection, Minnesota Historical Society, St. Paul, MN.

184   Whipple, *Lights and Shadows,* 194.

185   Cecelia McKeig and Renee Geving, *The 1898 Battle of Sugar Point: The Last Encounter Between the U.S. Army and the Indians of North America,* (Walker, MN: Cass County Historical Society, 2011), 2–6.

186   William Durbin, "Who Was George Bonga," *Minnesota Conservation Volunteer,* (November-December, 2010), http://files.dnr.state.mn.us/mcvmagazine/young_naturalists/young-naturalists-article/george_bonga/george_bonga.pdf.

Barry Babcock

The Real Story of the Headwaters
(pages 262-291)

187   Henry Rowe Schoolcraft, *Schoolcraft's Expedition to Lake Itasca: The discovery of the source of the Mississippi*, ed. Philip P. Mason, (East Lansing, MI: Michigan State University Press, 1993), 25.

188   Nicollet, *The Journals of Joseph N. Nicollet*, 86.

189   Walter O'Meara, *The Last Portage*, (Boston, MA: Houghton Mifflin, 1962), 261–262.

190   Schoolcraft, *Schoolcraft's Expedition*, 134–135.

191   Schoolcraft, *Schoolcraft's Narrative Journal*, 21–22.

192   Schoolcraft, *Schoolcraft's Expedition to Lake Itasca: The discovery of the source of the Mississippi*, APPENDIX C, "Journal and Letters of Lieutenant James Allen," (East Lansing, MI: Michigan State University Press, 1993), 219–220, 235–236.

193   Schoolcraft, *Schoolcraft's Expedition*, xx.

194   Cleve Stillwell, "Johnston: A 'Lost' Figure in the History of Itasca Park," *Park Rapids Enterprise*, Date Unknown.

195   Schoolcraft, *Schoolcraft's Expedition*, 82–83.

196   Nicollet, *The Journals of Joseph N. Nicollet*, ix–x.

197   Emeroy Johnson, "Was Oza Windib a Swede?" *Swedish American Historical Quarterly*, 35, no. 3 (July 1984), 207.

198   Zapffe, *Minnesota's Chippewa Treaty*, 253–255.

199   Luukkonen, *Between the Waters*, 205.

200   Johnson, "Was Oza Windib a Swede?", 217.

201   Edward D. Neill, *History of Washington County and the St. Croix Valley*, (Minneapolis, MN: North Star Publishing Company, 1881), 407.

202   Ibid.

203   C.J. Peterson, "The First Swedish Settler in Minnesota," in *Swedish Pioneer Centennial Celebration: Rockford Illinois June 1948*, (Rockford, Il: Swedish Pioneer Centennial Association Rockford Committee, 1948), 10.

204   Johnson, "Was Oza Windib a Swede?", 213.

205   Peterson, "The First Swedish Settler in Minnesota," 10.

206   Folwell, *A History of Minnesota*, Vol. 1, 206–207.

Bonga

207   Peterson, "The First Swedish Settler in Minnesota,"
10.

208   Ibid., 10.

www.ingramcontent.com/pod-product-compliance
Lightning Source LLC
Chambersburg PA
CBHW030401130626
46549CB00004B/1582